Fuller's eight principles of the
"inner morality of law"
"principles of legality."

Hohfeld
    Right — Duty

species of   Privilege — No right
rt "   (liberty - not)

    Power ⟷ Liability

  Immunity ⟷ disability

Legal Philosophies

Legal
Philosophies

by
J. W. Harris BCL, MA, PhD
Solicitor, Fellow of Keble College, Oxford

London
Butterworths
1980

England London	Butterworth & Co (Publishers) Ltd 88 Kingsway, WC2B 6AB
Australia Sydney	Butterworths Pty Ltd 586 Pacific Highway, Chatswood, NSW 2067 Also at Melbourne, Brisbane, Adelaide and Perth
Canada Toronto	Butterworth & Co (Canada) Ltd 2265 Midland Avenue, Scarborough, M1P 4S1
New Zealand Wellington	Butterworths of New Zealand Ltd 31–35 Cumberland Place
South Africa Durban	Butterworth & Co (South Africa) (Pty) Ltd 152–154 Gale Street
USA Boston	Butterworth (Publishers) Inc 10 Tower Office Park, Woburn, Mass. 01801

ISBN 0 406 859361 2

Photoset by Scribe Design, Gillingham, Kent
Printed by Billing and Sons Ltd,
Guildford, London and Worcester

Preface

This book is intended for the beginner in legal philosophy, legal theory or jurisprudence. It has been written with the needs of the law student primarily in mind. It may also be useful to students of politics, or of moral and political philosophy; for no detailed knowledge of any branch of the law is required in order to follow the lines of argument discussed.

Before they embark on a new legal course, such as contract or land law, law students are commonly recommended to read some introductory work which covers the ground of the course in outline. An overview of the terrain, before undertaking detailed study, is thought desirable. In the case of legal philosophy, legal theory or jurisprudence, there is even more need for such an introductory book; for, not only is the subject matter strange to the student, but he finds that he is now expected to employ critical criteria of a wholly new kind. In other law courses, he has learned that 'information' must be supported by citation of statutes or cases, and that 'critical comment' consists either in the analytical exposition of the implications of these same sources or else in matching them with 'policy'. Now, in 'jurisprudence', so much that was taken for granted or left unsaid about the law is put before him. 'Information' appears to consist in acquaintance with the views of a very heterogeneous collection of theorists and philosophers; and 'critical comment' appears to range from the minutiae of textual exegesis, to the deepest questions about the nature of man or society as to which – perish the thought! – he is expected to take up an overt moral or political stance. Besides these difficulties of method, jurisprudence is daunting because there is so much of it. There is no end to the literature of philosophy, politics and social theory which might have a bearing on the issues comprised in it. Oh for the security of a case and statute reading list which, if long, might at least be regarded as definitive!

This book may help to absorb the first shock. It can be read through as a survey of the ground. It covers a wider range of topics than most single courses in legal philosophy, legal theory or jurisprudence are likely to encompass. Selection will be essential for issues to be dealt with at all adequately, but a glance at the full menu may help.

Portions of the book may also be read, week by week, as an introduction to different topics in a course. Each chapter has been designed, so far as possible, to stand on its own — although cross-references have been made where crucial intersections of theme seemed to require them. There is a select bibliography for each chapter so that the subject can be more fully explored.

No introductory work can make legal philosophies simple, and this book does not try to do so. It attempts two things, apart from providing a general survey: first, to set out the major contentions on either side of a debate, leaving the student to pass his own judgment; secondly, to indicate by what sorts of criteria someone who knows something of the law, but little of philosophy, is supposed to judge jurisprudential issues.

J. W. Harris
Keble College
Oxford
September 1980

Contents

ellution

viii Contents

Table of abbreviations

The following is a list of the abbreviations used for periodicals referred to in this book.

Ad L Rev	Adelaide Law Review
AJ	*Acta Juridica* (South Africa)
Am Anth	American Anthropologist
Am J Comp L	American Journal of Comparative Law
Am L Rev	American Law Review
Am Phil Q	American Philosophical Quarterly
Am PS Rev	American Political Science Review
ARSP	Archives für Rechts-und Socialphilosophie
ASAL	Annual Survey of American Law
Br J L Soc	British Journal of Law and Society
Calif L Rev	California Law Review
Can Bar Rev	Canadian Bar Review
China Q	China Quarterly
CLJ	Cambridge Law Journal
CLP	Current Legal Problems
Colum L Rev	Columbia Law Review
Cor L Rev	Cornell Law Review
Crim LR	Criminal Law Review
Dal LJ	Dalhousie Law Journal
Duc U L Rev	Ducane University Law Review
Duke LJ	Duke Law Journal
Ga L Rev	Georgia Law Review
GST	Groetius Society Transactions
Harv L Rev	Harvard Law Review
ICLQ	International Comparative Law Quarterly
IESS	International Encyclopaedia of the Social Sciences
IJE	International Journal of Ethics
Ind LJ	Indiana Law Journal
Inter-Am L Rev	International-American Law Review
Is L Rev	Israel Law Review
JCL	Journal of Comparative Law

JLE	Journal of Legal Education
JL Econ	Journal of Law and Economics
JLS	Journal of Legal Studies
JPE	Journal of Political Economy
J Phil	Journal of Philosophy
JSPTL	Journal of the Society of Public Teachers of Law
Jur Rev	Juridical Review
LQR	Law Quarterly Review
LS Rev	Law and Society Review
McGill LJ	McGill Law Journal
Mich L Rev	Michigan Law Review
Minn L Rev	Minnesota Law Review
Miss L Rev	Missouri Law Review
MLR	Modern Law Review
Mod Sch	The Modern Schoolman
NLF	Natural Law Forum
NY U L Rev	New York University Law Review
OEP	Oxford Economic Papers
Phil Rev	Philosophical Review
PPA	Philosophy and Public Affairs
Rut L Rev	Rutgers Law Review
SALJ	South African Law Journal
Scand S L	Scandinavian Studies in Law
Stan L Rev	Stanford Law Review
Tas U L Rev	Tasmania University Law Review
Tul L Rev	Tulane Law Review
U Br Col L Rev	University of British Columbia Law Review
U Chi L Rev	University of Chicago Law Review
U CLA L Rev	University of California and Los Angeles Law Review
U G LJ	University of Ghana Law Journal
U Pa L Rev	University of Pennsylvania Law Review
U Tor LJ	University of Toronto Law Journal
Vand L Rev	Vanderbilt Law Review
Vill L Rev	Villanova Law Review
Virg L Rev	Virginia Law Review
W & M L Rev	William and Mary Law Review
Wis L Rev	Wisconsin Law Review
Yale LJ	Yale Law Journal

1 What is jurisprudence about?

Jurisprudence is a ragbag. Into it are cast all kinds of general speculations about the law. What is it for? What does it achieve? Should we
value it? How is it to be improved? Is it dispensable? Who makes it?
Where do we find it? What is its relation to morality, to justice, to
politics, to social practices, or to naked force? Should we obey it?
Whom does it serve? These are the questions of which general jurisprudence is comprised. They can be ignored, but they will not go
away.

In his daily round, the legal practitioner can usually push aside
such questions together with the office cat. But now and then they will
jump on his desk. Here is client Jones, storming in with some story
about his neighbour's appalling behaviour.

—Yes, well, we might try to take out an injunction – though it's
not certain that what he did amounts to what the law regards as a
nuisance.
—Not certain! Can't you look it up?
—The law isn't something you just look up.
—What have you got all those books for then?
—They help ... anyway, we'll have to convince the county court
judge that your neighbour was acting unreasonably.
—I know the judge. A sound man! He'll agree with me.
—But he's got to apply the law. It's not just a question of the
particular judge – or, at least ... you may be sure that you're in the
right, but we're not here concerned with questions of abstract
justice.
—What sort of justice, then?
—Look, I don't think you'll be entitled to legal aid, so you must
decide ...
—I know, the law's up for sale, unless some political do-gooder
has decided you're poor enough to have it on a plate. You'll be
asking me next: 'How much are your principles worth?' The law's
supposed to protect people like me against people like him.
—No it isn't. It is supposed to do equal justice to all.
—But you just said ...

1

—This sort of discussion is all very well, Mr Jones, and outside office hours I'd be glad to pursue it. Right now, we have to decide on your best course of action.

—I know what I'm going to do. I'll let down the tyres on that great monstrosity he parks outside.

—You can't do that, it's illegal!

—Why should I be the only one to obey the law? Anyway, I can't see the police bothering with a thing like that and he's not likely to waste his time coming to see someone like you.

—That's not the point. Just because you think your neighbour has been antisocial, that's no reason for you to be it too.

—So now you're preaching!

It is sometimes said that the justification for teaching jurisprudence to law students is that it will make them better lawyers. I have disagreed with this view, at least so far as general jurisprudence is concerned. People acquire those technical skills of legal reasoning and legal argumentation which make up the concept of 'good lawyer' by immersing themselves in substantive legal subjects. Jurisprudence has to do, not with the lawyer's role as a technician, but with any need he may feel to give a good account of his life's work – either to fellow citizens, or to himself, or to any gods there be. What is it that is so special about legal reasoning as against any other kind of reasoning? (see chapter 15, below). Does the lawyer contribute to the maintenance of the rule of law? If so, is the rule of law such a worthwhile ideal anyway? (see chapter 11, below). Does the lawyer's role vary from one kind of society to another? (see chapter 19, below). Of course, any lawyer may rest his case at the bar of conscience on his technique alone, and assert that it requires no justification. I recently heard a New York lawyer interviewed about his practice in advising suspected Mafia families, and that is what he did: 'I just do a job, like a surgeon.' Is that enough? Surgeons might not be flattered.

My view about good lawyers being those who have acquired special skills may be old-fashioned. A 'progressive' law teacher would insist that awareness of the social implications of law is of the essence of proper legal training. Whether for his craft or for his well-being as an informed citizen, we can all agree that a lawyer should be familiar with the social dimensions of law. But what are they? What does it mean to say that a thing like 'law' has a 'social context'? (see chapter 18, below). It is commonly urged that the lawyer should not be too parochial. He should not assume that the law of the modern state is the only kind of law. Why not? (see chapter 17, below).

The won't-go-away questions are not and should not be the lawyer's preserve. Everyone has a right to ask whether the ideal of the rule of law has value; whether there is any moral duty to obey the law (see chapter 16, below); whether the law ought to diminish our liberty for our own physical or moral good (see chapter 10, below); what it is, if anything, that justifies the institution of punishment (see chapter 5, below). 'Out of office hours', we all stand on the same (usually shakey) ground when we debate the merits of proposed legislation in terms of the public good (see chapter 4, below), or of justice (see chapter 20, below). By 'we' I mean lawyers and non-lawyers. It may be that moral and political philosophers are better informed. Jurisprudence has to entrench upon these disciplines at many points, as well as upon those of social and political theory. It is a scavenger, as well as a ragbag; having no perimeter to its field of inquiry, save that what is studied must have a bearing on some general speculation about law.

If jurisprudence has a heartland all its own, it is legal theory. Much discussion about the moral claims of the law, and the moral claims on the law, takes the concept of law itself for granted. Yet, answers to such questions may turn on what picture of law we have. Legal theory asks: What is the nature of law (everywhere, or just in the modern state)? Some would claim that this question deserves an answer in and for itself. For others, the question is important but subsidiary – when we have defined law, we can describe its functions and its values; or, we should choose between competing definitions of law by reference to the functions we believe it has or the values we wish it to serve. Writers make different assumptions about the proper relationship of legal theory to issues of legal philosophy – that is, between an investigation of the nature of law and a discussion of the value implications of law. For Bentham and Austin, law should be defined in terms of political facts, so that it may be laid bare for criticism in terms of utility (see chapter 3, below). For Hart, the diverse social functions of the law must be incorporated into our conception of law, so that any judgments we make about it are not deflected by a distorting mirror (see chapter 9, below). For Kelsen, pure information about legal prescriptions must be separated from intrusive value judgments of all kinds (see chapter 6, below). Despite the obscurities of his esoteric language, Kelsen is the true friend of the practitioner who wants to be called on to describe the law and nothing but the law *in office hours*. For the natural lawyers and for Fuller and for Dworkin – each in their very different ways – such a practitioner cannot be satisfied. What 'the law is' is so intimately connected with what, morally speaking, 'the law ought to be', that our picture of it must include some conception of moral truth (see chapters 2, 11 and 14, below). For the 'realist', all the pictures of law we have are illusions. We must reject them in the interests both of truth and of proper shouldering of the burden of subjective valuations (see chapter 8, below).

I have expressed the controversial opinion that general jurisprudence is not a necessary part of the training of a lawyer *qua* lawyer – it being, as I think, concerned with the more important matter of the training of the lawyer *qua* citizen and of the citizen *qua* legal critic. 'Particular jurisprudence' may, however, bear more directly on the professional lawyer's concerns. General jurisprudence deals with speculations about the law; particular jurisprudence, with speculations about particular legal concepts. Every lawyer has from time to time to analyse terms of art appearing in legal materials. When is a concept employed in the law fit for jurisprudential analysis as distinct from ordinary legal elucidation? I suggest that no line is to be drawn. There is a continuum from very concrete questions – like, what does this word mean in the context of this statute? – to very general questions – like, what is the essence of a legal right? Roughly, particular jurisprudence concerns itself with terms which are common both to different systems of law and to different branches of law. 'Base fee' is not such a concept, not because it is not difficult, but because it is peculiar to the common law. 'Rape' is not such a concept, because though it appears in all systems, it is peculiar to criminal law. Particular jurisprudence fastens on terms which are inter-branch and inter-systemic – like right, duty, possession, person and so on. Opinions vary as to the value of such analyses for the practising lawyer, but they were certainly intended to assist him (see chapter 7, below).

The two concepts investigated by particular jurisprudence which have the best claim to the attention of the practising lawyer – as indeed to that of the political scientist – are those of 'precedent' and 'legislative intention'. All modern legal systems have to deal with statutory interpretation and have some notion of precedent. The investigation of the version of these concepts employed by any particular system turns out to involve a special mixture of constitutional and conceptual issues (see chapters 12 and 13, below). That will not be news to anyone who has followed recent controversies in the United Kingdom about the law on picketing, which have forced onto the television screen those hardy old questions, of what it means to 'give effect to Parliament's intention', or what it means to be 'bound' by a decision of the House of Lords.

All these questions, then, are what jurisprudence is about. Whether the word 'jurisprudence' is a good baggage label for them matters not at all. Sometimes this word is used as a heavy word for the study or knowledge of the law. There was a time when it was used in England to stand merely for the analysis of legal concepts. In French, 'la jurisprudence' signifies what we call case law; and 'théorie générale du droit' covers much of the same ground as what is here called jurisprudence. I believe that use of 'jurisprudence' to stand for general speculations of all kinds about the law is now fairly common in modern English usage; that 'legal theory' is used to cover inquiries into the nature of law; and that 'legal philosophy' means that branch of practical philosophy which investigates the value implications of describing something as 'legal'. Whether labels matter when it comes to the word 'law' itself – a question which is highly controversial in the areas of 'primitive law' and 'living law' (see chapters 17 and 18, below) – it is surely the case that labels do not matter in assigning the proper fields for 'jurisprudence', 'legal theory' and 'legal philosophy'. It is the won't-go-away questions which count.

This book does not break up the subject according to a systematic plan. That would be impossible without prejudging crucial questions – such as whether 'the relations of law to morality' is a different question from 'the nature of law'. Some chapters deal with particular questions (like the duty to obey the law), some with topics involving clusters of questions (like statutory interpretation), some with schools of thought (like the historical school), and some with individual theorists. My object is to introduce the reader to a bill of fare. On controversial matters, I have tried to state both sides of a question leaving it to the reader to provide an answer; but one cannot always disguise one's own view. I hope at least to have exemplified how jurists argue so that, if he wants to, the reader can join in. Welcome to the feast.

2 Natural law

One facet of common discourse assumes a correlation between 'good' and 'what comes naturally'. Parental affection, heterosexual love, support for aged kin and comradely interdependence are natural and therefore good. That which ignores or distorts human nature is bad. Lawyers, on occasion, have been prepared to listen to such 'naturalistic' arguments, especially where an issue is not covered by the arguments from authority with which lawyers are more familiar. In a case of first impression in 1970, an English judge held that a 'marriage' between a man and a person who had undergone a 'sex change' was a nullity since it could not involve the natural, biologically-determined consequences of marriage.

> 'Since marriage is essentially a relationship between man and woman, the validity of the marriage in this case depends, in my judgment, upon whether the respondent is or is not a woman ... Having regard to the essentially heterosexual character of the relationship which is called marriage, the criteria must, in my judgment, be biological, for even the most extreme degree of transsexualism in a male or the most severe hormonal imbalance which can exist in a person with male chromosomes, male gonads and male genitalia cannot reproduce a person who is naturally capable of performing the essential role of a woman in marriage.'[1]

In another case of first impression in 1976, an injunction was issued to prevent the parents of a mentally defective girl from having her sterilised, as this would take away the child's fundamental human right to reproduce.[2] Conversely, in 1978 an injunction was refused to a husband to prevent his wife having an abortion on the ground that the courts can only enforce rights already recognised by positive law and neither an unborn foetus nor a father-to-be has any such right.[3] The jurists who developed the law of the Roman empire made frequent references to the nature of the case as a basis for settling matters

1 *Corbett v Corbett* [1971] P 83 at 106 per Ormerod J.
2 *Re D* [1976] Fam 185.
3 *Paton v British Pregnancy Advisory Service Trustees* [1979] QB 276.

not covered by authority. The compilers of the *Corpus Juris* of the emperor Justinian in 533 AD employed the adjective *naturalis* as a classificatory peg, distinguishing 'natural' obligations and transactions from their counterparts in the *Ius Civile*. Parallel with, and sometimes infusing, these lawyer-like references to the natural, the philosophy of the ancient world had evolved a conception of natural law.

The classical doctrine of natural law, though it would support the naturalistic arguments and classifications of the lawyers, has much more far-reaching implications. It speaks of a law of nature which has characteristics quite different from those of the ordinary laws familiar to practitioners. First, it is universal and immutable. In consequence, it is available at all times and in all places for those whose office it is to enact or develop law. In other words, it is one conception of 'justice', in the sense in which justice stands for the righting of wrongs and the proper distribution of benefits and burdens within a political community. Secondly, it is a 'higher' law. It has a relationship of superiority towards laws promulgated by political authorities. This means that it determines whether ordinary laws are morally binding on subjects. These first two characteristics emphasise the 'legal' quality of natural law. If it were merely a system of private ethics, it would not *eo ipse* be mete for enactment by legislatures and judges and would not set criteria for obedience. Thirdly, it is discoverable by reason. Herein lies the 'natural' quality of natural law. The stoics, the school which elaborated the doctrine, viewed all things, including man, as having natural essences or ends. The reflective intellect possessed direct knowledge of these qualities from which conclusions might be drawn, by rational steps, about what justice requires. Aristotle had claimed that it was natural to man to be a member of a *polis* – often crudely paraphrased as the view that man is a 'political animal' or 'social animal'. That being so, his nature requires rules setting up political organisations and imposing mutual forbearances for the common good.

The most famous summary of the classical natural law doctrine is the following statement of the stoic position given by Cicero in the first century BC.

'True law is right reason in agreement with Nature; it is of universal application, unchanging and everlasting; it summons to duty by its commands, and averts from wrong-doing by its prohibitions. And it does not lay its commands or prohibitions upon good men in vain, though neither have any effect on the wicked. It is a sin to try to alter this law, nor is it allowable to attempt to repeal any part of it, and it is impossible to abolish it entirely. We cannot be freed from its obligations by Senate or People, and we need not look outside ourselves for an expounder or interpreter of it. And there will not be different laws at Rome and at Athens, or different laws now and in the future, but one eternal and unchangeable law will be valid for all nations and for all times, and there will be one master and one ruler, that is, God, over us all, for He is the author of this law, its promulgator, and its enforcing judge.'[4]

Natural law was eventually prayed in aid by the Christian church. The New Testament spoke of divine grace and individual redemption, but was rather thin on political blue-prints. Some of the fathers of the church were pessimistic about human institutions. Given the sinful condition of man since the fall, his political arrangements were likely to be defective. St Augustine (354–430) asked rhetorically: 'What are states without justice but robber-bands enlarged?'[5] Medieval scholars were more optimistic. The fall had not taken away man's ability to appreciate his own good, and to reason therefrom to the good society. The Roman Catholic church eventually adopted the views of the Dominican jurist St Thomas Aquinas (1225–1274). Aquinas synthesised Christian revelation with the pre-Christian doctrine of natural law. His legal theory encompasses four types of law. 'Eternal law' comprises God-given rules governing all creation. 'Natural law' is that segment of eternal law which is discoverable through the special process of reasoning mapped out by the pagan authors – intuitions of the natural and deductions drawn therefrom. 'Divine law' has been revealed in Scripture. 'Human law' consists of rules, supportable by reason, but articulated by human authorities for the common good. As to the interrelation between these different types of law, two crucial propositions stand out in Thomist philosophy. First, human laws derive their legal quality, their power to bind in conscience, from natural law. Man's natural end being social, a community prescription which is, in reason, directed to the common good has, by nature, the quality of law. In some instances, the content of law is deducible from first principles of natural law; for the rest, the legislator has the freedom of an architect. Secondly, any purported law which is in conflict with natural or divine law is a mere corruption of law and so not binding by virtue of its own legal quality; nevertheless, even if an enactment is contrary to natural law and so 'unjust', obedience may still be proper to avoid bad example or civil disturbance.

---

4 *De Republica* III, xxii, 33.
5 *Confessiones* IV.

'But in human affairs a thing is said to be just when it accords aright with the rule of reason: and ... the first rule of reason is the natural law. Thus all humanly enacted laws are in accord with reason to the extent that they derive from the natural law. And if a human law is at variance in any particular with the natural law, it is no longer legal, but rather a corruption of law.

But it should be noted that there are two ways in which anything may derive from natural law. First, as a conclusion from more general principles. Secondly, as a determination of certain general features. The former is similar to the method of the sciences in which demonstrative conclusions are drawn from first principles. The second way is like to that of the arts in which some common form is determined to a particular instance: as, for example, when an architect, starting from the general idea of a house, then goes on to design the particular plan of this or that house ...

Man is bound to obey secular Rulers to the extent that the order of justice requires. For this reason if such rulers have no just title to power, but have usurped it, or if they command things to be done which are unjust, their subjects are not obliged to obey them; except, perhaps, in certain special cases when it is a matter of avoiding scandal or some particular danger.'[6]

Aquinas' theory gives political rulers quite a lot of room for manoeuvre. So long as what they lay down is guided by a reasoned assessment of the common good, it has the power to bind in conscience. Only the first principles of natural law – such as 'do harm to no man' – are immutable. Specific deductions from first principles might vary. Furthermore, natural law could be added to. Thus, although by nature all men were equally free and all things were held in common, positive law could introduce the legal concepts of slavery and private property. The effect of the theory is to clothe all legislation with presumptive moral status; and even where positive law conflicted with natural law, compliance might still be morally required.

As a topic in the history of ideas (in the fields of ethics and of political and legal philosophy), there can be no doubt of the importance of the doctrine of natural law. It is through the medium of this doctrine that the Roman Catholic church claims to be able to speak authoritatively on ethical questions to all men. In 1968, Pope Paul VI appealed to it as support for the view that artificial means of birth control are not allowable.

'The Church, calling men back to the observance of the norms of natural law, as interpreted by her constant doctrine, teaches that

6 *Selected Political Writings* (D'Entreves (ed)) pp. 121, 179.

each and every marriage act must remain open to the transmission of life ...

We believe that the men of our day are particularly capable of seizing the deeply reasonable and human character of this fundamental principle.[7]

So far as political philosophy is concerned, the Thomist version of natural law is seen as conservative compared with the revolutionary implications to which the doctrine later gave rise. Aquinas showed how the bindingness of positive law actually derived from natural law, so long as flexible notions like the rationally-conceived common good were not overstepped; and he thus threw over positive law a halo of moral sanctity. Later writers, using the same process of reasoning from nature, evolved the conception of natural rights, infringement of which entitled citizens to revolt. The American colonists in 1776 justified their overthrow of British rule on the ground that the colonial government had impaired rights to 'life, liberty and the pursuit of happiness', it being 'self-evident' that man was endowed with such rights. The French National Assembly in 1789 made a similar appeal to 'simple and indisputable' principles, which showed that men had natural rights to 'liberty, property, security and resistance to oppression'. Such rights were evident to reason, taking the nature of man as its starting-point. Intermingled with such naturalistic reasoning was 'contractarian' reasoning, that is, the view that political rights and obligations could be conceived of in terms of a social contract. But the two modes of philosophising must be distinguished, since writers who shared the concept of social contract took very different views of the significance of 'nature'. Thomas Hobbes (1588–1679) rejected the view that there could be some supra-state concept of justice based on man's natural qualities. On the contrary, he argued, in the state of nature the life of man is 'solitary, poor, nasty, brutish, and short'.[8] By the social contract, citizens surrendered natural liberty, and claims to just treatment must be based on the contract. John Locke (1632–1704) on the other hand, argued that there were natural rights which survived the social contract, and failure to protect them was a ground on which governments could be changed. The most complex amalgam of contract and nature is that of Jean-Jacques Rousseau (1712–1778). For him there were natural rights which nothing could take away; but, provided the social contract invested the 'general will' with all legislative power, there could be no question of positive law entrenching on rights. The general will subsumed all wills, so that every man willed what the law

7 *Humanae Vitae* paras. 11 and 12.
8 *Leviathan* ch 13.

stipulated – even if, on occasion, someone had to be 'forced to be free'. A natural rights argument as such, like a natural law argument, bases its claims about what ought to be done by governments on the nature of man. A contractarian argument, as such, bases such claims on what citizens did (or notionally would) agree to. These are rival conceptions of justice. The most celebrated modern contractarian theory of justice, that of Professor Rawls, is considered in chapter 20, below.

So far as legal philosophy is concerned, academic jurists up to the end of the eighteenth century commonly incorporated the doctrine of natural law. Generally, however, this was no more than a gloss without detailed implications, as it is in the *Corpus Juris* of Justinian. Sir William Blackstone (1723–1780) begins his *Commentaries on the Laws of England* with an assertion of all the leading tenets of the classical doctrine – natural law willed by God and discoverable by reason; positive law deriving its binding force from natural law; positive law in conflict with natural law being a nullity; and adds in the concept of social contract for good measure. Yet this acceptance of natural law had little effect on his detailed exposition of English law. On the European continent, however, whole expository statements of law purported to be based on natural law. This was of particular importance in the area of what we now call 'public international law'. Civilian academic lawyers were expounders of Roman law. In the sphere of private law, there were authoritative texts enough in the *Corpus Juris* and the commentaries written upon it to make appeals direct to naturalistic reason unnecessary – although the texts themselves contained such references. But the emergence of comity between sovereign and equal states gave renaissance lawyers a new problem. How could law, not made by princes, bind princes among themselves? The answer was to redeploy the classical Roman concept of *Ius Gentium*. This originally referred to the law which Roman authorities enforced in dealings between citizens and foreigners, or between foreigners, as opposed to the *Ius Civile* which was applicable between citizens. It now came to cover relations of war and peace, treaty-making and allegiance, and so on. But it is one thing to find a label, from where was to come the content? Only from natural law, that is, from propositions which, it seemed to these authors, no one in reason could dispute. In this way writers like Grotius (1583–1645) and Puffendorf (1632–1694) discovered or – if naturalistic arguments are inappropriate – created new law for a new era. Natural law was increasingly secularised, in that its rational (as distinct from re-vealed) basis was stressed. Even if God did not exist, Grotius said, natural law would have the same content; and just as God cannot cause that two times two shall not be four, so he cannot cause the intrinsically evil to be not evil.

Granted its historical importance, what is twentieth-century man to make of the classical doctrine of natural law? One's answer to that depends, in the first instance, on what one makes of two assertions about the relation of law to morality which together led to the eclipse of natural law thinking during the nineteenth century, and dissatisfaction with which has led, in some quarters, to its recent revival. These assertions generally go under the names of 'noncognitivism' and 'legal positivism'.

Noncognitivism is the view that there is no rational procedure by which we can objectively know what is morally right and wrong. We cannot derive an 'ought' from an 'is'. No amount of information about the facts of the world or of human nature provides proof that anything ought to be done or not done. In the English-speaking world, the paternity of this doctrine is generally attributed to the Scottish philosopher, David Hume (1711–1776). In his *Treatise of Human Nature*, first published in 1739, he wrote:

'In every system of morality, which I have hitherto met with, I have always remark'd, that the author proceeds for some time in the ordinary way of reasoning, and establishes the being of a God, or makes observations concerning human affairs; when of a sudden I am surpriz'd to find, that instead of the usual copulations of propositions, *is*, and *is not*, I meet with no proposition that is not connected with an *ought*, or an *ought not*. This change is imperceptible; but is, however, of the last consequence. For as this *ought*, or *ought not*, expresses some new relation or affirmation, 'tis necessary that it shou'd be observ'd and explain'd; and at the same time that a reason should be given, for what seems altogether inconceivable, how this new relation can be a deduction from others, which are entirely different from it. But as authors do not commonly use this precaution, I shall presume to recommend it to the readers; and am persuaded, that this small attention wou'd subvert all the vulgar systems of morality, and let us see, that the distinction of vice and virtue is not founded merely on the relations of objects nor is perceiv'd by reason'.[9]

For many jurists, Hume's point is a knock-down argument against all forms of natural law thinking; for does it not show that reason can tell us nothing about justice or political obligation? It must, however, be borne in mind that, according to the standard interpretation of the passage just quoted, Hume was making only a logical point – an assertion about the logically necessary relationship between

9 *A Treatise of Human Nature* p. 521.

propositions. It merely deprives natural lawyers of that most revered of philosophic weapons, the deductive syllogism.

A syllogism comprises three elements: a major premise, say, 'all men are mortal'; a minor premise, 'Socrates is a man'; and a conclusion, 'Socrates is mortal'. Given the premises, one cannot deny the conclusion without self-contradiction. Therefore, the conclusion follows, with logical necessity, from the premises. Since Hume, few would be prepared to defend the following syllogism: 'all animals rear their young'; 'men are animals'; 'therefore, men *ought* to rear their young'. Granted the first two steps, the conclusion does not follow for the simple reason that it contains a copula not contained in the premises, namely, the 'ought'. Thus, even if we accept all that Aristotle said about man's social nature as factually correct, it does not follow, logically, that he is under any kind of obligation to other members of his community. If we grant that, biologically, the primary function of sexual relations is begetting of offspring, it does not follow, logically, that artificial means of contraception are morally wrong.

Two matters must be taken into account in order to set Hume's point in a proper relationship to the whole field of human reasoning. First, if syllogistic, deductive demonstration is the only kind of acceptable 'proof', then one has to be sceptical, as Hume was, about all the assertions of natural science. Not only do *ought*-assertions not follow from *is*-assertions, but no proposition about the future follows from any number of propositions about the past. From the fact that the sun has always risen in the east, it does not follow as a matter of logical necessity, that it will do so tomorrow. Only mathematical deductions from definitional axioms meet the test of logical necessity. Philosophers have had to find other, nonsyllogistic criteria of proof to support the rationality of natural science. Secondly, and more importantly for our assessment of the claims of natural law, if those engaged in a discussion can begin by agreeing on some *ought*-proposition as major premise, then, given factual propositions as minor premises, they can go on to deduce *ought*-conclusions. If I say that killing the innocent is wrong and you disagree, we can get no further. But if we both accept the major premise, we may make progress. Perhaps there are normative premises about which all those who ever debate do agree – about the dignity of man requiring that all be provided with a minimum of security, clothing, food, freedom of self-expression and so on. Only if there are not does Hume's *is/ought* cleavage scupper natural law in port. Hume himself does not appear to have been a subscriber to the extreme relativism of later writers who contend that all our moral opinions are dependent on our personal experience and circumstances. His remark about reason being 'the slave of the passions' is sometimes cited in support of 'emotivism', the view that normative discourse is nothing more than an expression of feelings, equivalent to cries of 'ouch'. But it may have meant no more than that our emotions – which could be universally shared emotions – must give us the normative premises from which reasoning may then proceed.

'Tho' the rules of justice be *artificial*, they are not *arbitrary*. Nor is the expression improper to call them *Laws of Nature*; if by natural we understand what is common to any species, or even if we confine it to mean what is inseparable from the species.'[10]

In his recent comprehensive restatement of natural law theory, J. M. Finnis denies that the true classical doctrine ever purported to derive 'ought' from 'is'. He concedes that the stoic doctrine, renaissance theorists and indeed Catholic writers on natural law down almost to the present day, did claim to draw normative inferences from nature and in that sense confused fact and value. But he argues that this was not true of Aristotle – who, on the contrary, clearly differentiated between 'speculative reason' (reasoning about what is the case) and 'practical reason' (reasoning about what ought to be done); and it was not true of Aquinas – whose ethical theory was misunderstood by later writers. Basing himself primarily upon his interpretation of Aquinas, Finnis claims that the 'classical doctrine' takes as its first step towards normative conclusions, not some observation of human or other nature, but a reflective grasp of what is self-evidently good for men.

'When discerning what is good ... intelligence is operating in a different way, yielding a different logic, from when it is discerning what is the case (historically, scientifically, or metaphysically); but there is no good reason for asserting that the latter operations of intelligence are more rational than the former ...

The basic forms of good grasped by practical understanding are what is good for human beings with the nature they have. Aquinas considers that practical reasoning begins not by understanding this nature from the outside, as it were, by way of psychological, anthropological, or metaphysical observations and judgments defining human nature, but by experiencing one's nature, so to speak, from the inside, in the form of one's inclinations. But again, there is no process of inference. One does not judge that 'I have (or everybody has) an inclination to find out about things' and then infer that therefore 'knowledge is a good to be pursued'. Rather, by a simple act of non-inferential understanding one grasps that the

10 *A Treatise of Human Nature* p. 536.

object of the inclination which one experiences is an instance of a general form of good, for oneself (and others like one).'[11]

Expanding and clarifying Aquinas' approach, Finnis proceeds to set out his own theory of natural law. He argues that there are certain 'basic forms of human flourishing' which are in one way or another used by everyone who considers what to do, however unsound his conclusions. These include 'life', 'knowledge', 'play', 'aesthetic experience', 'friendship', 'practical reasonableness', and 'religion'. There are, secondly, a set of 'basic methodological requirements' of practical reasonableness which, taken together, provide the criteria for distinguishing ways of acting that are morally right or wrong. These include 'pursuit of goods', 'a coherent plan of life', 'no arbitrary preferences amongst values', 'no arbitrary preferences amongst persons', 'detachment and commitment', 'the (limited) relevance of consequences', 'respect for every basic value in every act', 'the requirements of the common good', and 'following one's conscience'. These basic goods and methodological requirements together constitute the universal and unchanging principles of natural law. Because of them, objective knowledge of morality is possible. 'Justice' consists of the concrete implications of the requirement to foster the 'common good' (in the sense of the set of conditions which enable the members of a community to realise the basic values for themselves and to attain any other reasonable objectives they may have). People may reasonably differ as to details, and the justice of arrangements varies with circumstances. Nevertheless, Finnis argues, the basic goods and methodological requirements are sufficiently precise to rule out many kinds of injustice. In their light one can arrive at certain absolute duties, with correlative absolute natural (human) rights – rights not to be tortured, not to have one's life taken directly as a means to any further end, not to be positively lied to (in situations in which factual communication is reasonably expected), not to be condemned on knowingly false charges, not to be deprived of one's procreative capacity; and the right to be taken into respectful consideration in any assessment of what the common good requires.

Finnis contends that most jurists have misunderstood classical natural law doctrine. It appealed, not to inferences drawn from our nature, but to judgments made with our nature 'from the inside'. One may wonder what difference this makes to practical reasoning. When we reflect on our own and other people's inclinations in order to gain self-evident knowledge about universal goods, are not assumptions of fact about human nature inevitably going to form part of the content

11 *Natural Law and Natural Rights* p. 34.

of the reflection? Perhaps the Thomist writers of the seventeenth century and afterwards, although they changed Aquinas' conceptual structure, were nevertheless drawing out the implications of his theory. Finnis himself appeals to facts of human experience and psychology when working out the requirements of 'practical reasonableness'. He gives two reasons for maintaining that a regime of private ownership (including of means of production) is in most times and places a requirement of justice. The first is the good of 'personal autonomy in community'. The second is the rule of human experience that resources are more productively exploited by private than by public enterprise. He argues that 'public morality' limitations on the exercise of rights are justified in the light of psychological facts about the egotistic nature of sexual drives. On the general question of specifying and demarcating rights, he says:

'There is, I think, no alternative but to hold in one's mind's eye some pattern, or range of patterns, of human character, conduct, and interaction in community, and then to choose such specification of rights as tends to favour that pattern, or range of patterns.'[12]

Finnis stresses that our knowledge of self-evident human goods is not innate. It comes to us, to all of us, only if we have had sufficient experience and are willing to engage in reasoning reflection. It may be that such reflection must embrace an indissoluble mixture of what human beings are like and what is good for them – at least if it is to yield principles sufficiently concrete to be useful guides to moral deliberation. Even if this process does affront the *is/ought* cleavage, that only shows that we are not dealing with logical necessities. We can still call the process 'reasoning'. If it will yield basic principles to which all who engage in it must reasonably assent, then there is a natural system of morality.

The second fundamental assault on natural law doctrine is 'legal positivism'. This expression is used in many ways, but most of its adherents would at least subscribe to the following two propositions. First, no element of moral value enters into the definition of law. Secondly, legal provisions are identified by empirically-observable criteria, such as legislation, decided cases and custom. Their contention is that there is no law but positive law, and therefore no such thing as 'natural law'. Whether or not there are criteria of morality or justice by which we can assess the merits of positive law, what law is is one thing, its goodness or badness another.

12 *Natural Law and Natural Rights* p. 219.

Legal positivists have appealed to two features of legal practice in support of their anti-natural law stance, one empirical, and one programmatic. When practising lawyers describe the law to clients, they do not give, and would not be thanked for giving, their views about what the law ought to be. They look up the books, and from them state what the law is. As to programmes of reform, we need to know what the law is before we can formulate ways of changing it. If, in stating the law, we base our reasoning on inferences from morality rather than on known source materials, we may smuggle in controversial moral claims. Better to set out the law as it is, and then go on to give our reasons why the law is right or in what ways it should be changed. The issues of justice and of the morally-binding nature of positive law raise questions as to which there is no specifically juristic answer. Lawyers, *qua* lawyers, have nothing special to say about them; so these issues should not be presented in the guise of a supposed higher law.

Bentham, the founder of English legal positivism, appealed in just this way to legal practice when refuting the natural law theory espoused by Blackstone. By insisting that human law derives its validity from natural law, Blackstone merely warded off criticism of the law. If the law could not be shown to conflict with natural law, it was valid. Although Blackstone repeated the classical view that laws contrary to natural law are a nullity, he gave no example of any such purported enactment in England, but only the hypothetical example of a law which allowed or enjoined us to commit murder. On this frail example, Bentham turned the heavy guns of his characteristic irony.

'Murder is *killing* under certain *circumstances.*—Is the human law then to be allowed to define, *in denier resort*, what shall be those *circumstances*, or is it not? If yes, the case of a "human law allowing or enjoining us to commit it", is a case that is not so much as supposable: if *no*, adieu to all human laws: to the fire with our Statutes at large, our Reports, our Institutes, and all that we have hitherto been used to call our law books; our law books, the only law books we can be safe in trusting to, are Puffendorf and the Bible.'[13]

The answer of natural lawyers to the positivists runs as follows. Issues of justice and of the duty to obey cannot be separated from legal science in the way positivists suggest. When we describe the law on many questions, we have to refer to moral considerations. And this is not just a matter of filling in gaps. It is systematically part of the function of lawyers, and especially of judges, to answer two questions in one: 'What is the law?' and 'What does justice require?' Certainly,

13 *Fragment on Government* ch 4, para. 18, n. 1.

one distinguished English judge, Lord Denning, appears to believe
that 'justice' is the judge's prime concern, and that an admission that
law conflicts with it is a confession of defeat. A. L. Goodhart has
argued that there is a general coincidence between English law and
'the moral law'. However, he denied that this moral law was derivable
from general principles, calling it a 'pragmatic natural law'. Lord
Denning, too, appeals to no higher law. Perhaps he should?

What Bentham says about burning law books is a travesty. The
classical doctrine distinguished *mala in se*, like murder and theft,
where the principles of positive law are deduced from or founded on
objective moral principles; and *mala prohibita*, regulatory offences
which are more or less at the discretion of the legislature. In the case of
the latter, we clearly find the law in the positive sources; and even
with the former, matters of definition and penalty are left to positive
law. Dr Finnis argues that the central claim about positive law
deriving its legal quality from natural law is a support, not an under-
mining of positive law. He maintains that his theory of natural law
enables one to found both the reasonable claims, and the limits, of
authority on objective moral principles; for it can be rationally
demonstrated that the problems of 'coordination in community'
require legislative determination. Similarly (he argues) the principles
of the rule of law, discussed in chapter 11, below, can be shown to be
based on 'practical reasonableness'.

'The tradition of natural law theorizing is not concerned to minimize the range and determinacy of positive law or the general
sufficiency of positive sources as solvents of legal problems.

Rather, the concern of the tradition ... has been to show that the
act of "positing" law ... is an act which can and should be guided by
"moral" principles and rules; that those moral norms are a matter
of objective reasonableness, not of whim, convention, or mere
"decision"; and that those same moral norms justify (a) the very
institution of positive law, (b) the main institutions, techniques,
and modalities within that tradition (e.g. separation of powers),
and (c) the main institutions regulated and sustained by law (e.g.
government, contract, property, marriage, and criminal liability).
What truly characterizes the tradition is that it is not content
merely to observe the historical or sociological fact that "morality"
thus affects "law", but instead seeks to determine what the requirements of practical reasonableness really are, so as to afford a
rational basis for the activities of legislators, judges, and citizens.'[14]

14 *Natural Law and Natural Rights* p. 290.

Finnis also claims that the slogan '*lex iniusta non est lex*' has been misrepresented by critics of natural law doctrine. An unjust law is not a 'nullity', in the sense of being something one can totally disregard. It merely lacks, prima facie, the power to bind in conscience which laws usually possess; and there can be a moral duty to obey even unjust laws if not doing so might lead to the weakening of a legal system which is on the whole just. Arguments for and against a prima facie duty to obey the law are considered in chapter 16, below. It should be mentioned, however, that some advocates of natural law would give a much more robust interpretation to the nullity doctrine. According to this view, *lex iniusta non est lex* is not merely a guide to conscientious disobedience, but also a moral blue pencil for use by legal science. Where laws are (or were) sufficiently heinous, lawyers, *qua* lawyers, can disregard them. This view gained adherents as the direct consequence of the Nazi nightmare. In some of the decisions of German courts since the establishing of the Federal Republic, Nazi legislation has been declared invalid, inter alia, because it was incompatible with fundamental justice. A majority of the House of Lords has indicated that it would refuse to recognise a Nazi law depriving Jewish citizens of German nationality even though it passed the normal criteria of recognition specified in the English rules relating to conflict of laws simply because it was flagrantly unjust.[15] The doctrine proclaimed at the Nuremberg war trials – that superior orders constitute no defence to 'crimes against humanity' – can also be understood as moral blue pencil; although there was no explicit appeal to natural law.

I have suggested that, in considering the value of natural law doctrine to twentieth-century man, the arguments from noncognitivism and from legal positivism must be considered 'in the first instance'. Even if these attacks can be parried, it does not follow that one has arrived at a higher law. To some extent, what one calls 'natural law reasoning' is a matter of words. But since many different ways of circumventing the gulf between 'is' and 'ought' have been suggested, it seems unhelpful to call them all 'natural law'. The classical doctrine asks us to do it by drawing inferences from human nature or, if Finnis is right, by grasping self-evident truths with our human nature. One is moving quite a distance from the classical doctrine when what is described as 'natural law' are the purely formal characteristics which all legal systems are said to possess – Stammler's conception of natural law with a changing content. And it can only lead to confusion to use the term 'natural law' to embrace either contractarian conceptions of justice, or psychologically-grounded utilitarianism, or 'scientific' Marxism, even though they all

15 *Oppenheimer v Cattermole* [1976] AC 249.

support normative claims by reference to the 'facts' of human experience.

The doctrine need not be accepted even by one who rejects both the propositions which I have attributed to legal positivism. Professor Dworkin, for example, does believe that morality enters into the definition of law, and denies that law can be separately identified by criteria of pedigree (see chapter 14, below). Those who classify all jurists as either positivists or natural lawyers would therefore place him in the latter category. But he reasons to normative moral/legal conclusions, not from nature, but from a conception of equality, without appeal to higher law.

Conversely, Professor Hart (an avowed positivist) claims to find useful work for the label 'natural law'. He argues against the natural law implications of the post-Nazi experience, contending that the best way to deal with 'offenders' who claim the shield of Nazi 'law' is frankly to enact retrospective legislation. He believes that the statement of law and its criticism should not be confused. However, he finds a 'core of good sense' in the natural law doctrine.

> 'For it is a truth of some importance that for the adequate description not only of law but of many other social institutions, a place must be reserved, besides definitions and ordinary statements of fact, for a third category of statements: those the truth of which is contingent on human beings and the world they live in retaining the salient characteristics which they have.'[16]

The most important characteristic is that men wish to survive. They are not members of suicide clubs. That supplies the 'ought' of a major premise. The minor premises come from certain indisputable observations ('truisms') about man and the world. First, men are mutually vulnerable. Second, unlike nation states, they are approximately equal in their abilities to help and harm each other. Third, they have limited altruism, being neither angels nor devils. Fourth, they live in a world with limited resources. Fifth, they suffer from weakness of intellect and will which means that achievement of their aims requires a special coordination of their activities. On the basis of these universal truths, Hart concludes that all human societies have, and must necessarily have, rules restricting violence, some property system which entails rules restricting theft, and some system of promising which entails rules restricting deceit. These are the 'minimum content of natural law'.

Is the 'natural law' label appropriately employed in this context? If all societies have these rules, then no society can ever be called unjust

16 *The Concept of Law* p. 195.

and no government legitimately resisted for not having them. The only normative mileage one could make out of this minimum content would be an argument against dispensing with social organisation altogether, a refutation of some forms of anarchism. The minimum content does not appear to require that the exercise of force be politically centralised. It is consistent with a system of rules that protects only one group (by institutionalising slavery or racial oppression); and with any kind of property regime, public or private – although not with the final stage envisaged by Marxist theory, in which there would be production to abundance and so no restrictions on any use of material things (see chapter 19, below). It has to be consistent with much variation in social organisation in order for its claim to descriptive universality to be true. One might call it a 'sociological' conception of natural law. Sociology provides generalisations based on proven information. The minimum content gives us generalisations based on 'truisms', facts so obvious that they need no proof. If a Martian came to earth, we might take him to one side and begin his sociological education as follows: 'Now I know that you Martian chaps are all armour-plated crabs and so couldn't hurt each other if you tried, and also that you are so rational and benevolent that you can plan your lives without cooperative institutions, and that you only eat red mud of which you have an inexhaustible supply. Things are, otherwise with us.'

There may be a lot to be said for sociology-for-Martians, precisely because it tells us humans basic truths our dreamers sometimes forget. But the classical doctrine of natural law goes much further. It requires us to look at man and his world in as much detail as we can, and to apply to the information we have a special kind of moral reasoning which we all share. If we do that, so the doctrine contends, we will arrive at concepts of man and of communities (national and international), which will provide a consistent critical touchstone for all political arrangements including laws. That system of justice arrived at in that way the doctrine calls 'natural law'. It is 'natural' by virtue of the sort of reasoning which reveals it. It is a higher 'law', both because it provides criteria of justice for legislatures and judges, and also because it tells us when we are morally required to obey the prescriptions of political superiors and when we are not. Whether there is such a system the reader must decide.

Bibliography

Aquinas St T.	*Selected Political Writings* (D'Entreves (ed), Dawson trans, 1959) pp. 103–180
Bentham J.	*A Fragment on Government* (Burns and Hart (eds), 1977)
Blackstone W.	*Commentaries on the Laws of England* (16th edn, 1825) vol I, intro., s. 2
Brown B. F.	'Natural Law: Dynamic Basis of Law and Morals in the Twentieth Century' (1957) 31 Tul L Rev 491
Buckland W. W.	*Some Reflections on Jurisprudence* (1945) chs 2–3
Chroust A. H.	'On the Nature of Natural Law' in Sayre (ed) *Interpretations of Modern Legal Philosophies* (1947)
Davitt T. E.	'Law as a Means to an End – Thomas Aquinas' (1960–61) 14 Vand L Rev 65
Denning Lord	*Due Process of Law* (1980) Pt 8
D'Entreves A. P.	*Natural Law* (2nd edn, 1970)
Finnis J. M.	*Natural Law and Natural Rights* (1980)
Friedmann W.	*Legal Theory* (5th edn, 1967) chs 7–17, 28, 30
Ginsburg M.	'Stammler's Philosophy of Law' in Jennings (ed) *Modern Theories of Law* (1933)
Goodhart A. L.	*English Law and the Moral Law* (1955) pp. 28–37
Haines C. G.	*The Revival of Natural Law Concepts* (1930)
Hall J.	*Foundations of Jurisprudence* (1973) chs 2–3, 5
Hart H. L. A.	*The Concept of Law* (1961) ch 9
Hook S. (ed)	*Law and Philosophy* (1964) Pt 2
Hume D.	*A Treatise of Human Nature* (Mossner (ed)) Book III
Jolowicz H. F.	*Lectures on Jurisprudence* (Jolowicz J. A.(ed), 1963) chs 2–5
Jones J. W.	*Historical Introduction to the Theory of Law* (1956) ch 4
Lloyd D.	*Introduction to Jurisprudence* (4th edn, 1979) ch 3
Locke J.	*Two Treatises of Government* (Laslett (ed), 2nd edn, 1970) Book II, ch 2
Lumb R. D.	'Natural Law and Legal Positivism' (1958–59) II JLE 503
Maine H. J. S.	*Ancient Law* (Pollock (ed), 1930) chs 3–4
Maritain J.	*The Rights of Man and Natural Law* (1954)
O'Connor D. J.	*Aquinas and Natural Law* (1967)
O'Meara J.	'Natural Law and Everyday Law' (1960) 5 NLF 83

Oppenheim F. E.	'The Natural Law Thesis' (1957) 51 Am PS Rev 41
Pollock F.	*Essays in the Law* (1922) ch 2
Richards D. A. J.	*The Moral Criticism of Law* (1977) ch 2
Ross A.	*On Law and Justice* (1958) chs 10–11
Samek R. A.	*The Legal Point of View* (1974) ch 11
Sklar J. N.	*Legalism* (1964) Pt 1
Stammler R.	*The Theory of Justice* (Husik trans, 1925)
Stone J.	*Human Law and Human Justice* (1965) chs 2–3, 6–7
Van Niekerk B.	'The Warning Voice from Heidelberg – the Life and Thought of Gustav Radbruch' (1973) 90 SALJ 234
Wild J. D.	*Plato's Modern Enemies and the Theory of Natural Law* (1953) chs 3–8
Wright R. A.	'Natural Law and International Law' in Sayre (ed) *Interpretations of Modern Legal Philosophies* (1947)

3 The command theory of law

We all know that from time to time the law makes demands of us. We may often think these demands reasonable; but sometimes we regard them as quirkish or arbitrary or even outrageous. Is there not then a difference between our perceptions of what the law requires, and our views as to what it would be reasonable to require? The assumption that there is such a difference, and the working out of the implications of the difference, have been the hallmarks of the theoretical tradition known as legal positivism. According to legal positivism, law is not some set of propositions derivable by reasoning from the nature of things, as the natural lawyers would argue. One version of this approach saw law as the commands of political superiors, of the state sovereign. This is the command theory of law.

The English founder of this theory of law was Jeremy Bentham (1748–1832). Bentham was a philosopher and reformer dedicated to the principle of utility: that every act or law should be judged, as to its goodness or badness, solely by reference to its consequences in terms of human happiness. He was anti-traditionalist from an early age, and was shocked to the core when in his 'teens he attended lectures by Sir William Blackstone and heard all the complexities and anomalous accretions of the contemporary common law defended in the name of reason. The root cause of all such unmerited praise seemed to him to be the confusion of law as it is with law as it ought to be, and for that the theory of natural law was largely to blame. It was necessary to define law in terms of facts, the political facts of power, human prescriptions, punishments and rewards. That done, one could devise a scientific theory of legislation based on the principle of utility.

Analysis for its own sake was never Bentham's aim. He believed that all law could be analytically reduced to a 'logic of the will', in which every human act could be seen either as commanded or prohibited, or not commanded or not prohibited, by the law. Where an act was commanded or prohibited, it was the subject of a legal duty. 'Duty' was the lowest common denominator of all laws. All other legal concepts, such as right, power and property, were to be translatable into their relationships to duties. Having decided, on the basis of utility, what acts ought to be made the subject of duties, and what

24

incentive to compliance (whether punishment or reward) was desirable, scientific codes could be worked out.

In fact, most of what Bentham wrote by way of explaining the
nature of law was not published in his lifetime. Elements of a command theory appeared in *A Fragment on Government* (1776) and *An
Introduction to the Principles of Morals and Legislation* (1782). But his
major work on legal theory remained in manuscript form until it was
discovered by Charles Everett more than a century after Bentham's
death. This work was first published in 1945 as *The Limits of Jurisprudence Defined*, and later in a definitive edition as *Of Laws in General*
(1970). Bentham's lifetime publications were principally concerned
with issues of moral and political philosophy and with programmes
for institutional and economic reform.

The popularising of the command theory of law was left to
Bentham's disciple, John Austin (1790–1859). Austin was appointed
in 1827 to the first chair of jurisprudence at the newly created University College in London. Six of his lectures were published in 1833 as
The Province of Jurisprudence Determined. This book is generally cited as
the standard exposition of the command theory of law. Austin's later
lectures were published posthumously. They applied the theory of
law set out in *The Province* to a wide range of legal concepts. For the
next half century and more, a series of writers sought to refine the
conceptual analysis appearing in these lectures, and they became
known as the 'analytical school of jurisprudence'. Today, analysis of
concepts flourishes, but the Austinian basis for it has largely been
rejected (see chapter 7, below).

Even if the law as it is can be apprehended separately from some
vision of what it ought to be – and that is a large question – in what
value-free 'facts' is our apprehension to be anchored? There are
books, judges, court officials, policemen, prisons. A factual definition
of law which purports to be universal, to apply in all countries at all
times – or at any rate, as Austin said, in all the 'maturer systems' – will
have to give us universal facts, broad sociological and political
generalisations about institutions. Where do we start?

Bentham and Austin started with concepts they found in political
philosophy. Since the renaissance, political philosophers like Bodin
and Hobbes had explained those traditional puzzles of their discipline
– the sources of political authority and political obligation – in terms
of a sovereign who gave commands. Bentham and Austin took over
these concepts and turned them to new purposes. In their hands, the
sovereign was not he who by divine or natural right could tell us what
we ought to do. The sovereign was identified by the fact that he was
obeyed, and his commands were those facts which people call 'laws'.

1 Laws as commands

Austin's book determines the province of jurisprudence. That is to say, it sets a fence round those sorts of entities whose terminology is worthy of analysis by anyone seeking enlightenment about standard legal processes.

①   The first step, in drawing the definitional boundary, was to exclude everything which was not deliberately laid down, everything which was not a 'command' as Austin defined that term.

> 'The ideas or notions comprehended by the term *command* are the following. (1) A wish or desire conceived by a rational being, that another rational being shall do or forbear. (2) An evil to proceed from the former, and to be incurred by the latter, in case the latter comply not with the wish. (3) An expression or intimation of the wish by words or other signs.'[1]

On this basis, so called 'customary law' was to be excluded from the province of jurisprudence, unless it had been adopted as the content of a wish by some state organ. The same was true of public international law and of conventional constitutional law.

②   The next step was to exclude those commands which were not laws. Only 'rules' (that is, general commands as opposed to particular commands) were 'laws properly so called'.

> 'Every *law* or *rule* (taken with the largest signification which can be given to the term *properly*) is a *command*. Or, rather, laws or rules, properly so called, are a *species* of commands[2] ... Now where it obliges *generally* to acts or forbearances of a *class*, a command is a law or rule. But where it obliges to a *specific* act or forbearance, or to acts or forbearances which it determines *specifically* or *individually*, a command is occasional or particular.'[3]

③   Finally, there must be excluded from the province of jurisprudence all those laws properly so called which are not 'positive laws', that is, which were laid down by someone other than the sovereign or his subordinates. This excluded divine laws (the general commands of God), and also laws laid down by private individuals (such as the general commands of an employer). Austin uses the expression 'positive morality' to stand both for general commands of non-sovereign human beings, and also for those so called 'rules' which are supported by public opinion but are not commands of anyone. In delimiting

1 *Province* p. 17.
2 *Province* p. 13.
3 *Province* p. 19.

↓positive law, he draws the line between those general commands of ↵ individuals which are to be attributed to the sovereign and those which are not, in terms of commands being issued 'in pursuance of legal rights'. This appears to mean that general commands issued for a man's own benefit are not positive laws, whilst those issued in a fiduciary capacity are; for Austin indicates that the term 'positive law' encompasses the commands of a guardian, but not those of a master.

'Positive laws, or laws strictly so called, are established directly or NB. immediately by authors of three kinds: – by monarchs, or sovereign bodies, as supreme political superiors:by men in a state of subjection, as subordinate political superiors: by subjects, as private persons, in pursuance of legal rights. But every positive law, or every law strictly so called, is a direct or circuitous command of a monarch or sovereign number ... to a person or persons in a state of subjection to its author.'[4]

Austin's underlying assumption seems to be that only general commands of the sovereign and his subordinates are enforced in courts and written about in law books. We must therefore demarcate them, analyse the terms they use, see how these terms relate to each NB. other – this is jurisprudence. The demarcation may be represented in ↵ the following diagrams.

DIAGRAM 1 *Commands*

Particular commands

General commands (otherwise called 'laws properly so called' or 'rules' simpliciter)

Commands of God ('divine laws')	Commands of the sovereign ('positive laws')	Commands of others ('positive morality') NB.

DIAGRAM 2 *Laws by analogy*

Laws by a close analogy ('positive morality' – for example, laws of honour, public international law, constitutional law, customary law)

Laws by a remote analogy (for example, laws of physics)

These diagrams show that Austin excluded from the definition of positive law many things which others have thought a proper subject

4 *Province* p. 134.

of jurisprudential inquiry, especially customary law, constitutional law and international law. His reason for excluding them was that they were not commands. Yet there were three other things which Austin wanted to reserve for the province of jurisprudence, even though he recognised that they did not meet his definition of 'command'. These were repealing laws, declarative laws and 'imperfect laws', that is, laws prescribing acts but without sanction. (The last mentioned, Austin believed, were to be found in Roman, but not contemporary, law). It would be inappropriate to charge him with inconsistency, since the three non-command types are expressly stated to be exceptions. But he can be charged with lack of largeness of aim, with providing too narrow a backcloth against which to depict law. Will we get a good picture if we only analyse the concepts used in statutes, judicial decisions and Roman law texts? Austin evidently thought we would, so repealing and declaratory statutes and imperfect laws came in, while the concepts of conventional constitutional law, international treaties and mere custom were out. Nowadays, many analytic jurists take the view that the concepts employed in familiar legal texts should be compared with, and explained in the light of, concepts found, not merely in conventional 'laws' of all kinds, but in morality, games and other rule-governed practices.

Less important criticisms concern terminology. It was rather odd of Austin to use the expression 'law properly so called' in a sense wider than 'positive law' or 'law simply so called', and even odder to use 'positive morality' in two senses, as standing for general commands of private people not given in pursuance of legal rights and also for all varieties of rules set by opinion. Call them what you like. What matters is: should they be within an illuminating model of law or without it? And if without, how related to it?

As for general commands of God ('divine laws'), Austin as a unitarian believed that God's law was the mark of what law ought to be; and as a utilitarian, he believed that God's law was discoverable by asking which rules would have best consequences in terms of human happiness. They were not part of the picture of law as it is. Whether he was right about that is part of the large positivist-versus-natural-lawyer controversy.

None of the criticisms of Austin, in terms of largeness of aim, have been as persistent and damning as attacks mounted against the cornerstone of the first diagram, the concept of command itself. Austin said that every command comprises three elements: a wish, a sanction, and an expression of the wish; and every command which is a law comprises a fourth element, generality. Some critics make the point that his definition of command does not square with the way the

word 'command' is used in ordinary language. Do we not speak of
'commands' in contexts where the commander owes his authority to
respect rather than the power to punish?

That criticism based on the true meaning of the word 'command' is
misplaced can be easily demonstrated. Supposing one accepted –
nobody does, but let's suppose – that the laws of the modern state do
have just those elements in terms of which Austin defines general
commands, and no others. Then Austin's legal theory would be
accurate and definitive and it would be a very small point that his own
use of the middle term 'command' diverged from any dictionary
definition. Conversely, if his use of 'command' matched ordinary
usage, but the laws of the state have none of the elements, his theory is
false. His is a command theory of law, using 'command' in his sense; it
is not a theory about what it is to 'command' in any other sense.

If his theory were right, then every positive law would contain the
four elements of wish, sanction, expression of wish, and generality – as
well as a fifth element of 'emanation from a sovereign person or body'
(to be considered in the next section). To test it, we must look to see
whether each of these elements is present in every law, or whether
laws contain further elements not specified by his definition.

When we say that something is required by law, are we committing
ourselves to the proposition that some political superior entertains a
wish that the conduct in question be performed? Certainly not, if
'conceiving a wish' is understood in a psychological sense. As many
critics have pointed out, no one has the psychological capacity to
make compliance with every legal duty the content of a separate wish.
Is there some other, non-psychological sense of conceiving a wish
such that the sovereign may be said to do it in regard to every law?
Austin says that the sovereign's wish that instructions emanating
from subordinates – like judges and deputy legislators – be carried out
is manifested by the fact that the sovereign punishes breaches.
Similarly, the sovereign shows his desire that the laws of previous
sovereigns should be obeyed by not repealing them and enforcing
compliance with them. This is his much criticised idea of 'circuitous'
commanding. So the sovereign's wish is not a brute psychological
fact. It is a construct made up out of other facts, like punishing or not
repealing. It may be urged in Austin's defence that the brute facts of
legal life are too complicated for the empirical basis of law to be
stateable directly in terms of them. We need simplified pictures made
up of constructive, second-order 'facts', that is, 'models'. But is
'circuitous commanding' a good model? That depends on how illuminating we find it in depicting the relationships between the
administration of law and political power. If we think that, in essence,
all law enforcement gives effect to the desires of political superiors,

maybe it is not so bad. But if the relationship between what the law achieves and the diffusion of political power among officeholders is much more complicated, the model distorts.

It is the second element of command/laws (the sanction) which has attracted most attention. Is it true that all laws have sanctions? Austin analyses all legal concepts in terms of wish, sanction and sovereign. Particular attention has been paid to his analysis of legal duty. He says that a person is under a duty if the sovereign has expressed a wish and has the power and purpose to inflict an evil. One has a legal obligation when one is, by virtue of threatened punishment, 'obliged' to act. Discussions of 'duty' typically give rise to three quite separate issues. First, when does a legal duty (as opposed to any other kind of duty) arise? Second, what motivates people to comply with legal duties? Third, ought one to act in accordance with one's legal duties? Austin is certainly not concerned with the third of these questions when he defines duty in terms of sanction – he does not say that might is right. Critics have accused him of confusing the first and second. Sometimes, it is true, he indicates that sanction is a motive. But he tells us that the smallest chance of the smallest evil is sufficient for a duty to exist, and it is reasonable to conclude that his primary concern is the first issue. One is under a legal duty when, and only when, the sovereign has stipulated a sanction; why one obeys, and whether one ought to obey, are different questions. In so far as positive law recognises duties where there are no sanctions, the command model is incomplete – as Austin himself recognised by stating that the province of jurisprudence should encompass 'imperfect laws'. ie. laws w/o us sanctions - one of his exceptions.

Much more important is the objection that there are many laws which do not impose duties at all, such as laws empowering people to make wills or contracts. Austin dealt with this difficulty by asserting that, in such cases, people are the addressees of conditional commands, subject to the sanction of nullity – if you want to make a will, sign it in the presence of two witnesses or it will have no legal effect. Such a rendering, argues Professor Hart, distorts the 'social function' of such provisions; for they empower people to do things, they don't make demands – they are 'power-conferring rules'. If a concept of law should capture, not merely the political and social facts enderlying all legal institutions, but also their typical functions, the command theory is undoubtedly deficient. The law does many other things apart from making demands on us. But whether one can type different sorts of laws by reference to different functions is more problematical. As we shall see in connection with Hart's concept of law (chapter 9, below), it is not historically accurate to regard the introduction of the Wills Act formalities as a measure designed to empower people to do what they could not do before. Whether the common perception of such formality provisions is one of 'the law's demands' or 'the law's assistance' is a complex issue about social attitudes. The general question of ascribing social functions to the law is discussed in chapter 18, below.

As to the third element of Austin's command conception of law – an expression of wish by words or other signs – it can be objected that much of the language of statutes and judgments does not look like wish-expressive language. If a section contains a definition, the language is very far from anything like: 'My desire is that people act in the following way'. Austin tells us that commands are distinguished from other significations of desire, not by their imperative form, but by the power and purpose to inflict a penalty if the desire be disregarded. But that does not seem to meet the objection that much legislative language is not expressive of any desire, imperative or otherwise. Perhaps we can extend Austin's point, and interpret the third element as entirely dependent on the second: if the legislator has penalties in mind, then (for that reason) any language he uses must be reconstructed as expressive of a legislative intention that people shall do or forbear. The third element thus means merely that, before there can be a command and hence a law, the legislator must have taken some overt step beyond conceiving in his own bosom a wish and a purpose to punish.

The fourth element (generality) can be attacked for excluding from the province of jurisprudence particular judicial orders and statutes dealing with a finite number of actions. Actual examples of the latter may be rare; but it is common enough for a judge to issue a one-off order requiring X to do Y. As we shall see in chapter 6, below, Kelsen argues that such 'particular norms' ought to be comprised within a theory of law.

2 The sovereign

Because positive laws are (according to Austin) a species of commands, they comprise the four elements of wish, sanction, expression of wish and generality. Because they all emanate from a sovereign person or body, there is a fifth element, that of identifiable political superiors who entertain and express the wish and purpose to inflict the punishment.

It is important to distinguish the use which the command theory of law makes of the concept of sovereignty from the employment of that concept within legal rules. Sovereignty is an important concept in constitutional law. Some constitutions vest supreme legislative power in a particular body, like the Queen in Parliament, and 'sovereignty' ✓ is the term used to stand for this vesting. Rules of public international law vest rights and duties in 'states', but only if they are 'sovereign and independent'. Austin was not seeking to explicate either of these particular legal conceptions of sovereignty – so that it is not enough to refute his theory to point out, for example, that some constitutions do not employ the conception. For him, the sovereign is a pre-legal political fact, in terms of which law and all legal concepts are definable. (Although occasionally, conceptions of 'sovereignty' similar to Austin's may be used to supplement English rules for the recognition of foreign law – as when the House of Lords recognised East German law, even though they were bound to accept that East Germany was not a sovereign state, by treating the East German government as a delegate of the recognised sovereign, the USSR.[5]

Austin defines the sovereign as a person or body of persons who receives habitual obedience within a political society – a society whose numbers are not extremely small – and who renders habitual obedience to no one else. Laws are defined as the sovereign's general commands. It ought to follow from these definitions that, if one wants to discover the positive law of Ruritania, all one has to do is find out who is habitually obeyed there and then collate his or their general commands. Finding out the sovereign person or body will be a sociological exercise. One will note that there are people giving directions to others, that there are people obeying others; but in any political society there will be discoverable one person or body whose orders are generally obeyed and who obeys orders from no other.

Since legal concepts are defined in terms of the sovereign's commands it follows, Austin argued, that there could be no legal limitation on the sovereign, and no division of sovereign power. Being under a duty is defined as being commanded by the sovereign; so no precept purporting to limit the sovereign could itself have the status of law. In particular, the sovereign could not be bound by laws promulgated by previous sovereigns. Austin's definitions exclude the idea of continuity of law from one sovereign to another. Anything which a former sovereign commanded is law today only if our present sovereign has re-commanded it.

'Even though it sprung directly from another fountain or source, it *is* a positive law, or a law strictly so called, by the institution of that present sovereign in the character of political superior. Or (borrowing the language of Hobbes) "The legislator is he, not by whose authority the law was first made, but by whose authority it continues to be a law".[6]

Although Austin correctly drew out the implications for illimitability and indivisibility which flowed from his assumed pre-legal sovereign, he did not himself apply the sociological test of habitual obedience in discovering who the sovereign was. His definition required him to look at the facts of command and obedience. His practice was to look at constitutional rules. This was his greatest inconsistency and points up the most important flaw in the command theory.

Imagine one were oneself asked to discover, by inquiry into the facts of political life, who is that person or body of persons who is habitually obeyed (gets their way) in Britain in our day or in Austin's. There would be no easy answer, and answers given by political scientists are likely to be equivocal or coloured by assumptions about the propriety of certain kinds of political power. Probably, there is not and was not any single group to fit the bill; or if there is or was some readily identifiable ruling class, it is not their general commands which are collated in law books and cited in courts.

Austin, ignoring his definition, sought the sovereign in the United Kingdom and the United States by reference to the constitution. In his early lectures, he assumed that the sovereign in the United Kingdom was that body composed of the king, all the peers and all the members of the House of Commons – that is, 'parliament' viewed as a collection of people, not a constitutional abstraction. Then he saw a difficulty, in that there would be no sovereign during prorogations. His final conclusion was that the United Kingdom sovereign was a body constituted of king, peers and all electors. In the United States, since not congress but the states have the power to change the written constitution, he found the sovereign body to be the combined members of the electors of all the states' governments. Some body!

If there were nothing else amiss with the command theory of law, the fallacy of the concept of a personal sovereign would alone necessitate its rejection. There are difficulties in spelling out how a legislative body (as such) can entertain and express wishes; but they may not be insurmountable, as we shall see when considering the conception of 'legislative intention' universally employed in statutory interpretation (chapter 12, below). A rule-free identification of a commanding body is, however, impossible, as Austin's own practice makes clear. He says that the members of the sovereign body, while acting in their sovereign capacity, might issue commands to themselves in their private capacity. But how is one to distinguish a man's

6 *Province* p. 193.

'acting like a legislator' or 'acting like an elector' from any other things he does except by reference to rules which tell you what counts as legislating or voting? Certainly, the distinction cannot be referred to others' habitual obedience. A child may habitually obey its father. The brightest child would find it difficult to say when his obedience was rendered to his father, *qua* father, and when it was not.

Even if laws are commands, their source is determined by constitutional rules and practices not capable of reduction to habitual obedience of a person. If these rules and practices (or some of them) are distinguishable as 'laws', then there is no need to predicate illimitability or indivisibility of legislative power. Rejection of Austin's simple sovereignty model is not now controversial. But, as we shall see in other chapters, there is no agreement as to whether laws are or are not in some sense 'commands', nor as to what the true test of legal pedigree is, or whether any such test is, can or should be applied.

Bibliography

Austin J.	*The Province of Jurisprudence Determined* (1954) lectures 1, 5–6
Bentham J.	*An Introduction to the Principles of Morals and Legislation* (Burns and Hart (eds), 1970) ch 17 *Of Laws in General* (Hart (ed), 1970) chs 1–2, 19, appendix (a)
Bryce J.	*Studies in History and Jurisprudence* (1901) vol II, ch 10
Buckland W. W.	*Some Reflections on Jurisprudence* (1945) chs 1, 5, 9–10
Eastwood R. A. and Keeton G. W.	*The Austinian Theories of Law and Sovereignty* (1929)
Friedmann W.	*Legal Theory* (5th edn, 1967) ch 22
Harris J. W.	'The Concept of Sovereign Will' [1977] AJ 1
Hart H. L. A.	*The Concept of Law* (1961) chs 2–4 'Bentham's *Of Laws in General*' (1971) 2 Rechtstheorie 55
Heuston R. V. F.	'Sovereignty' in Guest (ed) *Oxford Essays in Jurisprudence* (1961)
Jenks E.	*The New Jurisprudence* (1933) pp. 73–84
Jones J. W.	*Historical Introduction to the Theory of Law* (1956) ch 3

Lyons D. B.	*In the Interests of the Governed* (1973) chs 6–7
Manning C. A. W.	'Austin to-day; or "The Province of Juris-prudence" Re-examined' in Jennings (ed) *Modern Theories of Law* (1933)
Morison W. L.	'Some Myths about Positivism' (1959–60) 68 Yale LJ 212
Paulson S. L.	'Classical Legal Positivism at Nuremberg' [1975] PPA 132
Raz J.	*The Concept of a Legal System* (1970) pp. 5–43
Rees W. J.	'The Theory of Sovereignty Restated' in Laslett (ed) *Philosophy, Politics and Society* (1956)
Ruben E.	'Austin's Political Pamphlets' in Attwooll (ed) *Perspectives in Jurisprudence* (1977)
Samek R. A.	*The Legal Point of View* (1974) ch 6
Stone J.	*Legal System and Lawyers' Reasonings* (1964) ch 2
Stumpff S. E.	'Austin's Theory of the Separation of Law and Morals' (1960–61) 14 Vand L Rev 117
Tapper C. F. H.	'Austin on Sanctions' (1965) 23 CLJ 271

4 Utilitarianism and the economic analysis of law

The student of jurisprudence will, in many contexts, be referred to arguments deriving from utilitarian moral philosophy. Professor Rawls, in advancing a theory of substantive justice, seeks to refute the view that the rightness of social institutions is to be measured only by utility (see chapter 20, below). In the context of the philosophy of punishment, the two views generally contrasted are those of retribution and utility (see chapter 5, below). Utilitarian arguments are among those considered in assessing whether or not there is a moral duty to obey the law (see chapter 16, below), and whether the conventional morality of a community should be legally enforced (see chapter 10, below). In the context of legal reasoning, one of the criteria suggested for determining what rules judges should lay down is utility (see chapter 15, below). We saw in the last chapter that, in devising a command theory of law, Bentham was seeking a definition in terms of fact (in contrast to natural law) so that a proper basis might be laid for scientific legislation based on utility.

Moral philosophers have subjected utilitarianism to minute critical analysis. All that is attempted in this chapter is, first, a sketch of the classic theory put forward by Bentham, with a discussion of criticisms of utilitarianism based on that sketch; and secondly, an outline of the modern economic analysis of law which parallels the utilitarian approach, but in a form which is supposed to insulate it against some of these criticisms.

1 Utilitarianism

'The greatest happiness of the greatest number' is a maxim adopted by Bentham to popularise his philosophy. It is, however, as he recognised, somewhat inaccurate. A measure may be justified by utility which increases the happiness of a few greatly even though it marginally diminishes that of the many.

'By the principle of utility is meant that principle which approves or disapproves of every action whatsoever, according to the tendency which it appears to have to augment or diminish the happiness of the party whose interest is in question: or, what is the same thing in other words, to promote or to oppose that happiness.'[1]

The happiness of an individual will be augmented if there is an addition to the sum total of his pleasures greater than any addition to the sum total of his pains. The interest of the community is comprised of all interests of the individuals of which it is composed. Therefore, the happiness of the community will be increased if the total of all the pleasures of all its members is augmented to a greater extent than their pains. Bentham lists fourteen pleasures and twelve pains as a comprehensive account of happiness-relevant consequences. When assessing the rightness of any proposed action, one notes which items on this list will result from it, and measures the value of each particular lot of pleasure or pain by reference to seven criteria: intensity, duration, certainty, propinquity, fecundity, purity and extent.

> '*Intense, long, certain, speedy, fruitful, pure* – such marks in *pleasures* and in *pains* endure. Such pleasures seek, if *private* be thy end. If it be *public*, wide let them *extend*. Such pains avoid, whichever be thy view. If pains *must* come, let them *extend* to few.'[2]

Bentham advances the principle of utility as the sole proper basis for morality and legislation. Both the rightness of every act we do in private life, and the rightness of public measures of all kinds, should be tested by his 'felicific calculus'. His philosophy is anti-conventionalist and universalist. The mere fact that overwhelming opinion in a community has held something to be right or wrong is no warrant for moral approval or condemnation; only the test of utility can decide. And, although what the law is differs from one society to another, what it ought to be is in principle everywhere the same, namely, legislation which passes the utilitarian test.

He begins his advocacy of the principle of utility with some psychological assumptions which today look rather crude. He believes that all that men desire are pleasures and the avoidance of pains, and that men are motivated to do whatever they do by their desires.

> 'Nature has placed mankind under the governance of two sovereign masters, *pain* and *pleasure*. It is for them alone to point out what we ought to do, as well as to determine what we shall do. On the one hand the standard of right and wrong, on the other the chain of causes and effects, are fastened to their throne ... The *principle of*

1 *An Introduction to the Principles of Morals and Legislation* ch 1 (2).
2 *Introduction* ch 4(2)n.

utility recognises this subjection, and assumes it for the foundation of that system, the object of which is to rear the fabric of felicity by the hands of reason and of law. Systems which attempt to question it, deal in sounds instead of sense, in caprice instead of reason, in darkness instead of light.'[3]

It might be thought from this that Bentham is substituting his own natural law for other systems, that he is deriving an 'ought' from an 'is'. This he denies, saying of the principle of utility:

'Is it susceptible of any direct proof? It should seem not: for that which is used to prove every thing else, cannot itself be proved: a chain of proofs must have their commencement somewhere. To give such proof is as impossible as it is needless.'[4]

The object of Bentham's psychology is, therefore, not proof but advocacy. He commends the principle of utility as a moral principle which, he thinks, any reader will find preferable to any other, given the truth of his assertions about human nature. Three aspects of this advocacy can be distinguished. First, since men desire only happiness, they must approve a principle which affirms that they ought to have what they want. Secondly, if one will accept the principle of utility, then all disputes about right and wrong will be reduced to disagreements about future matters of fact, and hence morals and legislation become scientific. Utilitarians are concerned only with consequences; they will know how to value consequences; so all that any two of them can be at issue about are what consequences a certain act or measure will in fact bring about. Thirdly, since men are only motivated by pain and pleasure, properly drafted legislation can produce a coincidence between the interests of the individual and the interests of the community. Given appropriate rewards and punishments laid down by law, we can achieve a fortunate state of affairs in which a man will draw the same conclusions about the rightness of any proposed action of his, whether he calculates the effect only upon his own happiness or upon that of the community.

Benthamite utilitarianism was an important part of the political culture of the first half of nineteenth-century Britain, and reforms (creditable or otherwise) have been attributed to its influence. The sweeping away of archaic legal procedures and the pruning of pointlessly severe punishments may owe something to it. But so too may the new poor law introduced in 1834, with its notorious 'less eligibility' principle – workhouse conditions should always be worse than

3 *Introduction* ch 1 (1).
4 *Introduction* ch 1 (11).

those resulting from the least remunerative employment, otherwise there would be no incentive to work.

Utilitarians, after Bentham, have modified many of his assertions. John Stuart Mill was an avowed utilitarian, but rejected Bentham's view that all pleasures were to count the same. Since, Mill argued, people educated to appreciate intellectual and aesthetic pleasures always value them more than sensual pleasures, they should be counted as intrinsically of more worth. Probably no one today would wish to be tied to Bentham's list of pleasures and pains and no one would accept the grandiose simplicity of his psychological assumptions. Nonetheless, those who take utilitarian positions tend to reflect the spirit of his advocacy of the principle. Why should we accept that actions are morally required unless their consequences are good for people – meet their demonstrable needs and desires, or cater for their satisfactions? Why should we accept any principle as morally appropriate merely because someone or some body of people say it is right? And if two disputants have different moral philosophies or political programmes to recommend, is not the best ground for discussion achieved if each is required to set out what consequences he maintains will follow from acceptance of his view? And even if rationalistic motivation is not to be hoped for, should not public measures seek to balance conflicting aspirations by giving as much satisfaction to each as possible?

Bentham advocated the same test, the principle of utility, for both private acts and public measures. Yet his own definition speaks only of 'actions'. He was evidently not aware of the distinction which later philosophers have drawn between 'act-utilitarianism' and 'rule-utilitarianism'. For the former, an act is right if it has best consequences. For the latter, an act is right if required or permitted by a rule where the general following of that rule would have best consequences. Austin accepted the principle of utility, but believed it should be applied to rules. 'Our rules would be fashioned on utility; our conduct, on our rules.'[5] He regarded 'the laws of God' as the test of what positive laws ought to be. Where they are not revealed in scripture, they are those rules which will promote human happiness (it being assumed that God wills the welfare of his creatures). Creative judicial decisions generally are, and should be, dictated by the consequences any decision would have were it universalised into a rule.

In the context of legal philosophy, the version of utilitarianism most often appealed to is 'ideal rule-utilitarianism'. This stipulates that an action is right if required or permitted by a rule, where that

5 *Province* p. 47.

rule, if obeyed by all to whom it applies, would have better consequences (or at least as good consequences) compared with any
other rule governing the same act. It appears to have advantages over
act-utilitarianism. Where a judge is deciding whether liability-in-
damages should be imposed for some activity, if he views his decision
as a single act the relevant consequences might include the effect on
the particular defendant who is poor; and hence by act-utilitarian
reasoning the award should not be made. But it might be that a rule
requiring all judges to award damages in such circumstances would
have good consequences, so that the award would be right by rule-
utilitarian reasoning.

Many objections have been raised to utilitarianism of all kinds.
Here are a few.

First, the felicific calculus is impracticable. No one can know all the
consequences of his acts and it would often be foolish to try to assess
them. Received moral precepts provide more practical guides to
action. This objection tells less in the context of deliberate rule-
making by legislators or judges than in the sphere of private morality.
Even so, are not the results of research into expected consequences of
public measures commonly contradictory and often proved wrong?
Does that mean we should not try to calculate consequences?

Secondly, the pleasures and pains of different people are not intra-
commensurable. Supposing all agree that the effect of proposed legislation would be marginally to increase the average take-home pay, at
the cost of marginally increasing the number of those out of work.
How do we balance the satisfactions of the majority against the
different kind of distress caused to the minority? When a judge is
deciding whether or not to issue an injunction against an alleged
nuisance, how is the enjoyment of one who likes late-night noisy
parties to be weighed against the discomfort of his neighbours? We
shall see that those who advocate an economic analysis of law believe
that such problems are in principle soluble.

Thirdly, the principle of utility is unworthy. Satisfaction of all
human desires should not be the aim of our morality. Some pleasures
are gross and some forms of suffering are ennobling. Bentham was
aware that ruling out any particular kinds of pleasure or pain from the
calculus would entail making pre-utilitarian value judgments, and so
he tried to include them all. For example, his list includes 'the
pleasures of malevolence'. This led him into difficulties with his
theory of punishment; for he wanted to maintain the position that
punishment is in itself evil and can only be justified by the prevention
of greater evil. Why is not pure retribution a good by virtue of
satisfying feelings of vengeance? Bentham's answer was that 'no such
pleasure is ever produced by punishment as can be equivalent to the

pain.'[6] But is that not a distinct value judgment rather than a plausible generalisation from the facts of human experience? Some take the view that our satisfactions cannot be the only test of what is right, but must themselves be judged by some higher value, such as human dignity. Supposing it could be shown that women living in purdah would lead less happy lives were they to be allowed into the outside world – it might still be argued that it is right to free them.

Fourthly, are not human desires and satisfactions capable of manipulation? If so, how can the issue of how to mould them be decided by utility? If by education or advertising a person can be brought to desire things which he would not have desired otherwise, and to cease to want other things, can judgment be passed on the manipulation programmes in terms of a principle which merely refers us to maximising satisfactions? Is it an answer to say that the felicific calculus includes, not merely all the things we want, but all the things we might come to want given alternative measures of education and indoctrination?

Fifthly, whose interests are in question? There may be various utilitarian answers to a problem, depending on whether we include as relevant beneficiaries the members of a national community, all mankind, present and future generations, or all sentient creatures. Utility cannot itself dictate where to draw the line. On the issue of abortion on demand, for instance, if the interest of the foetus does not count, abortion ought clearly to be allowed; if it does count, very heavy considerations must weigh on the other side before the loss of future satisfactions involved in the destruction of the foetus can be justified. More bizarre problems have been raised by asking whether the persons whose interests are in question include all those who could possibly be begotten. If so, then so long as any addition to the population would give the new individual satisfactions which would outweigh the dissatisfactions to others resulting from his demands on resources, then there is a duty to beget him. Not merely is birth control ruled out, but we all have a duty to procreate to the maximum. Because of this argument, modern utilitarians often appeal to a principle of *average* utility – you maximise the average satisfactions of the people who now exist. It is not clear whether this justifies killing off the extremely miserable, provided this can be done without causing fear or other pains to the rest.

In the light of such objections and many others, there are not many today who base all their moral and political judgments on strictly utilitarian reasoning. Yet it is also true that utilitarian considerations are seldom ignored. Consequences are usually accepted to be among the morally-relevant considerations of private acts and public measures.

6 *Introduction* ch 13 (2)n.

2 The economic analysis of law

Some of the objections to utilitarianism can be met if, instead of
concerning ourselves with the messy business of actual human
psychology, we simplify our task with a few definitional assumptions.
This is what has been attempted in the economic analysis of law
which has grown up (principally in the United States) during the past
twenty years. The felicific calculus is difficult because one cannot be
sure how people will react to alternative measures. The answer of
economic analysis is to make an assumption. Man is a rational
maximiser of his satisfactions. The entire theory is premised on this
definition. If he will achieve more of what he wants to achieve by
taking step X rather than step Y, *homo economicus* will, by definition,
take step X; to do otherwise would, by definition, be acting irration-
ally. The felicific calculus is also problematic because of the empirical
difficulties in finding out what people do in fact want. No problem!
For the economic analysis of law, what I want is, by definition, what I
am willing to pay for – either in money, or by the deployment of some
other resource that I have such as time and effort. The utility calculus
is objectionable in principle because the advantages to some cannot
be measured against the disadvantages to others. But this is not so,
according to economic analysis; for all that happens to us can be
reduced to things we will pay to have or pay to be without, the solvent
of a hypothetical market. Should my neighbour be prevented from
having noisy parties which disturb me? He would pay X pounds for
the privilege, if there were a market in noisy parties; I would pay Y
pounds to be left in peace. If X is greater than Y, satisfactions are
maximised by allowing him to go ahead. That is the 'efficient' solution. Where Bentham spoke of the greatest happiness of the greatest
number, the economic analyst speaks of overall efficiency.

The economic analysis of law was first applied to specific areas of
law, such as anti-trust legislation and the law of nuisance; but it has
since been directed towards the legal system as a whole, both detailed
provisions and the process of law creation and administration. The
most systematic, across-the-board application of this approach is to
be found in Richard Posner's *Economic Analysis of Law*. Posner claims
for it the status of a general theory of law: it both explains why many of
the legal rules and institutions we have are what they are, and it has
normative implications for how the law should be improved. But he
denies that it is the same theory as that of classical utilitarianism. It
has the differences mentioned above. It explicitly makes simplifying
assumptions about rational action in a world of scarce resources,
rather than advancing empirical claims about human nature.
Furthermore, the theory does not purport, as Bentham's did, to be a

comprehensive moral philosophy. It is concerned with efficiency, meaning the maximising of satisfactions as defined by economic criteria. It leaves open the question of whether efficiency, so defined, is the highest ideal. Empirical-psychological and normative-philosophical issues are side-stepped by initial definitions. Nevertheless, Posner argues, the theory is, on the level of explanation, preferable to any other social-scientific approach to law because its conclusions have greater predictive power; and its normative implications cannot be ignored whatever one's philosophical stance, since, he implies, good reasons will have to be given why an inefficient solution to any problem is to be preferred to the efficient one.

Much of the common law, according to Posner, can be explained in economic terms. Occasionally, judges have expressly adverted to economic considerations. A favourite text for those who share this view is the formula propounded by Justice Learned Hand as a test for negligence.

'The defendant is guilty of negligence if the loss caused by the accident, multiplied by the probability of the accident's occurring, exceeds the burden of the precautions that the defendant might have taken to avert it.'[7]

Generally, it is true, the surface reasoning of judges and lawyers employs concepts with no obvious economic significance. But, Posner argues, if we look deeper we find that common law rules have resulted from arguments which are in reality economic in nature. Posner finds that the common law, in all its branches, exhibits a deep unity that is economic in character.

'The common law method is to allocate responsibilities between people engaged in interacting activities in such a way as to maximize the joint value, or, what amounts to the same thing, minimize the joint cost of the activities. It may do this by redefining a property right, by devising a new rule of liability, or by recognizing a contract right, but nothing fundamental turns on which device is used ... The Hand formula expresses a general test of liability at common law.'[8]

Whatever the surface vocabulary, economic considerations have been systematically at work in the development of the common law. In the field of competing uses of property, judges have spoken in terms of the causation of damage, reasonable use and so on. But the true

7 *United States v Carroll Towing Company* (1947) 159 F 2d 169 (2nd Cir) (cited by
   Posner *Economic Analysis of Law* (2nd edn) p. 122).
8 *Economic Analysis of Law* p. 179.

rationale has been something else. A favourite example for the school of economic analysts is the emission of sparks from trains which damage farmland. What view would one expect a court to take of this issue, supposing it to have economic analysis in mind? The cost of the potential damage to the farmers is the resource-cost involved in avoiding the damage, assuming they had no legal protection – perhaps the cost of moving crops back from the railway. If there were liability on the railway company, its cost would be measured in terms of resources which would have to be expended to avoid sparks. Having determined the comparative costs, we then apply a hypothesis of trading between the parties, on the assumption of zero 'transaction costs'. If the railway's costs are greater than the farmers' costs and the railway is made liable, then the railway will purchase a right to emit sparks from the farmers. It will give them something a little more than their damage-costs which they, being rational maximisers, will of course accept; whilst what the railway will pay will be less than its precaution-costs. Thus, whether the railway is made liable or not, emission sparks will fly. Conversely, if the farmers' costs are greater than the railway's costs, whether the railway is made liable or not, emission sparks will be prevented because, if the railway is not liable, the farmers will buy the right to protection. In a situation of zero transaction costs, it makes no difference, from the viewpoint of economic analysis, where property rights are located, so long as they are located somewhere. The analysis makes no pretensions to deal with issues of initial distribution of wealth. Property is necessary for efficient use of resources, and, once property rights are established, a free and notionally costless series of transactions will inevitably produce maximum efficiency. Here is a garage. Someone must own it, for otherwise inefficiency would result from competing unregulated use. If I own it, anyone to whom its use is more valuable will buy it from me. Transaction costs are low in the case of the garage, so the law makes no limitation on the absolute protection given to owners by the rules of trespass. Where transaction costs are low, let the market reign. But in the sparks case, transaction costs are high. The railway would have to negotiate with all those farmers, everyone employing surveyors, lawyers and other agents. So if liability were imposed on the railway even though its costs are greater than the farmers' costs, no purchase of the farmers' rights would take place, and an inefficient result would be produced – a greater cost incurred rather than a less. In such circumstances, legal decision-making has to take the place of the market. The court decides which party would buy out the other if there were no transaction costs, and awards liability accordingly to make no such transaction necessary. If the railway's costs are greater, then it is not liable; if the farmers' costs are greater, the railway is liable. This, so the economic analysts argue, is just what common law judges have tended to do, often without being conscious of the true economic rationale.

The layman might think that the law penalises conduct such as murder, assault, rape and theft because such things have always been thought to be morally wrong. In the language of natural law, such actions are termed *mala in se*, as distinct from *male prohibita* (regulatory offences created in the service of some particular policy goal). The true basis of legal prohibition is, Posner argues, quite different. Economic efficiency, not some other normative conception, is what determines legal prohibition. So-called *mala in se* are examples of *coerced transactions*. Some value is transferred from the victim to the delinquent without proper bargaining. The law penalises the thief, not because theft is in some non-economic sense 'wrong', but in order to persuade the thief to use the market. Posner concedes that there are problems with the assessment of damages in the case of some serious assaults, since there is no available market in maiming and mutilation. Nonetheless, he maintains that 'intentional torts' and serious crimes all fall foul of the overriding principle that, when transaction costs are low, people must use the market. Whether the law penalises through tortious liability or criminal sanction is merely a question of technique. The reason for punishment is that the cost to the delinquent needs to be greater than mere compensation in order to provide him with the necessary incentive to refrain. Posner expressly follows Bentham's cost-benefit analysis of punishment.

Posner goes through the common law, branch by branch, demonstrating its economic logic. When it comes to statutes, he finds, on the whole, that – although those manning legislative and administrative agencies are themselves motivated by utility – the rules they produce are inefficient. They are the result of pressures brought to bear by competing interest-groups, and the resulting compromises do not maximise total satisfactions. In particular, the substitution of administrative or adjudicatory processes for low-cost market transactions is inefficient. Posner casts a jaundiced eye on modern consumer law, whether originating from statute or cases. If manufacturers and sellers of products cannot contract out of liability, they will either take cost-unjustified steps to improve their products, raising the price more than the cost of the defects to the consumer; or they will add in the cost of anticipated damages and raise the price that way. The result will be that the total value of the transactions to all concerned is reduced – especially if the consumer is a 'risk preferrer', that is, someone who would like to pay less and take the chance of defects. Fraud, incapacity and duress are valid grounds for interfering with freedom of contract, for here the consumer is prevented from acting as a rational maximiser; but the other more comprehensive grounds of intervention recognised by modern law are unfortunate.

'If unconscionability means that a judge may nullify a contract if he considers the consideration inadequate or the terms otherwise one-sided, the basic principle of encouraging market rather than surrogate legal transactions where (market) transaction costs are low is badly compromised. Economic analysis, at least, reveals no grounds other than fraud, incapacity, and duress (the last narrowly defined) for allowing a party to repudiate the bargain that he made in entering into the contract.

Whether noneconomic grounds are available in this setting may be doubted. If a rule of contract law is inefficient, whatever its noneconomic merits, the parties will simply contract around it; if forbidden to do so, there will be a price adjustment.'[9]

Many lawyers will agree that the economic analysis of law does throw interesting light on particular areas. Critics have suggested, however, that its explanatory power is not as inclusive, even in relation to the common law, as its advocates suggest. Does the above explanation of the law's penalisation of serious offences in terms of 'coerced transactions' carry conviction? Is the following explanation of the no-duty-to-rescue rule fanciful? If I see someone drowning and could easily rescue him without risk to myself, I am morally blameworthy if I watch him drown but I incur no tortious or criminal liability – unless some prior special relationship existed between us. Posner gives the following economic explanation. With no liability, strong swimmers often do rescue people. This increases total values, because the person drowning would pay a large sum to be rescued if there were a market; and the rescuer achieves satisfactions through being recognised as an altruist. If strong swimmers were liable for failure to rescue, there would be an incentive to keep off the beach. They would no longer receive recognition as altruists, and they would avoid situations in which they would be forced either to incur the resource-costs of rescue, or pay damages or fines. There would consequently be less rescues, and so a diminution in total values. The no-liability rule is therefore efficient.

The normative implications of economic analysis are challenging. Because nothing but efficiency is taken into account, other moral criteria are thrown into sharper relief. Posner argues forcefully that the law prohibiting a market in the production of babies for adoption is inefficient. The demand and supply would eventually equalise. Poor adopters would be better off, because the prices charged by producing mothers in circumstances of open competition would be less exacting than criteria of wealth currently applied by adoption agencies. Such an analysis at least requires us to ask why it is that this proposal is, at present, generally looked on with horror. The strength of economic analysis, as of its utilitarian parent, is its appeal to the intuition: other things being equal, why not give people what they want? Its weakness, some would argue, is its artificial equation of 'what people want' with 'willingness to pay', and its assumptions about rational maximisers. Is the law's only function that of ministering to the market? Does it not have to balance competing claims to power and influence by people who are bound to lose out in any competition based on market competence? And, above all, can any philosophy of law be adequate which side-steps the crucial questions of substantive justice involved in the distribution of wealth?

Bibliography

Utilitarianism

Austin J.	*The Province of Jurisprudence Determined* (1954) lectures 2–4
Bentham J.	*An Introduction to the Principles of Morals and Legislation* (Burns and Hart (eds), 1970) chs 1–5
Brandt R. B.	*Some Merits of one Form of Rule Utilitarianism* (1967)
Hare R. M.	'Ethical Theory and Utilitarianism' in Lewis (ed) *Contemporary British Philosophy* (4th series, 1976)
Hodgson D. H.	*Consequences of Utilitarianism* (1967)
Lyons D. B.	*Forms and Limits of Utilitarianism* (1965)
	In the Interests of the Governed (1973) chs 1–5
Mill J. S.	*Utilitarianism* (1960)
Quinton A. M.	*Utilitarian Ethics* (1973)
Ross A.	*On Law and Justice* (1958) ch 13
Sartorius R. E.	*Individual Conduct and Social Norms* (1975) ch 2
Smart J. C. and Williams B.	*Utilitarianism: For and Against* (1973)
Stephen L.	*The English Utilitarians* (1900)
Stone J.	*Human Law and Human Justice* (1965) ch 4
Wasserstrom R. A.	*The Judicial Decision* (1961) chs 6–8

The economic analysis of law

Baker C. E.	'The Ideology of the Economic Analysis of Law' (1975) 5 PPA 3
Becker G. S.	*The Economic Approach to Human Behaviour* (1976) Pt 3
Bowles R.	'Creeping Economism: a Counter-view' (1978) 5 Br J L Soc 96
Buchanan J. M.	'Good Economics – Bad Law' (1974) 60 Virg L Rev 483
Calabresi G.	'Some Thoughts on Risk Distribution and the Law of Torts (1961) 70 Yale LJ 499
Calabresi G. and Melamed A. D.	'Property Rules, Liability Rules, and Inalienability: One View of the Cathedral' (1972) 85 Harv L Rev 1089
Coase R. R.	'The Problem of Social Cost' (1960) 3 J L Econ 1
Cranston R.	'Creeping Economism: Some Thoughts on Law and Economics' (1977) 4 Br J L Soc 103
Epstein R. A.	'A Theory of Strict Liability' (1973) 2 JLS 151
Leff A. A.	'Economic Analysis of Law: Some Realism about Nominalism (1974) 60 Virg L Rev 451
Mishan E. J.	'Pareto Optimality and the Law' (1967) 19 OEP 255
	'Evaluation of Life and Limb: a Theoretical Approach' (1971) JPE 687
Nozick R.	*Anarchy, State and Utopia* (1974) pp. 57–87
Posner R.	*Economic Analysis of Law* (2nd edn, 1972)
Storey D. J.	'The Economics of Water Pollution Law: an Application of Posner's Law' (1976) 3 Br J L Soc 76

5 Punishment

In *Crime and Punishment*, Dostoevsky puts the following views in the mouths of his characters:

Marmeladoff: Mr Lebeziatnikoff, who is up to all the ideas of our day, explained lately that pity is now actually prohibited by science, an opinion current in England, the headquarters of political economy.

Sonia (to Raskolnikoff): You must make atonement, so that you may be redeemed thereby ... You shall have it (her cross) at the moment of your expiation.

Porphyrius (to Raskolnikoff): *You cannot do without us* ... I am even of opinion that, after careful consideration, you will make up your mind to make atonement ... In truth, Rodion Romanovitch, suffering is a grand thing ... There lies a theory in suffering.

The 'theory' to which Porphyrius refers is that of retributive punishment. According to this theory, justice requires that a man should suffer because of, and in proportion to, his moral wrongdoing. The political economists in England, to whom Dostoevsky was passionately opposed, were the utilitarian disciples of Bentham, who had written (as we saw in the last chapter), that all punishment was in itself an evil, and could only be justified as far as it prevented some greater evil. From a utilitarian point of view, the pain of punishment may be outweighed by its good consequences if it deters the offender from offending again, or if it deters others from committing the like offence, or if it can be made the occasion for reforming the offender, or if it results in a dangerous person being removed from society. For retributivists, whatever other purposes are served by a penal system, it only exacts justice so far as it gives an offender his moral deserts. Welfare consequences are irrelevant from the point of view of retributive justice. Kant expressed the matter graphically:

'Even if a Civil Society resolved to dissolve itself with the consent of all its members – as might be supposed in the case of a People inhabiting an island resolving to separate and scatter themselves throughout the whole world – the last Murderer lying in the prison

49

ought to be executed before the resolution was carried out. This ought to be done in order that every one may realise the desert of his deeds, and that bloodguiltiness may not remain upon the people; for otherwise they might all be regarded as participators in the murder as a public violation of Justice.'[1]

Thus, the philosophers and moralists have divided themselves on the issue of punishment: retributivists versus utilitarians. The numbers on each side vary. Thirty years ago there were very few confessed retributivists in the English-speaking world; now they are perhaps in the majority. Not that every writer takes his stand firmly at one end or other of the tug-of-war, and there are many combinations and variants. The discussion is not exclusively jurisprudential since plenty of punishment goes on outside the law. It bears on legal institutions in four contexts: legislation; judicial 'legislation'; sentencing; and institution-evaluation.

First, in debating the merits of proposed legislation which seeks to penalise or de-penalise some activity, one may ask whether the measure is supposed to be justified by its good consequences, or whether it is aimed at more perfectly realising the state's duty to punish wrongdoing. Such discussion overlaps with issues raised in chapter 10, below, about freedom and the enforcement of morals.

Secondly, in the judicial elucidation of the criminal law, conceptions of what punishment is for play a role. In this context, no consistent commitment to utilitarian or retributive views emerges. On one view, as we shall see, the insistence on proof of intent or recklessness (*mens rea*) in serious crimes, and the admissibility of exculpatory defences (like capacity or duress), are justified on retributive but not on utilitarian grounds. Certainly the judges commonly speak of both as 'requirements of justice'. In two recent decisions, senior English judges have been divided about the relative weight to be given to such 'retributive' considerations as compared with general consequentialist arguments. In 1975, a majority of three to two of the House of Lords laid down, for the first time, that duress could be a complete defence to a charge of murder as a principal in the second degree.[2] A year later, the Privy Council, again by a majority of three to two, refused to extend the defence to those charged with murder as principals in the first degree.[3] The minority judges in the first case and the majority in the second stressed the bad consequences of allowing people to go free on the ground that, when they killed or assisted in killing, they were acting under the threat of death

1 *The Philosophy of Law* p.198.
2 *Director of Public Prosecutions for Northern Ireland v Lynch* [1975] AC 653.
3 *Abbott v R* [1977] AC 755.

from a terrorist or gang leader. To do this would be a 'terrorist's charter'. It would mean that any such leader could comfort his followers: 'If you are caught, you need only tell the truth, that I would have shot you if you had not obeyed; and they will have to let you go'. Each acquitted killer could be employed again and again. The majority in the first case and the minority in the second took the view that such considerations were outweighed by the injustice of convicting a man who was not, by non-heroic standards, morally blameworthy. Lord Wilberforce said:

RETRIB. VIEW

> 'The judges have always assumed responsibility for deciding questions of principle relating to criminal liability and guilt, and particularly for setting the standards by which the law expects normal men to act. In all such matters as capacity, sanity, drunkenness, coercion, necessity, provocation, self-defence, the common law, through the judges, accepts and sets the standards of right-thinking men of normal firmness and humanity at a level which people can accept and respect ... A law, which requires innocent victims of terrorist threats to be tried for murder and convicted as murderers, is an unjust law.'[4]

So far as drunkenness is concerned, the House of Lords has recently preferred general arguments of utility to specific arguments based on retributive justice. Before the decision in *Director of Public Prosecutions v Majewski*,[5] the predominant view among academic writers was that one who was too drunk to know what he was doing should not be convicted of a crime whose definition included *mens rea*. 'Logic' – that is, the consistent application of the *mens rea* principle – required that he could not be justly held accountable. The House unanimously rejected this view. Men who got into such dangerous conditions could not be left at large. Since we have no crime of 'getting dangerously drunk', the only way to protect the community was to convict a man of a crime of 'basic intent' (such as an assault) even though he had no control at the time of the offence. Lord Edmund-Davies said:

> 'It is at this point pertinent to pause to consider why legal systems exist. The universal object of a system of law is obvious – the establishment and maintenance of order.'[6]

UTIL. VIEW

The third jurisprudential context for conceptions of what justifies punishment is the area of sentencing. In the great majority of crimes, the courts have a wide discretion up to a statutory maximum. English

4 [1975] AC 653 at 684–685.
5 [1977] AC 443.
6 Ibid at 495.

judges adopt both retributive and utilitarian considerations. The Court of Appeal has laid down four principles to be applied in sentencing: retribution, deterrence (as regards both the offender and others), prevention, and rehabilitation – retribution being required so that society through its courts can show its abhorrence of particular types of crime.[7] The reasons for pronouncing sentence given by first instance judges contain variants of all these criteria: 'You have shown no remorse', that is, you are especially wicked and deserve heavy punishment (retribution); 'You broke a special relationship of trust' (ditto); 'I am not unsympathetic, having regard to the circumstances which led you to act as you did, but it must be made clear that this sort of thing is not to be tolerated' (deterrent); 'It is to be hoped that you take advantage of this further period of probation to undertake a proper training course' (rehabilitation); 'Such people as you are a danger to the community if left at large' (prevention). Superior courts vary sentences on appeal, sometimes because they take a different view of the deterrent, reformatory or preventative consequences, sometimes because the sentence is out of line with other sentences and so retributively unjust.

The three contexts so far considered presuppose a typical background of a criminal law and a criminal enforcement process. Could we not have something radically different, a system of 'treatment' rather than punishment, or no organised state force at all? As we shall see in chapter 19, below, Lenin envisaged a future classless society where such delinquents as remain will be dealt with by the spontaneous reaction of their fellows. Our fourth type of question considers whether 'punishment' is justifiable at all.

At this point, we are liable to run up against a 'definitional stop' argument: 'That system might be better, but it wouldn't be punishment, so it is not relevant to the philosophy of punishment.' Definitions ought not to block off fundamental questions in that way. Nevertheless, we have to pay some attention to the definition of punishment expressed or implied in some arguments about justification of punishment, just to see whether all alternatives have been considered.

Professor Rawls offers the following definition:

'A person is said to suffer punishment whenever he is legally deprived of some of the normal rights of a citizen on the ground that he has violated a rule of law, the violation having been established by a trial according to the due process of law, provided that the deprivation is carried out by the recognised legal authorities of the State, that the rule of law clearly specifies both the offence and the

---

7   *R v Sargeant* (1974) 60 Cr App Rep 74.

attached penalty, that the courts construe statutes strictly, and that the statute was on the book prior to the time of the offence.'[8]

Rawls, using this definition, purports to avoid the retributive/ utilitarian dilemma. He argues that, whatever justifies punishment in general, a punishment in a particular case is justified simply by reference to the practice of punishment. He conjures up an alternative practice – for which he coins the word 'telishment' – in which officials would have discretion to subject any individual they thought fit to deprivation if that would (in their view) advance the general good. He argues that, not merely would telishment be incompatible with retributivism, but that utilitarian considerations are likely to favour 'punishment' as against 'telishment', because the consequences of the latter practice would be so bad.

Might it not be possible, however, to devise a system of 'punishment' which lacks some of the features contained in Rawls' definition, but is still quite different from 'telishment'? Whether it would be preferable to Rawlsian punishment might depend on the importance we attach to the rule-of-law elements incorporated into his definition (see chapter 11, below). In 1974, the House of Lords declared that the crime of 'conspiracy to effect a public mischief' was unknown to the law. Lord Simon of Glaisdale said:

> 'In effect the concept enjoins an English criminal court to act like a "people's court" in a totalitarian régime, and to declare punishable and to punish conduct held at large to be "extremely injurious to the public".'[9]

'Punishment' by a 'people's court' need not be telishment. There may be no precise rules defining offences, but there may be fairly well-established criteria of 'guilt'. A Marxist revolutionary court may have a clear programme for delineating 'class enemies' who are to be eliminated or subjected to special disadvantages. An Islamic revolutionary court is more likely to justify its penalties directly by reference to considerations of retributive justice – punishment meet for evildoers.

In considering whether we need criminal law in order to perform what Lord Edmund-Davies calls 'the universal object of a system of law', viz. 'the establishment and maintenance of order', one spectacular non sequitur must be got out of the way. It is sometimes argued that, since most offenders continue to commit crimes after serving their sentences, it follows that deterrents do not work. But of course,

---

8 'Two Concepts of Rules' in Acton *The Philosophy of Punishment* pp. 111–112.
9 *Director of Public Prosecutions v Withers* [1975] AC 842 at 870.

the conclusion does not follow. Other people may have been deterred from committing their first crime. Such evidence as there is, for instance from police strikes, suggests that crime would be much greater were there no criminal law enforcement at all. This still leaves open for debate the Marxist contention that, if only people were properly re-educated, there would be no need for institutionalised law enforcement. Acceptance of that view must at present rest on faith.

Consider a much more modest departure from our present punishing practices, that of Lady Wootton. The system she advocates would be one of universal strict liability. Pre-announced rules would define the external manifestations of antisocial conduct, and a court would have to find whether these had been met in any particular case. But whether or not the person before the court had acted 'intentionally' would not be considered at the 'conviction' stage. The court, having found that a person had performed the prohibited conduct, would hand him over to sentence commissioners, trained social scientists who would be qualified to decide on the appropriate treatment – taking into account, if they thought fit, the fact that he had acted deliberately or accidentally. This system would be far removed from 'telishment'. It is not clear whether it would come within Rawls' definition of punishment, but Lady Wootton is clear that she would not wish it to be called 'punishment' precisely because of the retributive associations of that word. She would like what she regards as the essentially religious concept of responsibility to 'wither away'. She believes that her system would be preferable, on utilitarian grounds, to our present punishment practices. It would be forward-looking towards treatment, and not backward-looking towards moral guilt at the time of the offence. It would enable suitable treatment measures to be taken in the case of people who, under our present system, are not prosecuted because *mens rea* cannot be proved.

> 'If the object of the criminal law is to prevent the occurrence of socially damaging actions, it would be absurd to turn a blind eye to those which were due to carelessness, negligence or even accident.'[10]

Whether the requirement of *mens rea* is based on retributive grounds is a question which has provoked much controversy. Bentham argued that *mens rea* and the general defences were required by utility. His point was that, since the object of laying down penalties was to threaten just enough harm to deter from harm, it would be pointless to threaten those who could not help acting as they did. Professor Hart rejects this 'economy of threats' argument, on the ground that, although one who did not deliberately break the law could not himself

10 *Crime and the Criminal Law* p. 52.

have been deterred, punishing him might deter others. To that some would rejoin that the especially acute suffering involved in being punished for what you could not help would outweigh any deterrent advantages. Hart himself believes that *mens rea* is supportable on a modified retributive basis. He argues that the 'justifying aim' of punishment is utilitarian, the protection of society and so on; but this aim should be limited by reference to what he calls 'retribution in distribution'. Even if punishing one who was not at fault would produce a net utility gain, we should not allow it. We should defer to the popular conception of justice which requires that only the blame-worthy should be subjected to state penalising. He further concedes that a rough retributive scale of maximum punishments should be used to limit sentences even where longer sentences would be justified on utilitarian grounds. Does this concede too much to the retribu-tivists? If we are sure that burglars are deterrable, but that baby-batterers are not, is there not a (utilitarian) case for giving the former much longer sentences than the latter even if we think that their crimes are morally less culpable?

Issues raised in the debate between retributivists and utilitarians bear on all the four contexts we have been discussing. They cannot be ✳ NB. eliminated, as some philosophers appear to suggest, by focusing attention on 'decisions under a practice', where the judge has merely to perform his role-duty of applying the law. In sentencing, and in hard cases where the issue is what the law should be held to be, retributive justice and social consequences offer their competing allures. Nevertheless, if Hart and English judges are correct, it is not ⚓ necessary to come down bang on one side or the other. What are the general arguments for each view? Perusal of the writers may give the impression that the chief arguments are brick-bats thrown at the other party. Utilitarians argue that retributivists are cruel. They favour infliction of suffering when it cannot be proved that any good will be done by it. They believe, says Bentham, in a 'vengeful and splenetic deity'. Or else, they talk in mysterious metaphysical terms, as Hegel does when he speaks of punishment as the 'annulment' of a crime. They rely on loose language about 'paying one's debts to' society', in order to draw an inappropriate analogy between repara-tion and retribution – whereas, although it is true that someone who damages another has a duty to make good (a duty supportable on utilitarian grounds), moral wrongdoing, as such, does not give rise to a 'debt'. Above all, not only do retributivists regard infliction of punishment as justified simply by being morally deserved, but they hold the curious belief that it is possible to measure such desert by reference to the harm done and the degree of responsibility – witness the *lex talionis*, 'an eye for an eye, a tooth for a tooth'.

To such charges retributivists reply in various ways. Retribution is ✳
not cruel, because it treats a man with dignity, regarding him as a
responsible agent. It gives him a chance to expiate his crime by
suffering, so the analogy with debts is not inappropriate. Alternatively far from being cruel, retribution is the offender's right. How else
is the breach between him and society to be healed? Or, at least
retribution is not needlessly cruel, since society must denounce crimes
in an emphatic way, and the only available method is retributive
sentencing. As to *lex talionis*, of course the exact equivalent of harm
cannot be meted out to most offenders – you cannot defraud the
defrauder, or rape the rapist. But you can insist on proportionality: ✳
that is, given that punishments of a certain magnitude are customarily imposed for certain offences, you can insist on less for lesser
offences and more for graver ones. Above all, the retributivist appeals
to 'justice' as understood by the overwhelming majority of mankind
through all ages.

This latter appeal is particularly effective when the retributivist
swings into the attack. 'Justice' is held up as a shield against those
who would coerce us for what they consider to be community good.
Any coercion going beyond our deserts is unjust. Furthermore, the
retributivist may have a multi-principled ethic which allows him to
temper justice with mercy, whilst the strict utilitarian must decide
what is best, all things considered, by reference to consequences, and
thereafter regard any 'mitigation' as morally unacceptable.

Utilitarians, argues the retributivist, would support 'punishing'
the innocent if that could be seen to produce the greatest good. Here is
Lady Wootton, a utilitarian, suggesting that we ditch responsibility.
This would mean that, if a semi-illiterate widow inserts incorrect
information in her supplementary benefits claim form, she could be
brought before a court even though all concerned have no doubt that
she did not mean to defraud. She would, of course, be told that this
was not 'punishment', that she was not liable to 'conviction' but
merely to be found a suitable case for treatment. She could tell the
sentence commissioners about her mistake and, if they believed her,
they would probably require no more by way of treatment than that
she attend literacy classes: 'It's for your own good, dear!' The retributivist believes that no such assurance would meet her complaint
that 'It's not just; it wasn't my fault!'

Why should we stop with strict liability? If medical science
advances to the point where it can accurately predict that a certain
kind of individual is biologically predisposed to commit serious crime,
why wait for him to do so? Would not utilitarianism recommend his
humane incarceration? The retributivists might raise a similar point
in the context of what one might call 'social defence arguments'. It is

sometimes contended – for example, with criminal damage or petty theft by members of disadvantaged groups – that society is to blame, not the offender. What follows? From a retributivist point of view, if it is really true that what was done was not morally wrong, there should be no punishment; or if it was less wrong than would have been the case but for the social conditions, less sentence. But from a utilitarian point of view, perhaps, since such acts are harmful, those who are inevitably (because of their background) going to offend should be removed from society forthwith – into humane labour colonies or retraining camps. We would explain to the members of the disadvantaged group: 'It's not your fault that you will inevitably inflict damage; this is best for everyone'. Will they not reply: 'Who says I will? It's unjust.' Kant's major argument against a utilitarian theory of punishment is that it treats men as mere means, not both as means and ends. Only a conception of retributively just punishment accords with respect for men as autonomous individuals. Apart from this point of principle, are utilitarians in any better case, in the matter of being able to calculate consequences, than are retributivists in being able to provide objective scales of desert?

NB

To all of this utilitarians might answer that a careful calculation of social consequences will take proper account of the distress which would be caused to people by what the retributivists call 'unjust' measures. As the economic analysis of law demonstrates (see chapter 4, above), things like 'distress' are in principle measurable, by asking what people would pay to have them removed; whereas no measure is even in principle available for the retributivists' notion of subjective moral guilt. In any case, scientific progress is impossible if we insist on haltering it by untutored conceptions of 'justice'. It was necessary to fly in the face of popular retributivist sentiment in order to abolish the death penalty. We must do so again to get rid of the idea of personal responsibility.

Utilitarians are generally against the death penalty because there is no satisfactory evidence of its deterrent effect. Retributivists are divided about it. The traditional view, supported by Kant and Hegel, was that executing murderers was a clear case of just deserts. On the other hand, Dostoevsky, with his more individualistic view of the redemptive quality of punishment, ruled it out.

The retributivist-utilitarian debate will not go away. Even a radical critic who takes the view that nothing justifies our present punishing practices is still likely to employ the language of retributive or utilitarian justification in the context of particular decisions. Both have infused our political and moral language: 'He couldn't help what happened, so it's unjust to keep him inside. What's more, it's useless; no one will be deterred, and he's unlikely to do it again.'

Bibliography

Acton H. B. (ed)	*The Philosophy of Punishment* (1969)
Bedau H. A., Hirsch A. V., Wasserstrom R. A.	'The New Retributivism (A Symposium)' (1978) 85 J Phil 601
Bentham J.	*An Introduction to the Principles of Morals and Legislation* (Burns and Hart (eds), 1970) ch 13
Care C.	'Retributive Penal Liability' Am Phil Q Monograph no. 7 (1973)
Clarke M. J.	'The Impact of Social Science on Conceptions of Responsibility' (1975) 2 Br J L Soc 32
Gibbs J. P.	*Crime, Punishment, and Deterrence* (1975)
Haag E. van Den	*Punishing Criminals* (1975)
Hart H. L. A.	*Punishment and Responsibility* (1968)
Hegel G. W. F.	*Philosophy of Right* (Knox trans, 1942) pp. 66–74
Hirsch A. V.	*Doing Justice: The Choice of Punishments* (1976)
Honderich T.	*Punishment: The Supposed Justifications* (1969)
Kant I.	*The Philosophy of Law* (Hastie trans, 1887) pp. 194–205 *The Metaphysical Elements of Justice* (Ladd trans, 1965) pp. 99–107
Klenig J.	*Punishment and Desert* (1973)
Lucas J. R.	*On Justice* (1980) ch 6
Morris H.	'Persons and Punishment' (1968) 52 Monist 475
Murphy J. G.	*Retribution, Justice and Therapy* (1979)
Piper A. M. S.	'Utility, Publicity, and Manipulation' (1978) 88 Ethics 189
Ross A.	*On Guilt, Responsibility and Punishment* (1975)
Summers R. S.	Summers and Howard—*Law: its Nature, Functions, and Limits* (2nd edn, 1972) ch 2
Walker N.	'The Efficacy and Morality of Deterrents' [1979] Crim LR 129
Wootton B.	*Crime and the Criminal Law* (1963)

6   Kelsen's pure theory of law

Soon after the first world war, news in the philosophic world was coming out of Austria. In Vienna, thinkers were suggesting new ways of looking at old problems – demarcating factual (verifiable, scientific) statements from other kinds of assertion. One of these was Hans Kelsen (1881–1973), who applied this technique to the law. He developed what he called a 'pure' theory of law. The bricks out of which he built his model of law were not political events, like legislating, adjudicating or obeying. They were statements of a particular kind, those which purported to describe conduct as legal or illegal, or to ascribe to someone a legal duty or a legal right. These were not statements directly about the world of cause and effect. No lawyer asserting that such-and-such conduct was a crime was committing himself to the view that, if someone acted in that way, he would be punished; he would be asserting that, by law, he 'ought' to be punished, so the 'science of law' was not a science of nature. Its subject matter was a series of ought-relationships. The law must be understood as a system ('order') of 'norms'.

Kelsen's long career witnessed many restatements and refinements of this central tenet, that laws are not part of natural reality but norms by which reality may be measured. From that tenet he never deviated. On many other matters he changed his mind. In particular, he fluctuated about the value for understanding the normative science of law of certain analogies with the intellectual processes of natural science contained in the writings of Immanuel Kant (1724–1804). Kant had developed an epistemology (theory of knowledge) according to which we can only comprehend nature if we apply to it certain categories of thought not themselves given in nature – such as time, space and causality. Similarly, Kelsen argued during most of his career, legal science can only describe the law by making certain presuppositions – such as that valid norms could not conflict, that there is a hierarchy of norms within a legal order from the more abstract to the more concrete, and, above all, that description of the law is only possible if we presuppose a basic norm from which all norms within the system derive their validity. During the last decade of Kelsen's life, this Neokantianism fades, to some extent, from his

59

writings – certainly, the idea of non-contradiction is abandoned. The most that can be done here is to sketch the main lines of the theory as it stood before this last decade of revision.

Even so, it is not possible to give an account of the theory which would be uncontroversial. Apart from acknowledged changes of mind, there are many obscurities in Kelsen, and an army of scholars who debate what it was he was really trying to say. Without entering into such questions, one can still make some assessment of the theory's merits and demerits. Commentators would probably agree that it is the most internationally famous theory of law this century has so far produced.

1   Why 'pure'?

Kelsen believed that statements of positive law were not statements of moral or political value, nor yet statements of fact. The 'law', then, which such statements describe must not be defined in terms of morals, politics or sociology. Theory must make articulate the subject matter of discourse. A theory of law must be pure, in that it must construct a concept of law with these other things excluded. He did not suppose that lawyers could be trusted to keep their own information pure. On the contrary, he found that much legal text-writing tended to smuggle in the writer's own value judgments, and part of the explanation for that was that legal language used concepts which morals and politics and social sciences also employ – like duty, state and person. The thing to do was to isolate the norms of positive law, which alone could be the subject matter of objective (scientific) description, and then define 'legal' uses of such concepts in terms of those norms. A legal norm characteristically provided that if certain conduct was performed, an official should apply some measure of coercion. To say that someone has a legal duty is therefore to say no more than that some norm of positive law makes the opposite conduct the condition for coercion to be applied to him. The 'state', as a legal concept, means just the personification ('hypo-statisation') of all the legal norms valid within a territory. A 'person', as a legal concept, means some entity (human or otherwise) to whose actions or existence legal norms attach consequences.

It is, said Kelsen, not the business of the science of law 'to approve or disapprove its subject'.[1] Let lawyers stick to their last. If asked for information about the law, they can, scientifically, only describe

---

1   *Pure Theory of Law* p. 68.

norms – the circumstances under which, by law, coercion is stipulated. Whether conduct is, by any other criterion, right or wrong is a private and wholly subjective value judgment; the lawyer's attitude as to that is no different from everyone else's. If it is not clear whether, by existing norms, conduct is the condition of sanctions, but the law empowers judges to decide the question at their discretion, then legal science must report just that – the law authorises the court to create a particular norm ordering a sanction in this case. Whether the judge ought so to 'legislate' is a question of legal politics. He has the authority, but how he exercises it is beyond science to lay down.

Legal commentators commonly support their descriptions of the law by reference to the purposes or functions of the law. They suggest that a particular interpretation is correct, having regard to the motives of the legislature or the social function the law is supposed to serve. Such psychological and political matters cannot be objectively known and should therefore, Kelsen argues, not be part of objective legal science. The only 'function' which can, objectively, be attributed to all legal systems is that which appears on the face of legal norms. Reading the legal texts will show that coercive acts by one man against another are always either the condition for the application of sanctions ('delicts'), or else they are prescribed by legal norms ('sanctions'). So the only universal function is the monopolisation of force within the legal order – not justice, but peace. The purpose of legislators are multifarious. The technique for achieving them is always the same – the discouraging of conduct by attaching a sanction to it. This overall technique breaks down into three particular techniques, typical of different branches of the law or of particular economic regimes. The penal technique makes conduct (offences) the condition of sanctions to the delinquent. The administrative technique stipulates that coercive measures should be taken – such as the internment of the insane or those considered politically undesirable – without any particular conduct by the person against whom the measures are applied being laid down as a condition. The civil technique stipulates as the conditions for coercive measures (like awards of damages) both the conduct of the delinquent (breach of contract or tort) and the decision of some party to sue. This latter technique is typical of capitalist economic regimes. The term 'legal right', in its strict sense, refers to the fact that some norm makes the application of coercion conditional on someone's choice to sue.

Thus, the 'pure' theory recommends that all positive law should be viewed as a system of norms stipulating that, under certain conditions, a coercive measure ought to be applied. Is such a view practicable, and, if practicable, is it desirable?

Can all the products of legislation – provisions setting up institutions, rules about formalities for transactions, conceptual definitions, and so on – be reduced to the Kelsenian canonical form of: 'if ... then a sanction ought to be applied'? Kelsen's major works, *General Theory of Law and State* and *Pure Theory of Law*, seek to demonstrate how this can be done. Procedural requirements relating to legislation can be rewritten for example: 'if a bill has been duly voted on and promulgated ... then the court should order (the sanction stipulated in the bill)'. Rules relating to the formation of contracts or wills may be rendered: 'if there has been an offer and an acceptance, and if there was consideration, etc., and if breach and suit followed, then ... sanctions'; or: 'if a will has been validly made and the executors will not deliver the property to the legatee, and he has claimed it, then the court should order them to deliver'.

Kelsen recognises that there may be products of legislation which cannot be reconstructed in this way. If an act contains congratulatory remarks about a statesman, or purely 'ideological' provisions about the existence of God or the sovereign will of the people, it is unlikely that civil or criminal wrongs will only be punishable if such provisions are complied with. If a statute provided: 'Winston Churchill was a great man', but did not go on to make the denial of this the condition for punishment, the provision would, for that reason, be what Kelsen calls 'legally irrelevant material'. Legislation, and particularly constitutions, do contain ideological pronouncements, as well as indications of the conditions under which state force is to be applied, but only the latter are part of positive law. The Kelsenian canonical norm-structure is supposed to provide a litmus paper test for distinguishing the legally relevant from the legally irrelevant.

Is this reconstruction desirable? If we think that the overall function of law is not the monopolisation of force but rather, say, the maintenance of just relationships or just allocation of resources, then of course the raison d'être of Kelsen's enterprise falls away. But even if we concede primacy to the maintenance of peace, does a model of law exclusively centred on this facet of legal regulation not leave out of account other aspects of social life which are, in some sense, 'legal'? Principles which cannot be represented as parts of sanction-stipulating norms may, some would argue, still be 'legal' in the sense that they can be used by judges to justify decisions in 'hard cases' (see chapter 14, below). There may be 'legal' sentiments which are a separable sub-set of social attitudes, constituting part of a 'living law' (see chapter 18, below). They would be left out of Kelsen's formal definition of law. The popular notion of what is a 'crime' may be more important than any formal definition of it. Supposing I am told that there is a law in the statutes of Redland which makes it punishable for a parent to allow his son to sleep with a girlfriend under the parent's roof. Provided that the law is occasionally invoked, such conduct will be a crime by Kelsen's theory – if it is never invoked it will, as we shall see, lose its validity by desuetude. Kelsen's critics would point to this as an illustration of the unilluminating formalism of the theory. If it is true that the vast majority do not think this sort of conduct 'really criminal', and would have no sympathy with, and give no assistance to, authorities seeking to restrain it, then it is not truly an offence. We need some theory of law based on social attitudes, which enables us to distinguish real from purely technical offences. One has to choose, in the light of issues ranging across the entire field of jurisprudence. Shall we conceive of law as a system constructed out of what is in the books, or as something integrally connected to a larger social order?

2 Sanctions

For Kelsen, the coercive measures stipulated by legal norms are the deprivation of life, liberty, health or property – that is, capital punishment, imprisonment, corporal punishment, or fines, damages, and other orders about handing over specific property. Unlike Austin (see chapter 3, above), he is quite clear on one point. It is no part of his theory that sanctions in fact provide a motive for compliance. Law is not distinguished from customary morality by the fact that it is enforced by coercion. It is distinguished in that it stipulates that coercion ought to be applied. Both legal and moral norms contain 'oughts', but a moral norm stipulates, for example, 'people ought not to steal'; whereas a legal norm stipulates 'if people steal, they ought to be punished'. Moral norms are addressed directly to citizens. Legal norms are addressed only to officials. It may be that people would comply with the conduct which is the content of a legal duty even if there were no sanctions. It may be that people comply with moral norms out of fear of social reactions. Sanctions (coercive measures) are the hallmark of law because they appear on the face of legal norms, not because of their supposed psychological effectiveness.

At the same time, legal science is not totally unconcerned with whether sanctions in fact occur. Although, by stating that such and such is a legal norm, the lawyer does not commit himself to a prediction that anyone will be punished, his statements about the validity of legal norms presuppose effectiveness in two ways. First, although a legal norm is valid from the moment of its enactment, it will (Kelsen argues) lose its validity if it has been ineffective for a long time – this is a generalisation of the civil law doctrine of 'desuetude' which, as it happens, does not apply in common law countries.

Secondly, no norm can be valid unless it is a member of a system of norms which is, by and large, effective. In these two ways, effectiveness conditions validity. But how do we measure effectiveness? By two criteria: first, is the norm 'obeyed' (in the sense that conduct conditioning the sanction is not performed); secondly, when disobedience occurs, is the sanction applied? A legal scientist, performing his proper objective role, cannot describe laws emanating from the government of Taiwan as the law of mainland China, because disobedience of Taiwanese laws is never matched by the application of sanctions on the mainland.

This much impurity appears to be unavoidable. Although descriptions of the law are not recordings or predictions of any events in the world, they take place only against a background of coercive measures by and large applied by officials. Some version of this effectiveness test appears in all positivistic theories of law.

Unlike Austin, Kelsen did not limit his theory to the laws of modern states. He asserted that everywhere at all times the word 'law' is used to stand for a system of coercive rules. In the context of primitive societies, the laws stipulated blood revenge. In public international law, the sanctions are war and military reprisals. Everything which is distinctly 'legal' about primitive societies or the international community must be slotted in as conditions for norms requiring kinship groups, or states, to take these drastic measures. Few would follow Kelsen here. The organisers of tribal initiations, or the instructors of diplomats, would be sorely perplexed if they were asked to sieve through the information they give and pick out only that which had a bearing on the propriety of killing. In these contexts, then, because Kelsen's theory cannot separate out any significant system of rules, the theory distorts.

Many critics would assert that the theory also distorts the positive law of modern states, by virtue of the overemphasis on sanctions. Even conceding that positive law is distinguished from other systems of rules by its coercive nature, do we really have to conceive of every rule as directing officials to take away life, liberty, health or property? One objection is based on cumbersomeness. Given Kelsen's reconstruction, you could not make a small point e.g. that a contract relating to land needs to be evidenced in writing, without placing it alongside the rest of the law on contract-formation and breach, all as the conditions for a direction to a judge to award damages or specific performance. Assessing this criticism is one of those things which turns on what one thinks Kelsen was really trying to say. If he meant that law books, solicitors and counsel should rewrite what they say in this cumbersome form, he was recommending what in practice cannot be done. If instead, as seems more plausible, he meant only that the deep structure of sanction-stipulating norms must be kept in mind, so that, on demand, any information about formalities or whatever could be related to circumstances in which damages or an order for specific performance would or would not lie, the objection from cumbersomeness is misplaced.

A second objection runs like this. The legal system is overall coercive, true. But the law has many functions wherein coercive enforcement is very much in the background, such as the enunciation of new standards – for example, in the areas of racial or sexual discrimination. A citizen will ask, and a lawyer will tell him, when it is or is not lawful to discriminate. The matter of sanctions will often never arise. We should split up laws into different types, depending on different legal functions. To this criticism we shall return in discussing Hart's concept of law (see chapter 9, below).

A third criticism fastens on the subsidiary role which Kelsen's coercive form gives to the concept of legal duty. If legislative material in terms makes conduct 'obligatory', but stipulates no sanction for failure to perform the conduct in question, then, by Kelsen's theory, there is no legal duty. If a statute stated that a public authority is to provide certain facilities, but there was in the law no sanction should they not, the duty is merely political-ideological – has the same status as if contained in a manifesto. But can that be right? Surely, the criticisms to which an authority will be subjected if it breaches what a statute ordered it to do will be of a different kind from those which will be made if, for any other reason, the critic thinks it has acted inadequately. It will be said to be 'flouting the law'. Is not the value of legality, as such, a cornerstone of the roles of public officials in modern states, which entails that a theory of law must be able to distinguish things they are legally bound to do from those they are not (even if there are no sanctions)? Judges themselves frequently speak of their 'duties', although they are not usually subject to deprivation of life, liberty, health or property if they fail to comply. That makes it necessary, according to Kelsen's theory, to call these duties 'non-legal'. But if they are merely moral or political, they are distinguishable from other moral or political duties which the same man may have, and the simplest way of distinguishing them is to say that they are 'legally' required.

Furthermore, so critics argue, specific conduct may be made the condition for a sanction when it is not thought of as the subject of a 'duty'. If the law states that, should anyone import canned octopus, an official shall levy on him a payment of £1 per ton, the non-importing will be termed a 'duty' and the £1 per ton a 'fine', only if the object of the legislation was to prohibit the importation. If the legislature had revenue-raising in mind, neither importing nor not importing will be said to be the subject of an obligation, and the payment will be termed a 'tax'. The purity of the theory, as represented in its canonical sanction-stipulating form, prevents us from inquiring into the motives of the legislature; so law conceived in terms of the theory cannot account for these differences in duty-terminology.

Kelsen might have replied to this charge – though I think he never did – 'so much the worse for your slipshod, ideologically-loaded terminology!' If a man is told that, by law, if he imports so much, he must pay so much, that is all the legal information he requires. Compare the situation with library or parking 'fines'. If I return my book late, am told how much is owing and pay up, and then the attendant tells me: 'You were at fault, acting wrongly, not doing your duty, when you kept the book over time', may I not answer: 'Mind your own business. You've told me the rules, and applied them.'

What Kelsen did say was that the primary legal norm stipulates a sanction. Sometimes, we infer a 'secondary norm', prohibiting the conduct which is the condition of the sanction. But this adds nothing to the legal information given in the primary norm. Saying that X is under a legal duty to Φ is the same thing as saying that if X does not Φ the law stipulates a sanction against X. Some judicial treatments of legal duty square with this view, as when the question whether the Crown's duty to protect overseas subjects is a legal duty or only a political duty is equated with the question whether non-performance of that duty is justiciable in the courts.[2] On the other hand, the sanction-stipulating conditions of some legal rules presuppose a legal duty, like the rule which states that a police officer who wilfully and without reasonable excuse or justification neglects to perform any duty imposed on him by common law or statute is indictable for the common law offence of misconduct in a public office.[3] References to duties in this rule cannot be translated in Kelsenian fashion, since it contemplates that the duty may be broken otherwise than wilfully, in which case there will be no sanction. More generally, judicial reasoning in instances where the law is not clear commonly starts from the assumption that X had a legal duty to do something, and then goes on to discuss whether any particular failure to perform it should be made the subject of a sanction. The reasoning would be circular if duty were defined as liability to sanction. Similar objections may be raised against Kelsen's reductionist analysis of other legal concepts in terms of sanctions. It will not work if the concept is presupposed as a step in reasoning leading to a conclusion about sanctions.

2   *Tito v Waddell (No. 2)* [1977] Ch 106; *Mutasa v A-G* [1979] 3 All ER 257.
3   *R v Dytham* [1979] QB 722.

Moreover, a major internal weakness in Kelsen's theory comes to light when we relate his sanction-dependent concept of duty to his concept of effectiveness (the latter being, as we have seen, a condition of validity). In the case of the importer of canned octopus, or that of the library or parking fine, how are we to measure the effectiveness of the norms unless we can say, as a matter distinct from the sanction, that the intention was to prevent the conditioning conduct, or merely to tax it? If importation, parking or late returning increase, but the payments are always collected, the rules are effective if intended to tax, but not so if intended to prohibit. The attaching of coercion to certain types of conduct is not a mere 'technique' designed to achieve *any* purpose. Often it has an immediate purpose of making the conduct illegal, something one is duty-bound not to do. The concept of 'duty' must therefore stand on its own feet, as something distinct from the concept of sanction. A theory of law must define duty and sanction separately.

3 The basic norm

Kelsen said that there were two things universally true of law, that it was coercive, and that it was a system of norms. For a legal norm to be described as 'valid' it must be a member of a system. (As to whether 'validity' entails anything besides system membership, such as 'bindingness' or 'moral worth', Kelsen was notoriously ambiguous.) The reason for the validity of a norm was always another norm. If it were said that a byelaw was valid, the reason for that would be a statute. The reason for the statute's validity might be a written constitution conferring legislative power on the legislature. The constitution might be valid because it had been promulgated in accordance with some historically prior constitution. Eventually, one must get back to a historical starting-point for norm-creation, beyond which the chain of validation cannot go. At that point it was necessary, Kelsen said, to presuppose a basic norm which authorised those who promulgated the historically first constitution. The coercive system constituting the law is founded on a 'presupposition', or 'hypothesis', that:

> 'coercive acts ought to be carried out only under the conditions and in the way determined by the "fathers" of the constitution or the organs delegated by them. This is, schematically formulated, the basic norm of the legal order of a single State.'[4]

4 *General Theory* p. 116.

If public international law is regarded as law, then, says Kelsen, legal science must interpret it as forming one system with national law. Either it is subsumed under national law, or national law is subsumed under it. In the latter case, the effective constitution of a state is authorised by the principle of effectiveness, a principle of customary international law; and the only true basic norm is that which authorises the creation by states of customary and treaty-made international law – that coercive measures should be applied in ways states have customarily recognised as 'legal'.

Just as validity is traced up, so authority may be traced down. The basic norm authorises the promulgators of the constitution, the constitution authorises the legislature, and so on. The law is a 'dynamic' system not a 'static' one, in that the content of norms lower in the hierarchy is not logically deduced from that of norms above them – as would be the case in a moral system in which, say, 'people ought not to harm their neighbours' was deduced from 'people ought to love their neighbours'. Dynamic derivation means that the contents of lower norms are within limits, chosen by the norm-creator. But the norm is only valid because the choice is authorised by a higher norm. The process of dynamic derivation produces gradually increased 'concretisation' as one moves down the ladder. For Kelsen, contracts, wills and settlements produce legal norms. So long as their makers act within legal powers, they create particular concretisations of higher norms. So too with judges. When a judge passes a sentence he creates an individual norm. Indeed, every act of norm-application is an act of norm-creation, except the final carrying out of a coercive measure.

In a country without a written constitution, like the United Kingdom, Kelsen tells us that the basic norm authorises the norm-creating effect of custom. I have suggested the following simplified model of norm-concretisation as an example of how Kelsenian reconstruction would apply to a particular case.

Concretisation of Kelsenian norms

(1) Basic norm of United Kingdom legal order: Coercive acts ought to be carried out only in ways customarily recognised as constitutional.

(2) Constitutional norm created by custom: Coercive acts ought to be carried out in accordance with statutes enacted by the Queen in Parliament.

(3) General norm created by statute: Where, pursuant to a contract of sale of goods, the seller neglects or refuses to deliver the goods to the buyer, and the buyer elects to sue, the seller ought to be condemned to pay damages.[5]

5 Sale of Goods Act 1979, ss. 2, 51.

(4) Particular norm created by contract between Smith and Brown: If Smith neglects or refuses to deliver his prize rabbit Wundabun to Brown, and Brown elects to sue, Smith ought to be condemned to pay damages.

(5) Particular concretised norm created by county court judge on Brown's suing Smith: If Smith fails to pay damages of £50 within twenty-eight days of this order, and Brown issues a warrant of execution, the bailiff ought to levy execution upon the goods of Smith.

(6) Particular fully concretised norm created by Brown's issuing warrant of execution: Bailiff, levy execution upon the goods of Smith.

For Kelsen, legal science gives information in terms of norms at many levels of generalisation. Smith and Brown and the bailiff will be informed of, and act against the background of, 'law' at the level of concreteness indicated by norms (4), (5) and (6). The textwriter on sale of goods will describe the law at the level of norm (3), and the constitutional lawyer that of norm (2). It is the theorist alone who is concerned with norm (1), the basic norm itself.

The concept of the basic norm has given rise to four kinds of question: What is its nature? What is its content? What is its function? How do we choose between competing basic norms?

Kelsen used a variety of nouns to describe the basic norm – 'presupposition', 'hypothesis', 'fiction'. He asserted that the basic norm differs from all other legal norms in that it is not posited by an act of norm-creation. It is not the product of legislation, but is assumed by anyone who purports to describe valid law. Just as the countryman who tells you that if you leave your mangel-wurzels out in the rain they will rot is presupposing a law of cause and effect which he may never have consciously articulated, so anyone stating that doing X is legal while doing Y is not is presupposing that legal duties can only emanate from certain sources. If he is speaking of American law, he assumes that the rules must derive only from the constitution promulgated by the fathers of the constitution in the eighteenth century, and so presupposes a norm which confers ultimate legislative power upon that body of men. If he is speaking of English law, he is assuming that the laws can only originate in the sources hallowed by the United Kingdom customary constitution, and so is presupposing a norm which confers ultimate legislative power on custom. The basic norm is not a psychological or sociological phenomenon. It is a logical category which makes 'cognition' of law possible. By articulating it, we introduce nothing new but merely make explicit intellectual processes which are always with us.

Some critics suggest that we can make explicit all that is presupposed in legal science without employing such a concept. Is it not enough to point out that lawyers derive laws from constitutional sources? Does the construct of the basic norm provide a satisfactory logical picture of the way in which this is done? Many would urge that some legal-science presuppositions are left out of account by the concept. Like other positivist theories, it does not explain how the law can be said to be X, not by reference to a particular source, but by reference to arguments based on justice or purpose.

As to content, why should we write the basic norm in terms either of a single historical date (when the written constitution was promulgated), or in terms of custom? Lawyers presuppose various independent sources of law – like legislation and precedent – and a ranking amongst these sources – statutes prevail over precedents and so on. Would it not be best to conceive of the basic norm as a rule listing all the sources in a ranked order?

Most discussion concerns the function of the basic norm. What is it for? Within Kelsen's writings, two functions can be distinguished. The basic norm explains how lawyers interpret law as a system. When the lawyer comes to his work, he assumes (before he starts) that he can produce a conclusion about the legality or illegality of conduct, and this means that he assumes that the products of legislation and precedent can be fitted together in some way. Just how they are to be fitted together varies from jurisidiction to jurisdiction, but universally some such systematising process is taken for granted. Thus, lawyers presuppose some rule from which all rules derive and which indicates how conflicts between rules are to be resolved.

The second function of the basic norm is that it explains how anyone, not just a lawyer, can interpret commands of particular individuals as objectively binding norms. The command of a gangster may have the same content as the command of a tax officer, but we only regard the latter as a valid (binding) norm. The explanation is that in the latter case we presuppose the validity (bindingness) of the basic norm underlying the legal system.

The two functions can be distinguished by reference to what Kelsen says about communists and anarchists. A communist will make no distinction (in terms of validity) between the demands of a capitalist legal order and those of gangsters; and an anarchist will not attribute bindingness to any legal system, any more than to a highwayman's orders. Yet: 'Even an anarchist, if he were a professor of law, could describe positive law as a system of valid norms.'[6]

It is the business of lawyers to systematise the effective order, which they do by presupposing a basic norm and referring to each norm derived from it as valid in the sense of 'existing'. It is for each individual, according to his political lights, to choose whether to accept the effective law as valid in the sense of 'binding'; if he does, he

6 *Pure Theory* p. 218.

presupposes the basic norm. The second function of the basic norm has been attacked for confounding the positivist distinction between law and non-law with moral and political questions about whether we ought to obey law. By referring 'bindingness' to the basic norm, Kelsen reduces the question of duty-to-obey to an all-or-nothing issue. If you presuppose the basic norm, all laws are binding; if you do not, none are. This means that, conceptually, we cannot even raise the question: Should we obey some laws but not others? or the question: Is there a prima facie duty to obey the law which can be displaced by particular moral or political considerations? (See chapter 16, below.) If we think that these questions should not be ruled out of court on conceptual grounds – as 'silly' or 'meaningless' – then we cannot follow Kelsen in his second function of the basic norm.

The issue of choosing between competing basic norms arises from the efficacy pre-condition of its presupposition by legal science. Kelsen says that when a revolution occurs, when the old laws cease to be effectively enforced and laws promulgated by the rebels are enforced instead, then lawyers presuppose a new basic norm authorising the revolutionary constitution. Kelsen does not say that it is right or desirable that lawyers should do this, but merely that they do do it. His is a descriptive theory. It has been criticised for making efficacy the only test for legal recognition of revolutions. Surely, it has been argued, lawyers take other things into account – such as the justice of the revolutionary cause, or the approval or disapproval of the populace – not just the fact of enforcement? Whether Kelsen, or his critics, correctly describe what lawyers do in such contexts is an issue of history.

Much more controversial has been the implication drawn from Kelsen's theory by judges in revolutionary situations. The theory was expressly cited, following a coup in Pakistan in 1958, one in Uganda in 1965 and the Rhodesian Unilateral Declaration of Independence in 1965, as justifying judicial recognition of new regimes. The judges in all three countries cited with approval the following passage:

'*Change of the basic norm.* It is just the phenomenon of revolution which clearly shows the significance of the basic norm. Suppose that a group of individuals attempt to seize power by force, in order to remove the legitimate government in a hitherto monarchic State, and to introduce a republican form of government. If they succeed, if the old order ceases, and the new order begins to be efficacious, because the individuals whose behavior the new order regulates actually behave, by and large, in conformity with the new order, then this order is considered as a valid order. It is now according to this new order that the actual behavior of individuals is interpreted as legal or illegal. But this means that a new basic norm is presupposed. It is no longer the norm according to which the old monarchical constitution is valid, but a norm according to which the new republican constitution is valid, a norm endowing the revolutionary government with legal authority. If the revolutionaries fail, if the order they have tried to establish remains inefficacious, then, on the other hand, their undertaking is interpreted, not as a legal, a law-creating act, as the establishment of a constitution, but as an illegal act, as the crime of treason, and this according to the old monarchic constitution and its specific basic norm.'[7]

These decisions, and the theory they purport to apply, have had a bad press. In general, it has been said that, so interpreted, Kelsen's theory amounts to 'might is right' – actually, it should be 'might is law'. In particular, the unpopularity of the Smith regime in Rhodesia has been reflected by distaste for the whole idea of measuring legality by effectiveness. Apart from the attacks of juristic critics, some courts have repudiated the theory. In 1970, the Supreme Court of Nigeria refused to apply Kelsen's theory of revolutions. It held that a military coup of 1966 was not a true revolution, so that the legislative capacity of new institutions was limited by reference to the pre-existing constitution.[8] In 1972, the Supreme Court of Pakistan rejected Kelsen's theory, repudiating its earlier decision. It held that it was through judicial recognition alone that a new legislative organ acquired competence; and that this should be accorded only if a revolutionary constitution embodied the will of the people.[9] In the

---

7 *General Theory of Law and State* p. 118 – cited and applied in *State v Dosso* [1958] 2 Pakistan SCR 180 at 185–186 (per Muhammad Munir CJ), 195 (per Shahabuddin J); and in *Uganda v Commissioner of Prisons, ex parte Matovu* [1966] EA 514 at 535–536 (per Sir Udo Udoma CJ; cited in *Madzimambuto v Lardner-Burke NO* [1968] 2 SA 284 at 315 (per Beadle CJ); applied in *R v Ndhlovu* [1968] 4 SA 515 by the Appellate Division of the High Court of Rhodesia, after the Privy Council's decision that English constitutional law knew no relevant doctrine of necessity, so that an all-or-nothing choice must be made between the old and the new regime: *Madzimambuto v Lardner-Burke NO* [1969] AC 645. United Kingdom courts were constitutionally bound to accept the validity of parliamentary legislation which purported to apply to Rhodesia: cf. *Adams v Adams* [1971] P 188; *Re James (an insolvent)* [1977] Ch 41. Occasionally, judges have suggested that laws of effective regimes might be recognised in our courts, even though their governments are not recognised by the executive: *Carl Zeiss Stiftung v Rayner and Keeler Ltd* [1967] 1 AC 853 (per Lord Wilberforce); *Hesperides Hotels Ltd v Aegean Turkish Holidays Ltd* [1978] 1 All ER 277 (per Lord Denning MR).

8 *E. O. Lakanmi and Kimelomo Ola v A-G (Western State)*: see A. Ojo 'The Search for the Grundnorm in Nigeria: the Lakanmi Case' (1971) 20 ICLQ 117.

9 *Asma Jilani v Government of Punjab* (Pak. Leg. decisions 1972, Supreme Court of Pakistan); see T.K.K. Iyer 'Constitutional Law in Pakistan: Kelsen and the Courts' (1973) 21 Am J of Comp L 759. The Court of Appeal in Ghana has refused

Nigerian case, the court's decision was immediately overturned by new legislation declaring that the 1966 coup had been revolutionary. In the Pakistan case, the court was in the happy position of adjudicating on the legality of one coup after it had been superseded by another.

There is no doubt that Kelsen did not expressly authorise judicial use of his theory. However, if he was right in saying that lawyers, *qua* lawyers, always accept efficacious systems, would it not follow that lawyers who refused to do this would be acting in some non-lawyer-like way? We must distinguish the position of legal advisers from that of judges. Supposing, during the Smith regime, one Zimbabwean freedom fighter had asked another for advice: 'I am going on a secret mission to Salisbury. As I don't want to be conspicuous, could you fill me in on the present currency and traffic law?' His colleague would be less than helpful if he replied: 'I can't do that, because that would be presupposing the validity of Smith's legislation.'

With judges, it may be another thing. It all depends on the relationship we hold to exist between efficacy and the judicial role. One view might be that a judge should always stick to his judicial oath. But that might not solve the problem where the oath speaks of upholding 'the law', and the question now is 'which law?' Another view is that judges must do justice, come what may, and 'justice' gives them criteria for choosing between competing governments. The 'will of the people' is one such criterion; 'necessity' is another. Would not the application of such criteria, however, inevitably involve a judge in making some 'political' (and therefore non-judicial) choice? Alternatively, drawing out the implications of Kelsen's view that efficacy is a pre-condition of legal validity, should we not say that the judge who stays in office will inevitably render support to the effective regime, since, be it good or bad, the only law is effectively enforced law? If that is right, then when an effective revolution occurs, the only true choice for judges or other officials is either to resign or to stay on and – like the French traffic police who remained on duty after the German invasion – inevitably to consolidate the new regime. This would mean that the British Government in 1965 gave (through its Governor) inconsistent directives to Rhodesian officials when they were told to carry on with their normal tasks, but not to recognise the new regime. If effectiveness is a pre-condition for law, then the British Government was disingenuous when it said to the black majority, in effect: 'We will not use force to oust the rebel authorities; but, don't worry, they are not legal.'

to apply Kelsen's theory that, when a basic norm changes, all norms are made new: *E.K. Sallah v A-G* [1970] CC 54 at 55; see T. and F.S. Tsikata 'Kelsen and others in the Court of Appeal' (1970) 7 U G LJ 142, and S. K. Date-bah 'Jurisprudence's Day in Court in Ghana' (1971) 20 ICLQ 315.

Bibliography

Brookfield F. M.	'The Courts, Kelsen, and the Rhodesian Revolution' (1969) 19 U Tor LJ 326
Dias R. W. M.	*Jurisprudence* (4th edn, 1976) ch 16
Dworkin R. M.	'Comments on the Unity of Law Doctrine (a Response)' in Kiefer and Munitz (eds) *Ethics and Social Justice* (1970)
Ebenstein W.	*The Pure Theory of Law* (1945)
Eckhoff T. and Sunby N. K.	'The Notion of Basic Norm(s) in Jurisprudence' [1975] Scand S L 123
Eekelaar J. M.	'Principles of Revolutionary Legality' in Simpson (ed) *Oxford Essays in Jurisprudence* (2nd series, 1973)
Finnis J. M.	'Revolutions and Continuity of Law' in Simpson (ed) *Oxford Essays in Jurisprudence* (2nd series, 1973)
Golding M. P.	'Kelsen and the Concept of "Legal system"' in Summers (ed) *More Essays in Legal Philosophy* (1971)
Harris J. W.	'When and Why Does the Grundnorm Change?' (1971) 29 CLJ 103 'Kelsen's Concept of Authority' (1977) 36 CLJ 353 *Law and Legal Science* (1979) ss. 5, 9–17
Hart H. L. A.	'Kelsen Visited' (1963) 16 U CLA L Rev 709 'Kelsen's Doctrine of the Unity of Law' in Kiefer and Munitz (eds) *Ethics and Social Justice* (1970)
Hughes G. B. J.	'Validity and the Basic Norm' (1971) 59 Calif L Rev 695
Kelsen H.	*General Theory of Law and State* (Wedberg trans, 1945) *What is Justice?* (1957) 'Professor Stone and the Pure Theory of Law: a Reply' (1965) 17 Stan L Rev 1128 'On the Pure Theory of Law' (1966) 1 Is L Rev 1 *Pure Theory of Law* (Knight trans, 1967) *Essays in Legal and Moral Philosophy* (Head trans, 1973)
Lloyd D.	*Introduction to Jurisprudence* (4th edn, 1979) ch 5

MacCormick D. N.	'Legal Obligation and the Imperative Fallacy' in Simpson (ed) *Oxford Essays in Jurisprudence* (2nd series, 1973)
Moore R.	*Legal Norms and Legal Science* (1978)
Morineau O.	'The Individual Norm' (1963) 5 Inter-Am L Rev 31
Munzer S. R.	*Legal Validity* (1972) pp. 15–25, 45–50
Nino C.	'Some Confusions Around Kelsen's Concept of Validity' [1978] ARSP 357
Paulson S. L.	'Material and Formal Authorisation in Kelsen's Pure Theory' (1980) 39 CLJ 172
Raz J.	*The Concept of a Legal System* (1970) pp. 93–120 *The Authority of Law* (1979) ch 7
Samek R. A.	*The Legal Point of View* (1974) ch 7
Stone J.	*Legal System and Lawyers' Reasonings* (1964) ch 3
Tur R.	'Positivism, Principles and Rules' in Attwool (ed) *Perspectives in Jurisprudence* (1977)
Woozley A. D.	'Legal Duties, Offences and Sanctions' (1968) 77 Mind 461

7 Legal concepts

1 Hohfeld's analysis

A little jurisprudence can be a dangerous thing. Not long ago, I was taking a short cut across a field. A young lady riding a horse politely asked me never to do so again, as this was private property so I was a trespasser. I knew that she had no possessory rights herself in the field, being neither owner nor lessee but merely one of several people licensed to keep a horse there. So, bethinking me of my Hohfeldian analysis, I replied: 'I may be a trespasser as against the lessees, but as against you I owe no duty not to cross this field.' Her rejoinder was that a trespasser was a trespasser – which is to say: 'It's all very well reducing legal rules to bilateral legal relations for some purposes, but when we are discussing the demands which honour makes of a law-abiding citizen, such reductionism is inappropriate.' On another occasion, I was attending a seminar given by radical social scientists on welfare rights. I asked whether the rights one should press for should be seen primarily in terms of the will-theory or the interest-theory of rights – that is, were we concerned to give the disadvantaged more dignity by making their choices the determinants of how official action should affect their lives, or was the idea simply to see that certain basic needs were met. The reaction was that such pettyfogging analysis was not called for. 'Welfare rights' was an ideological commitment, a slogan. It was an on-going movement, to whose wheels every good man and true should simply put his shoulder.

Chastened by these and similar experiences, I turn in this chapter to the immense jurisprudential literature which has been devoted to the analysis of leading legal concepts. As mentioned in chapter 3, above the modern approach to this enterprise in English-speaking countries began with Bentham and Austin. Bentham believed that 'expository jurisprudence' should turn its hand to explaining the significance of the basic building bricks used in legal prescriptions – such as 'right', 'duty', 'power', 'property' and so on; what Austin was to call 'the principles, notions and distinctions' common to 'mature systems'. For Bentham, the objective was purely practical. We should NB not only explain the part played by these concepts in the law, but we should reconstruct – where necessary, stipulating how words should be used – in the interests of greater clarity of thought and with a view to reform and codification. Later exponents of the method have sometimes appeared to overlook this pragmatic side of analytic endeavour, and have taken the view that scientific analysis was an end in itself. The most celebrated of English-speaking twentieth-century analysts, however, was fully conversant with the pragmatic objective. In the early years of the century, the American jurist, Wesley Newcombe Hohfeld, sought to reduce all legal quantities to their lowest common denominators. In doing this, he (unlike Bentham) did not have codification in mind; but he did believe that his analysis would facilitate the resolution of practical problems in judicial reasoning.

In *Fundamental Legal Conceptions as Applied in Judicial Reasoning*, Hohfeld expounds the lowest common denominators of the law in terms of legal relations. These consist of two squares of correlation and opposition.

Right	Duty	Power	Liability
Privilege	No-Right	Immunity	Disability

Within these squares, every horizontal represents a correlation, and every diagonal an opposition. To say that X has a duty to Φ entails that he has this duty as against someone, Y, who has the correlative right; and also that he has no privilege not to Φ as against Y. To say that A has a power entails that he can by his voluntary act change the legal relations of some other person, B, who has the correlative liability; and that it is not true that A has a disability as against B's legal relation, correlating with an immunity of B.

It is implicit in Hohfeld's analysis that the universe of discourse, which is the subject matter of judicial reasoning, consists of two things only: either some other-regarding act or omission of a person, or some relation-regarding voluntary act of a person. Here is a man putting an envelope into a pillarbox. For the purpose of judicial reasoning, ask not: 'Is this act unlawful?', for it might be a tort against one person – for instance, if it represents the publication of a libel – but be perfectly lawful as against everyone else; ask: 'Was this act the subject of a duty as against some other individual – say, the man's employer – or was it privileged as against that other individual?' It must be one or the other; for, as between A and B, every act of B must either be the subject of a duty – when A has a right that it be done – or it must be the subject of a privilege – when A has a 'no-right' that it be done. The only other question one can ask about the posting of the letter is: 'Was it the exercise of a power as against the legal relations of some other person?' If the person posting the letter is A, and B had previously posted a letter making A an offer, then the posting of the letter is an exercise of a power by A. It creates a contract. That means that, whereas before the posting of the letter of acceptance B did not have certain contractual rights and duties, afterwards he did. A's power to create these contractual relations is correlative to B's liability to have them created. Either A has this power or he does not, power being the opposite of a disability. If, for instance, the offer had been effectively revoked before the letter was posted, then, as to posting the letter and its effect on the relations of B, A would have a disability correlating with B's immunity.

Hohfeld gives many examples of the application of this analysis, both hypothetical, and related to the facts of reported cases. From his treatment of these examples, it becomes apparent that three kinds of advantage are being claimed for the analysis. First, it enables real normative choices to be disentangled from verbal confusions. Hohfeld cites cases having to do with trade competition and labour disputes. In such areas, he says, there is a temptation to move from the proposition that 'I have a right to trade' to 'so you have a duty not to impede my trading'. Such false logic would be avoided if we realise that the word 'right' is used loosely to stand for the four dissimilar relations of right-duty, privilege-no-right, power-liability, and immunity-disability. What people mean by 'I have a right to trade' is that, in carrying on my business, I do no man any legal wrong. As against every other person, each of my trading activities is privileged; as regards each such activity, every person has a no-right that I shall not do it. From that nothing follows about my rights regarding other people's actions. My privilege (my absence of duty) concerns my actions only. Any alleged 'rights' I may have, in the strict sense of that term, concern other people's activities. From my privilege to trade, it does not follow that I have a right that X shall not commit a certain act even if that act makes it more difficult for me to trade. It may be desirable that there should be such a right, but we should beware of thinking that there must be merely because my trading activities are privileged. Hohfeld would have approved of the distinctions drawn – though not necessarily of the normative choices made – in English cases on the 'right to picket'. It was pointed out that legislation which provided that picketers commit no tort or other unlawful act did not entail that picketers had any enforceable claim that those going to work should stop and listen.[1]

---

1 *Broome v Director of Public Prosecutions* [1974] AC 587; *Kavanagh v Hiscock* [1974] QB 600.

The second claimed advantage relates to change in judicial language. Hohfeld believed that his terminology was not too far removed from that employed in the cases. Within the eight basic terms, the only invention was the hyphen in 'no-right'. If judges (and lawyers in general) would only employ his terminology, clarity would reign. As to this hope, he has had no more success than other stipulators about use of legal terms. In the picket cases just referred to, a Hohfeldian point was made, but not in Hohfeldian language. The picketers were said to have been clothed with an 'immunity' not a 'privilege'. For Hohfeld, 'immunity' should only be used where we have in mind a situation in which X's legal relations cannot be changed by Y – for example, constitutional 'immunities' covering those relations which the legislature is disabled from altering. Of course, the fact that judges, legislators and lawyers in general have not used his words does not establish that things might not have been clearer if they had. Some American writers have deliberately employed his terminology, both in the analysis of private law, and in analysing the laws of primitive communities. *The American Law Institute's Restatement* also makes use of it.

The third advantage concerns the activity of other jurists. In the light of his analysis, so Hohfeld believed, juristic problems concerning the nature of such compound concepts as rites *in rem* and legal personality, and the problem of the relation between law and equity, could be dissolved. 'Rights *in rem*' should not be distinguished from 'rights *in personam*' by being thought of as rights over things, nor even as rights against the world. Every notion in the law must be reduced to combinations of bilateral relations. Every such relation has three elements: X, X's act or omission so far as it affects Y or Y's legal relations, and Y. Thus, a so called 'right *in rem*' was one of a bundle of similar relations between a property owner and each and every other member of the community. If I own Blackacre, this means that I have a right that X not enter on Blackacre without my leave, and a similar right against Y, Z and everyone else. It also means that I have a privilege myself to walk on Blackacre (or do any of an indefinite class of other acts in relation to Blackacre), correlating with X's no-right that I shall not walk, and a similar privilege correlating with Y's, Z's and everyone else's no-right. I also have a power to change X's legal relations by conveying Blackacre to him, correlating with his liability to have his relations changed. I have a similar power in relation to Y, Z and the rest. I have an immunity against having my relations changed by someone else conveying away Blackacre, which correlates with X's disability, and a similar immunity correlating with Y's, Z's and everyone else's disability. 'Ownership' then turns out to be constituted by a bundle of rights, privileges, powers and immunities.

Hohfeld recommended the term 'multital' relation for any relation
forming part of such a bundle, indicating that it was accompanied by
an indefinite class of similar relations. Where I have rights of a certain
tenor against only a finite class, we should speak of a 'paucital'
relation; and if only against one individual, a 'unital' relation. Such a
treatment of 'rights *in rem*' will dispose of two sorts of juristic puzzles.
It will enable us to understand how ownership can be limited or
fragmented, and it will dissolve the problem about having property in
non-tangible things. If I have licensed X to walk on my land, or
granted him a right of way, then, as against him, I have no right that
he shall not enter; but my multital rights about entry subsist against
everyone else. If the law prohibits me from developing the land
without planning permission, then, as to those actions comprised in
'development', I no longer have multital privileges so far as planning
enforcement officers are concerned. So far as non-tangible things are
concerned, we need not worry ourselves about questions like: Is a
reputation, or a marital status, 'property'? If I can sue anyone, or
most people, who defame me, then I have a multital right that each
person is not to defame me. In the days when it was possible to sue
anyone who alienated my wife's affections, I had multital rights
regarding such conduct. Knowing the bundles of legal relations
involved, it matters not a whit how we classify 'property'. In a similar
way, Hohfeld argued that there was no problem about the concept of
legal personality, once we recognised that rules relating to so-called
'juristic persons' actually create bundles of relations between
stockholders and company officers. And the problem about the
simultaneous existence in one piece of property of legal and equitable
ownership could be side-stepped by asking of any particular action: Is
it the breach of a duty owed to X at common law and/or in equity? If
both systems give the same answer, there was no conflict. If the
common law said 'no' and equity 'yes', then the common law was *pro
tanto* repealed. A tenant for life who is not impeachable for waste
commits no breach of duty to the remainderman at common law if he
cuts down ornamental trees; but he does in equity. Since equity
prevails over common law, the common law rule on this point has
been abrogated.

Is Hohfeld's analysis an accurate description of, or an acceptable
prescription for, the use of concepts in judicial reasoning? Should
judicial reasoning be the sole focus of an analysis of legal concepts?
These two questions interweave, in an often confusing way, the
particular charges levelled at Hohfeld's analysis.

Two minor matters need not detain us long. First, perhaps Hohfeld
could have picked better words, departing less from ordinary usage.
'Liberty' might be preferable to 'privilege'. 'Liability' sounds odd

when applied to a situation of material advantage – like my 'liability' to have my legal relations changed by someone's leaving me a fortune. Second, as Professor Glanville Williams points out, the accurate opposition (logical contradictory) to 'duty' should be 'liberty not'. Either I am under a duty to Φ as against someone, or I am privileged or at liberty 'not' to Φ. More important criticisms concern three matters: first, Hohfeld's insistence on correlativity; second, his failure to make clear the relationship between 'primary' ('antecedent'), 'secondary' ('remedial') and 'tertiary' ('adjectival') legal relations; third, his failure to investigate the essence of concepts, particularly that of a 'right'.

Older analytical jurists, like Bentham and Austin, took the view that there were some legal duties as to which there were no correlative rights. Critics of Hohfeld have asked whether the duties imposed by the criminal law or other areas of public law necessarily correlate with rights of individuals to claim performances of those duties. As to 'privileges', what is the point of insisting that every act which the law does not prohibit me from performing correlates with someone's 'no-right'? The law permits me to blow my nose. Why describe this legal situation in terms of multital privileges correlating with every other citizen's no-right that I should not do so? As to 'liabilities', my legal relations may change because of some occurrence which is not another's voluntary act – for instance, if a tree set on fire by lightning brings about a new duty to take care. Before the lightning struck, was I not subject to a 'liability' which did not correlate with a 'power'?

Nothing in Hohfeld's writings meets these sorts of criticism directly, but the implicit answer is clear enough. Correlativity is essential, as part of the law's lowest common denominators, because every judicial question concerns two people. The notion of a tax law imposing duties without correlative rights does not arise because, in court, someone or other (some revenue officer perhaps) must be claiming that a man ought to have paid so much tax. The only question the court has to decide is: Did this defendant owe a duty to this plaintiff? English courts in recent years have had to decide whether duties imposed by the criminal law, or duties of public authorities to provide facilities like housing, education, health care, amenities for the disabled and television programmes, are enforceable at the suit of private individuals.[2] The issue has always been,

2 *London Borough of Southwark v Williams* [1971] Ch 734; *Coote v Stone* [1971] 1 All ER 656; *A-G (on the relation of McWhirter) v Independent Broadcasing Authority* [1973] QB 629; *Apple Corps Ltd v Lingasong Ltd* [1977] FSR 345; *Gouriet v Union of Post Office Workers* [1978] AC 435; *Wyatt v Hillingdon LBC* [1978] 76 LGR 727; *Ex Parte Island Records Ltd* [1978] 3 All ER 824; *Thornton v Kirklees Metropolitan BC* [1979] 2 All ER 349; *Mead v London Borough of Haringey* [1979] 2 All ER 1016; *R v Secretary of State for Social Services, ex parte Hinks* (1979) 123 Sol Jo 436.

Hohfeld would argue, whether *as regards the plaintiff* the defendant's conduct was obligatory or privileged. Whether I am at liberty to blow my nose will never come to court; but if it did – say, I was an actor claiming compensation for unfair dismissal and my inappropriate nose-blowing was alleged as a proper ground for my dismissal – then the issue would be whether as to some other person I was or was not privileged to do it. Lightning cannot be joined as a defendant. It is only where my legal relations have been allegedly changed by someone's voluntary act that the question whether they were validly changed or not will arise; and the issue will always be between two persons, deciding whether there was power/liability, or disability/immunity.

Is that defence of the insistence on correlativity sustainable? Do judges ever say 'duty', 'right' and so on, where the concept is not being employed dispositively as to an issue between X and Y? One possible example concerns summonses for directions by trustees. Trustees may ask the court: 'Given this rather obscure settlement and the facts which have arisen, what should/may we do now?' Can that question (must that question) and its answer be translated into: 'What can one or more individual beneficiaries insist that we do, or as to which of the things we do can some (but perhaps not others) raise no complaint?' Similar questions can be raised about declaratory judgments, or any other proceedings not based on a straightforward *lis*.

Even where litigation is wholly adversary, judges employ terms like 'right' and 'duty', not merely in announcing their conclusions, but in the reasoning leading to such conclusions. In the latter context, it seems impossible to interpret such terms as correlations. The rule which has emerged from the cases on public duty mentioned above is that private citizens have no right to sue in respect of breaches of the criminal law unless they affect 'private rights'. Supposing a judge concludes: 'This breach infringed the plaintiff's private right; accordingly, he has a right to demand that the defendant desist from further breaches and I grant him an injunction.' If we interpret the first reference to 'right' in Hohfeldian terms, we would achieve the tautology: 'The plaintiff has a right to demand compliance because he has a right to demand compliance.' Where 'private right' is referred to as a reason for allowing a right to sue, what must be meant is something like 'private interest', a non-Hohfeldian, non-relational conception of right.

Similar non-Hohfeldian analysis of terms is required where reference to a general, uncorrelated 'duty' is given as a reason for recognising a certain relationship. In *Johnson v Phillips*[3] the duty of the

3 [1975] 3 All ER 682.

police to promote free flow of traffic was a reason for holding that a constable could (in an emergency) order a man to drive the wrong way down a one-way street. In *Kent County Council v Batchelor*,[4] a local authority's statutory duty to protect areas of natural beauty was a reason why it should be granted an interim injunction to restrain breach of a tree preservation order. It might be argued that, in the interests of clarity, different terms should be used as substitutes for 'right' and 'duty' where the context is not that of correlation. Is that practical? Or is judicial reasoning necessarily infused with moral and political ideas about private right and public duty, for which some non-Hohfeldian analysis is essential?

One might try to meet objections of this kind by restating Hohfeld's position in the light of American legal realism (see chapter 8, below). M. Radin takes this course. He insists that judicial reasoning is always to be read backwards. The court concludes (for inscrutable motives) that one party can or cannot make a claim against another. Anything it says about the pre-litigation legal position in purported justification of its decision can only be relevant so far as it concerns the two parties. Consistently with realist premises, there is no law but the law for the parties to a litigated dispute.

Whether Hohfeld would have accepted this characterisation of his analysis is unclear. He indicated that 'primary' relations are replaced by 'secondary' relations once a breach of duty occurs, and the latter by 'tertiary' relations once litigation begins. However,

'All primary, or antecedent, relations and all secondary, or remedial, relations can, in general, be ascertained only by inference from the purely adjective judicial processes, that is, by inference from either affirmative or negative action regularly to be had from the particular court from which a judgment or decree may be sought.'[5]

The first major criticism of Hohfeld concerns correlativity, the second concerns these levels of legal relations. Is the content of primary relations dependent on that of secondary and tertiary relations? Hohfeld says that if X is under a duty to deliver goods to Y and fails to do so, then secondary relations arise under which X is under a duty to pay damages to Y. But since contracts of this kind are not specifically enforceable, why did he not reach the 'realist' conclusion advocated by Holmes, that X's duty from the start was merely either to deliver or to pay damages? Further, Hohfeld does not make clear whether the replacement of primary by secondary

4 [1978] 3 All ER 980.
5 (1913) 11 Mich L Rev 537, 569, n.34.

relations is itself a 'change' in relations capable of being the subject of a power/liability, or disability/immunity, relation. If it is, then every duty-breaking act is itself the exercise of a power, since it converts someone's primary right into a remedial right. So is every filing of a defence, or other step in pleadings, which turns remedial into adjectival relations – the latter involving, apparently, legal relations between litigants and judges and other officials. Conversely, on this reading, every 'privilege' involves an 'immunity'; since if I am free, as against you, to act in a certain way, then I am immune from having this primary relationship changed into a remedial relationship by your suing me. In that case, the courts do employ Hohfeldian terminology when they speak of picketers' 'immunities'.

We do not know how realist Hohfeld meant to be. Most of his examples, however, suggest that he intended substantive legal relations to be analysed as a distinct field of discourse from remedial and adjectival relations. In that case, his analysis is unacceptable to the extent (if at all) that judicial reasoning does employ concepts like right or duty in a non-relational sense. Hohfeld claimed that failing to see concepts his way may obscure normative choices. I have myself made the converse claim in the context of the English law of trusts, namely, that insisting on seeing concepts Hohfeld's way has obscured normative choices – that insisting that the sort of 'duty' in terms of which a trust is defined is a relational duty has miscued judicial reasoning.[6]

So far we have discussed criticisms within the bounds of Hohfeld's own particular context, that is, concepts 'as applied in judicial reasoning'. He can be attacked, not for technical error, but for lack of largeness of aim, in that the fundamental conceptions examined are employed in many other contexts. Legal rights and duties are spoken of outside courts. If a man asks his solicitor: 'Do I break the law by doing such and such?' he might be surprised to receive the answer: 'Break it, as against whom?' Furthermore, the significance of legal concepts is not limited to their use by lawyers. When we criticise the law, or use it as a model for right conduct, we do not have to (and commonly do not) reduce it to paired relations. If we debate whether the law should make the wearing of seat-belts compulsory, we conceive of 'duty' as something required, not as something due to some particular individual or individuals. Those who think that one ought to obey the law make similar assumptions about the non-relatedness of duty – that was the point of the young lady equestrian's comment mentioned at the beginning of this chapter: 'A trespasser is a trespasser!' One of the matters which concerns a legal sociologist is

6 (1971) 87 LQR 31.

whether points of legal duty actually correspond to how people behave, or how they think they should behave. There is no question here of reducing duty rules to relational pairings.

The third type of criticism mentioned above concerns Hohfeld's failure to investigate the essence of concepts. The charge is one of arbitrary reductionism. Hohfeld insists that concepts like 'property' and 'corporate person' must be understood in terms of multital paired relations. But that means that we do not even ask whether there is something essential in the idea of property or legal personality – which might explain why legal reasoning has taken the form it has and point to the kinds of political philosophy which underpin it. Hohfeld assumes that all legal concepts belong to one kind of legal system:

> 'Since, in any sovereign state, there must, in the last analysis, be but a single system of *genuine law*, since the various principles and rules of that system must be consistent with one another, and since, accordingly, all *genuine* jural relations must be consistent with one another, two conflicting rules, the one "legal" and the other "equitable", cannot be valid at the same moment of time; one must be valid and determinative to the exclusion of the other.'[7]

I have argued (in *Law and Legal Science*) that the total significance of legal concepts cannot be expressed in terms of legal material frozen at a point of time in 'momentary legal systems'. Legal reasoning deploys legal concepts as part of the 'doctrine model of rationality'; and in that context the concepts exist as part of non-momentary (historic) legal systems, in which the pull of liberal conceptions of property rights and the tension between legal and equitable ownership may be permanent features.

In particular, it can be urged that Hohfeld's analytic squares fail to bring out the essence of the concept of a legal right. He says that we should distinguish four senses in which the word 'right' is sometimes used – right, privilege, power, immunity – but does not pose the question whether there is some underlying idea which explains all these uses. He does not take sides in the time-honoured debate between those who favour a 'will' or an 'interest' conception of 'right'. These schools are represented in modern British legal philosophy by Professor Hart and Professor MacCormick. Hart argues that the essence of a legal right is a legally protected 'choice'. He bases this contention largely on its utility to legal science. When lawyers are giving information about the law, they may be able to say all that needs saying in terms of duties. But sometimes the existence or

7 (1913) 11 Mich L Rev 537, 557.

operation of a duty is made dependent on the choice of an individual.
This special feature needs to be conveyed by some characteristic
terminology, and the word 'right' is apt for the job. In the context of
criminal and public law, what is required of someone is not usually
dependent on another's choice; so there is no special point in talking
about 'rights' not to be murdered or 'rights' that others should pay
taxes. On the other hand, in the typical civil law context, I may
release someone from their duty under a contract, or agree not to sue
for a tort, so that I am made mini-sovereign over his legal duty. 'Legal
right' should normally be reserved for this situation.

Professor MacCormick replies: first, there are sometimes rights
without duties; second, evaluative and critical discourse about the
law presupposes an interest conception of rights (for example,
'children's rights'). As to the first point, he cites Scottish legislation
concerning intestate succession which refers to the 'rights' of
successors in situations where the corresponding duty-holding
executors have not been appointed. To this it might be rejoined that,
even before the executor is appointed, the 'right' correlates with a
duty-shaped gap; and that it is called a right precisely because, once
the executor is appointed, it is for the successor to choose whether to
enforce or waive it.

MacCormick's second point raises more fundamental issues about
the nature of analytic enterprise. Should we analyse legal concepts by
reference to the use of words in the law, or also by reference to use of
the words in discourse about the law? Can one separate the tasks, for
example, by speaking of 'legal rights' as one sort of thing, and
'moral/political rights' as another? Philosophers have recently
distinguished 'concepts' from 'conceptions' in the following way. A
'concept' is that essential thing for which a word stands, though
different people may have conflicting 'conceptions' or 'ideas' about it.
Thus, the debate between will theorists and interest theorists assumes
that there is some notion to be sought to which the word 'right'
corresponds, though they have competing conceptions of what that
notion is. The other view, that you can have quite different concepts
which, for reasons of the history of language, just happen to be
represented by the same word, is at present unfashionable. As
Hohfeld never saw the issue in these terms, we cannot be sure what he
would have said to it. But a modern apologist for him might take the
view that there is no need to assume any underlying essence for the
four terms he distinguished as right, privilege, power and immunity,
merely because usage commonly terms them all 'rights'.

2 Analysis in general

General jurisprudence raises questions of all kinds about law, which may involve analysis of the concept of law and of other legal concepts. Particular jurisprudence is concerned with the analysis of legal concepts other than the concept of law itself. Substantive legal commentaries and legal arguments also engage in the analysis of legal concepts. It was suggested in chapter 1 that there is a *continuum* between particular jurisprudence and ordinary critical legal science; but that, as a rough guide, an analysis is 'jurisprudential' if a term is investigated, not with a view to ascertaining its meaning within a particular context, but on the basis that it stands for a concept which is common both to different legal systems and to several branches of the law. It therefore encompasses terms like 'right', 'duty', 'possession', 'ownership', 'contract', 'person', 'intention', 'fault', 'cause' and so on.

Hohfeld's is the most celebrated of modern essays in particular jurisprudence. It is not possible here to survey the issues which have been raised by other analyses of particular concepts. What needs to be stressed is that some other kinds of analysis presuppose quite different procedures. Hohfeld followed in the tradition started by Bentham, of analysing a legal concept by asking how it is employed in the law and how it ought to be employed in the interests of greater clarity. This is the tradition of logical atomism. The law is dissected into logically distinct packets of information, and our problem in analysing different concepts is to decide what labels to give the different packets.

Another older tradition seeks the essence of legal concepts by asking for true definitions. This is the tradition of 'real' essences. It used to be fashionable, for example, to debate whether or not there was some reality to which the concept of corporate personality corresponds. If there was not, the concept must be 'fictional'. Professor Hart attacked this approach in his 'Definition and Theory in Jurisprudence'. We must beware, he said, of theory raised 'on the back of definition'. The metaphysical connotations of the 'real essences' approach is uncongenial to the modern mind. But it can be defended by anyone prepared to take up an avowed ideological stance. Supposing one holds that there are good political-philosophical grounds for according to certain groups – those which exhibit a certain kind of internal cohesion and which play an important role in political life – rights and duties similar to those which one's philosophy accords to human beings. Then one may give voice to this view by a conceptual dogma: that sort of cohesion and that sort of importance is the real essence of legal personality.

A third tradition is that of 'nominal essences'. Legal concepts have essences, but these depend solely on the function of words in language. Hart suggested that the right sort of question to ask about concepts should not be of the form: 'What is a ...?' but rather: 'What functions are performed by sentences containing the word ... ?' During the 1950s, he brought to bear on the analysis of legal concepts the methods of 'ordinary language philosophy' which were then dominant among Oxford philosophers. Followers of this approach seek insights into the nature of legal concepts by careful attention to all the subtle variations of language, comparing uses of the same word inside and outside the law. Hart himself appears to have moved away from this approach in the direction of logical atomism. In 'Bentham on Legal Rights' (1973), he seems to assume that the most important criterion for testing the analysis of a legal concept is usefulness in giving legal information – although he still accepts that employment of the one word 'right' must indicate some underlying unity between the senses he so carefully differentiates.

I can suggest no reason why any one of these three traditions – logical atomism, real essences, or nominal essences – should be adopted to the total exclusion of the others. What matters is to know what we are about in any particular analytic enterprise. If we are analysing 'intention', are we recommending a clearer terminology, reflecting some prior breakdown of legal categories? Or are we relating the law to psychological reality? Or are we exploring the functions of the word 'intention' and its cognates? With 'contract', are we slotting a term into an overall breakdown of the law of obligations? Or are we anchoring it to that central device which, as the economic analysis of law reveals (see chapter 4, above), really maximises efficiency? Or are we drawing on the wealth of philosophic literature which deals with the function of expressions like 'I promise'? As for 'property', should that be a term given technical stipulative use within a code? Or is analysis of it dependent on its proper place within a philosophy of justice? (See chapter 20, below.) Or shall we look for its essence by collating uses of the word? In the case of 'rights', Hohfeld, as we have seen, wanted different senses clearly distinguished in the interests of clarity; and one criticism was that 'right' must have an essence. But is it a nominal or a real (ideological) one? As we shall see in chapter 14, below, Professor Dworkin believes NB it is the latter. He makes no claim that his analysis of 'rights' corresponds with the way that word is used by lawyers or non-lawyers. He advocates a liberal, individualistic philosophy, and believes that this same philosophy already infuses legal reasoning; on that basis he produces an answer to the question: 'What are legal rights?'

Perhaps one should give up particular jurisprudence altogether?

Two sorts of argument might tend to this conclusion. It might be contended that the meaning of a legal term varies from context to context, so that any general analysis of it is unwarranted – as D. Harris argues is the case with 'possession'. Or it might be contended that words simply do not stand for ideas at all. This is the view put forward by Professor Glanville Williams, on the basis of a semantic theory popularised by Ogden and Richards. He agrees with Olivecrona (see chapter 8, below) that the function of words is to influence action: we find out what words 'mean' by asking what pictures they bring to the mind and what impulses they stimulate.

Alf Ross advances a more specific argument for the view that words like 'ownership' stand for nothing. We could, he says, rewrite all the rules of law which employ this term without using it. The law says: 'If X has completed a valid purchase, he is owner'; and: 'If X is owner, he can sue for recovery'. One could eliminate the middle man and rewrite the law: 'If X has completed a valid purchase, he can sue for recovery'. This would be inconvenient, but the fact that it would be possible proves that it is 'nonsense' to attribute meaning to the term 'ownership', that it is 'without semantic reference'. Ross cites, as illustration, an island community where people believe in a magical form of contamination known as 'tu-tu'. If you eat the chief's food you become tu-tu. If you become tu-tu, you have to undergo a purification ceremony. Now, says Ross, one could rewrite the rule: 'If you eat the chief's food, you must undergo a purification ceremony'. So, just as tu-tu is meaningless, so is ownership.

In response to these objections to particular jurisprudence, consider the following argument in favour of analysing general legal concepts. Legal terms may be used, not merely to express legal rules, but as steps in reasoning towards legal decisions. We cannot grasp the significance of a legal concept without placing it in a dynamic as well as static context. If the rules of Ross's islanders are all clear, no doubt his suggested rewriting would be possible. But supposing some new issue arose? Supposing someone ate food belonging to the chief's son and some said that that made him tu-tu, while others denied it. The elders – or whoever settled disputed issues of law – would argue out the question in terms of what tu-tu really is. We outsiders consider tu-tu meaningless, but for them it is not; and, understanding the magical metaphysic from the inside, their 'lawyers' would know what sorts of argument were relevant to it. Similarly, open questions in our law are sometimes settled by reference to what the judges think 'possession', or 'ownership' or 'person' mean. Arguments of many kinds push the law into developments which stretch the meaning of terms. But if the terms themselves impose limits on such develop-ments, they cannot be meaningless. The common law of larceny was nailed to the concept of 'possession'. To be a thief, a person had to acquire possession of goods feloniously, and so theft could not be committed by one who was in possession before he formed a felonious intent. The judges were able to bring dishonest servants within the net, by asserting that someone who was entrusted with goods by his master did not acquire possession but merely detention. But where goods were entrusted to a servant by a third party for the master, it was felt that one could not deny that the servant (rather than the master) was in possession; so that if the servant dishonestly appropriated he did not steal. The crime of embezzlement had to be invented to plug a hole created by nothing except the outer limits of a concept.

Certainly, dogmatic particular jurisprudence has been overdone in the past. Sometimes it has been argued that a ... just is ... and so any legal rule employing the term must be given a particular interpretation. Furthermore, jurisprudence textbooks have tended to collate uses of terms without any very clear indication of the purpose of the exercise. But so long as legal reasoning by reference to conceptual doctrine continues, broad-scale conceptual analysis is likely to have its place.

Bibliography

Hohfeld's analysis

Attwooll E.	'Liberties, Rights and Powers' in Attwooll (ed) *Perspectives in Jurisprudence* (1977)
Campbell A. H.	'Some Footnotes to Salmond's Jurisprudence' (1940) 7 CLJ 206
Feinberg J.	'Duties, Rights, and Claims' [1966] Am Phil Q 142
Finnis J. M.	'Some Professorial Fallacies About Rights' (1972) 4 Ad L Rev 377
Haksar V.	'The Nature of Rights' (1978) 64 ARSP 183
Harris J. W.	*Law and Legal Science* (1979) s. 3
Hart H. L. A.	'Bentham on Legal Rights' in Simpson (ed) *Oxford Essays in Jurisprudence* (2nd series, 1973)
Hohfeld W. N.	*Fundamental Legal Conceptions as Applied in Judicial Reasoning* (1946)
	'Relations between Equity and Law' (1913) 11 Mich L Rev 537
	'Supplemental Note on the Conflict of Law and Equity' (1917) 26 Yale LJ 767

Honoré A. M.   'Rights of Exclusion and Immunities Against
                            Divesting' (1959–60) 34 Tul L Rev 453
Kamba W. J.   'Legal Theory and Hohfeld's Analysis of a
                            Legal Right' (1974) Jur Rev 249
Kocourek A.   *Jural Relations* (2nd edn, 1928) chs 1–2
Lyons D. B.   'Rights, Claimants and Beneficiaries' [1969]
                            Am Phil Q 173
MacCormick D. N.   'Childrens' Rights' (1976) 62 ARSP 305
                            'Rights in Legislation' in Hacker and Raz
                            (eds) *Law, Morality, and Society* (1977)
Radin M.   'A Re-statement of Hohfeld' (1938) 51 Harv L
                            Rev 1141
Ross A.   *On Law and Justice* (1958) chs 5–7
Stone J.   *Legal System and Lawyers' Reasonings* (1964) ch 4
Stone R. L.   'An Analysis of Hohfeld' (1963) 48 Minn L
                            Rev 313
Williams G. L.   'The Concept of Legal Liberty' in Summers
                            (ed) *Essays in Legal Philosophy* (1968)

Analysis in general

Auerback C. A.   'On Professor H. L. A. Hart's Definition and
                           Theory in Jurisprudence' (1956) 9 JLE 30
Baker G. B.   'Defeasibility and Meaning' in Hacker and
                           Raz (eds) *Law, Morality, and Society* (1979)
Bodenheimer E.   'Modern Analytical Jurisprudence and the
                           Limits of its Usefulness' (1955–56) 104 U Pa L
                           Rev 1080
Bronaugh R.   'Agreement, Mistake, and Objectivity in the
                           Bargain Theory of Contract' (1976) W & M
                           L Rev 213
Cohen J.   'The Value of Value Symbols in Law' (1952)
52 Col L Rev 893
Dias R. W. M.   *Jurisprudence* (4th edn, 1976) chs 10–13
Fitzgerald P. J.   *Salmond on Jurisprudence* (12th edn, 1966)
                           Book 3
Harris D.   'The Concept of Possession in English Law' in
                           Guest (ed) *Oxford Essays in Jurisprudence* (1961)
Hart H. L. A.   'The Ascription of Responsibility and Rights'
                           in Flew (ed) *Logic and Language* (1951)
                           'Definition and Theory in Jurisprudence'
                           (1954) 70 LQR 37
                           'Analytical Jurisprudence in Mid-Twentieth
                           Century: a Reply to Professor Bodenheimer'
                           (1957) 105 U Pa L Rev 953

Hart H. L. A. and
Honoré A. M.   *Causation in the Law* (1959)
Honoré A. M.   'Ownership' in Guest (ed) *Oxford Essays in
                      Jurisprudence* (1961)
Kelly D. St L.   'Legal Concepts, Logical Functions and
                      Statements of Fact' (1968) 3 Tas U L Rev 43
Lloyd-Bostock S.   'The Ordinary Man and the Psychology of
                      Attributing Causes and Responsibility'
                      (1979) 42 MLR 142
Paton G. W.   *A Textbook of Jurisprudence* (4th edn, 1972)
                      Books 4–6
Ross A.   'Tu-tu' (1957) 70 Harv L Rev 812
Simpson A. W. B.   'The Analysis of Legal Concepts' (1964) 80
                      LQR 535
Williams G. L.   'Language and the Law' (1945) 61 LQR 71,
                      189, 293, 384; (1946) 62 LQR 387
Wolff M.   'On the Nature of Legal Persons' (1938) 54
                      LQR 494

8 Legal realism

One suspects that cynicism about the law and lawyers has always been common among non-lawyers. Novelists and playwrights have attested to it. Dickens, in *Bleak House*, stated that the one great principle of English law was to provide work for lawyers. Molière's plays pillory lawyers and doctors alike; but whereas medical science now has a measure of awesome respect, the layman is generally still cynical about the law. In this century, two traditions of legal writers have come to the fore, many of whose conclusions are grist to the mill of those who suspect that, beneath a panoply of rhetoric, judges do what they like; or that a lot of legal words are jargon designed to bamboozle and impoverish the average citizen.

These traditions, one in the United States and one in Scandinavia, have been called 'realist'. As it happens, this is an inept label in the context of the history of philosophy. The term 'realist' was applied to followers of Plato, who taught that the things of everyday life are but imperfect copies of 'real' (ideal) forms which transcend our senses. The legal 'realists' are in the opposite camp. They attack what they claim to be only too prevalent in traditional legal science, the conception of law as a 'brooding omnipresence in the sky'. They say that lawyers commonly talk of 'rules' as though they were genuine entities, occupying some world other than the world of time and space (the universe of 'law'); and that legal concepts, like 'right', 'duty' or 'possession', are treated as if these words had some metaphysical essence as their counterpart in that same other legal world. Such mythology must be dispelled, and the scientific truth brought to light. Like other truth-seekers, however, they find it easier to agree on the falsity to be dismissed than on the 'reality' which is to be substituted.

1 American legal realism

The intellectual inspiration of the realist movement in America is generally credited to Oliver Wendel Holmes (1841–1935), who was a Justice of the Supreme Court from 1902. Holmes was no cynic. He did not believe that judges can do what they like, for he delivered judgments in which he pronounced himself bound to hold that the law was not as he would like it to be. He was a great expert in the common law and in American constitutional law, and a moderate, liberal reformer. But aphorisms of his have been cited again and again by those who wish to debunk over-conceptualism in legal thinking: 'The life of the law has not been logic, it has been experience.' Law should be viewed 'from the stance of the bad man'. 'The prophecies of what the courts will do in fact, and nothing more pretentious, are what I mean by the law.'

What Holmes was attacking was the idea that all inherited legal provisions could be rationally defended, and any tendency to expound 'law' which did not have a direct bearing on courts' decisions. Much of the law, he believed, had been invented in a historical context which had now been superseded, and the real purposes it served under changed conditions should be constantly reviewed. In no circumstances should it be claimed that the law, according to some conceptually deductive process, was one thing, if the practice of the courts suggested that it was something else.

A similar court-centred bias for American jurisprudence was insisted upon by Holmes' academic contemporary, John Chipman Gray (1839–1915). Gray, too, was no legal revolutionary. He wrote books about property law of a fairly traditional kind. But, as a theorist, he insisted that the law was comprised of the rules laid down by the courts, and that statutes and other legal materials were merely 'sources' of this law.

Succeeding members of the movement, like Karl Llewellyn (1893–1962) warned readers against 'paper rules', against merely reading the law off from the books. Law, said Llewellyn, was 'what officials do about disputes'. We should have regard to different styles of judicial interpretation of source materials prevalent at different places and in different epochs, and to all information that social research might provide about actual decisions. Mere 'rules' would often not tell us much about decisions, because they are often capable of being construed in different ways, and because different rules could be selected from the mass available to support decisions arrived at for reasons which had nothing to do with rules.

The writer commonly considered to be the most extreme of all the American realists was Judge Jerome Frank (1889–1957). Frank criticised authors like Llewellyn for what he called their 'upper courtitis'. They were merely 'rule-sceptics', whereas he, Frank, was a 'fact-sceptic'. What he meant by this was that, even if rules are clear as to interpretation, in lower courts they may have precious little determining effect on decisions because a tribunal of fact, particularly a jury, can always find the facts as it pleases so that a rule will give the decision it wants. What actually causes the tribunal to decide the way it does are conscious and subconscious attitudes, beliefs and prejudices, which are peculiar to the parties, the witnesses and the facts of each case. Rules are little more than pretty playthings. Frank's conclusion was:

> 'For any particular lay person, the law, with respect to any particular set of facts, is a decision of a court with respect to those facts so far as that decision affects that particular person. Until a court has passed on those facts no law on that subject is yet in existence.'[1]

Critical discussion of American realism, as a movement, has often been bedevilled by questions about how seriously we are supposed to take statements like that just quoted from Frank. Frank himself tells us that he is not intending to give a definition of 'law' suitable for all ✳ purposes; and also that his case is deliberately overstated. Minimally, realists say only that 'rules' are not all that matter in the administration of justice, and there has probably never been a theorist who denied that. More positively, the movement has had some influence in directing research towards non-rule-governed operations – towards studies of the personal background of judges, the actual workings of the jury system, the practical importance of availability of legal representation, and the consequences of formality in procedure. But these matters were not altogether neglected before the movement began.

In so far as the pronouncements of leading members of the movement have a general significance for our picture of law, this must be demonstrated by taking such definitions as Frank's at their face value. Two crucial theses emerge: first, rules *by their nature* cannot ⌐ control decisions by courts and other officials; second, the overriding function of law is the settlement of disputes. ⌐

These theses are connected. Viewed from the standpoint of a court, there is a dispute and legal rules are supposed, in most cases, to provide the answer. Frank asserts that judges and others delude themselves about this. They have a psychological need for security, a childish hang-over, which is satisfied by a belief that 'the law' (a father figure) dictates what is to happen. This must be a delusion, because decisions are actually caused by a multiplicity of motives operating on the finder of facts, which leads him to find suitable facts to fit the rules that will support the decision. These motives would ?? produce the same decision whatever the rules. Accordingly, in the

1 *Law and the Modern Mind* p. 50.

NB.   interest of truth, the idea that there is 'law' before the decision should be dropped.

The anti-rule causal thesis is almost impossible to test by experiment. You would need, say, ten motorists, all charged with speeding at more than 30 miles per hour in a built-up area, but charged before tribunals whose prejudices were thought to vary. Let five actually have been driving at 60 miles per hour, and five at 20. One would note variables, like the appearance of the witnesses, their class accents and so forth. Given that rules have no effect, there is no likelihood that those who were in fact speeding will be convicted, whilst those who were not will be acquitted. Is this plausible?

It might be thought that this would not be a fair test of Frank's position, because he is concerned with cases where issues of fact or law are likely to be raised, and in my example the excess over the speed limit or the falling short of it would be so patent that the speeders would plead guilty and the non-speeders would never be prosecuted. Such a suggestion raises another difficult issue, this time of evaluation. Are all those occasions on which rules have an effect without producing a dispute less important, and so not indicative of the true function of the law, than those occasions on which a dispute arises? The court-centred view of American realists is to be compared with the view that the function of law is to guide or coerce behaviour through rules, and that settling disputes is only a subsidiary function.

Further, precisely how is it that a decision settles a dispute? Presumably, through some order being made by the judge requiring a party to pay damages, to give up property, to desist from some activity, to go to gaol and so on. But if rules of the legislature have no determinative effect over disputes, ought we not also to assume that orders of judges have none over later disputes involving the same issue – for example, if a judgment creditor alleges that he has not been paid? If a statute is not a pre-existing rule for judge X, why is judge X's order a pre-existing rule for judge Y or sheriff Z? Perhaps Frank's realist definition could be taken further. 'For any particular lay person, the law, with respect to any particular set of facts, is some coercive measure by a state official actually being applied to that person.'

NB.   If one is merely a rule-sceptic and not a fact-sceptic, one could be a 'realist' only about difficult cases. The thesis would be that, although clear cases are governed by rules, whenever the law is uncertain we should abandon 'legal reasoning' in favour of behaviour-prediction. As we shall see in chapters 14 and 15, below, the nature of judicial reasoning in unclear cases is highly controversial. Legal standards other than rules evidently play some part. A 'realist' approach to this problem would require us to concentrate, not on the reasons judges give for their decisions, but on the motives which actually influence them; not on what they say, but on what they do. In an extreme form, it would regard all legal reasoning as mere surface talk. I have come across practitioners who, in their cups, talk about judges in just this way: 'You wouldn't get very far with that argument before judge X, given the way he feels about deserting husbands (or trade unions, or whatever)!' If it is systematically true that, whenever there is an arguable point, arguments based on the purpose of a rule, or Parliament's intention, or some legal principle, might as well not have been made because the judge's prejudices alone determine his decision, then perhaps law is (as F. Rodell argues) a 'high-class racket'. When teased with this inference, your cynical practitioner may well pull up, and say that it is of course only in relation to some kinds of dispute that judges reach the conclusions they wish whatever the arguments, and that for the most part decisions are influenced by well-reasoned advocacy. If that were not so there would, for example, be no agitation for the extension of legally-aided representation to tribunals. Do we believe him?

There remains the difficulty, which many critics of realism have pointed out, that if legal science is to be transformed into a science of prediction, just what are judges supposed to do? Practitioners may predict judicial decisions, but judges themselves cannot. They must purport to justify. The best advice which Frank could offer was that they should be as conscientious as possible in introspecting about their motives. At least they should be clear that justice in the case at bar (whatever 'justice' means, see chapter 20, below) is their goal, not some solution dictated by 'justice according to law'.

If the belief that rules matter, inside and outside courts, were to be totally discredited, it would not merely confirm the cynicism that many share about the law; it would also lead to total pessimism about the utility of law reform. Why bother to change the rules? The only possible 'law reform' would be to substitute officials with desirable prejudices for those officials we have. Judges, old or new, would automatically have complete discretion, but we might as well make this plain by giving it to the new ones expressly – for rules to guide them would not guide them.

Another criticism commonly advanced against realists is that, without rules, how do we know who are officials, for are they not appointed according to rules? To this it might be answered that we have psychological triggers of various kinds which make us view individuals acting in certain formal ways as dispute-settling officials. The topic of 'jurisdiction' should be concerned with deference reactions to wigs and gowns, not with rules. Would this mean that, if we were ever unsure whether a court had jurisdiction, these kinds of reactions, not the paper rules, would settle the question?

But then the realist case was never intended to be as extreme as it sounds. This makes an assessment of its contribution to theory difficult. Llewellyn denied that it had theoretical implications of any kind.

> 'Realism is *not* a philosophy, but a technology ... What realism was, and is, is a method nothing more.'[2]

The 'method' employed by members of the movement was a mixture of recording data about judicial practices, and intuitions based on what Llewellyn called 'horse sense'. As we shall see in chapter 18, below, it is questionable whether sociological research related to law presupposes any conception of law different from that the realists so vehemently denounced.

2 Scandinavian legal realism

If we are unhappy with the idea that rules are abstract entities, alleged to 'exist' as part of some legal system, one way of anchoring 'the law' in 'reality' is to equate it with the behaviour of officials – that is the approach of extreme American realism. Another way is to identify the law with psychological occurrences – the sensations produced in people's minds as the result of legal words. The latter is the course taken by a school commonly called 'Scandinavian realists'. This school derives its inspiration from the Swedish professor, Axel Hagerstrom (1868–1939).

Hagerstrom's own contributions to jurisprudence and moral philosophy were largely destructive. He was at pains to point out the 'metaphysical' elements in others' theories. He found suspect all accounts of law and morals which included assertions that a moral or legal rule actually exists; for such talk must assume that there is some non-natural sense in which things could exist, and therefore presupposes a world alongside or superior to the physical world. In fact, he said, value judgments about right and wrong are purely emotive. They merely express our feelings of like or dislike. Similarly in law, an assertion that there exists a binding rule mystifies the truth, for 'bindingness' as a quality has no counterpart in sense-experience. His historical researches convinced him that, in primitive law, men really believed in magical powers and bonds to which the words 'right' and 'duty' (or 'obligation') corresponded. As law developed, belief in these magical entities faded away but still people went on using these nouns with the same psychological effect as they had had over their more credulous ancestors. The assertion that one has 'a right' produces a sensation of power; and the assertion that someone has 'an obligation' typically produces in him feelings of constraint.

This sceptical approach to legal rules and legal concepts has been developed by writers of the school, the two most well-known of whom in the English-speaking world are the Swede, Karl Olivecrona (1897–1980), and the Dane, Alf Ross (1899–1979). Each of these authors seeks to build up a picture of law, starting with the insights which Hagerstrom provided. They share with him the assumption that the only 'reality' to which 'law' may correspond is a psychological reality.

Olivecrona equates law with 'independent imperatives'. It is false, he argues, to think of the law as the commands of an actual person, for no human being could go about commanding all that is contained in the law; and to identify the commander of the law with the 'state' or the 'people' is to deal in abstractions and therefore in unrealities. What actually occurs when legislation is enacted is that a proposal, such as a bill, is subjected to certain formal acts of voting, signing and promulgation. Because of the hold these formalities have over people's minds, the contents of the bill acquire a special psychological effectiveness. A legal provision contains two elements: an idea of an action ('stealing'), and some imperative symbol ('ought', 'duty', 'offence'). The provision itself is just words on paper. The 'reality' to which 'scientific' discourse about law must correspond consists of the psychological reactions of individuals – the ideas of imaginary actions and the sensations of compulsion and restraint produced when a provision is brought to our auditory or visual attention.

> 'In reality, the law of a country consists of an immense mass of ideas concerning human behaviour, accumulated during centuries through the contributions of innumerable collaborators. These ideas have been expressed in imperative form by their originators, especially through formal legislation, and are being preserved in the same form in books of law. The ideas are again and again revived in human minds, accompanied by the imperative expression: "This line of conduct *shall* be taken" or something else to the same effect.'[3]

Olivecrona takes the same view of the overall function of the law as does Kelsen, namely, the monopoly of force in the hands of state officials (see chapter 6, above). But in order to understand how this really works, he says, we must reject Kelsen's conception of law as

3 *Law as Fact* (1st edn) p. 48.

'norms' set over against reality. Legal rules must be placed within the world of cause and effect, and this is only possible if they are understood as psychological phenomena. He envisages a society in which it is felt desirable by those in power to make some new form of activity the subject of prohibition. Rules will be promulgated forbidding the conduct in question, coupled with the threat of sanctions. Initially, those to whom the prohibitions are addressed will calculate, on each occasion of temptation, whether the gains of disobedience are worth the risk of sanction. But the human personality cannot withstand constant warring between temptation and fear; so eventually both will be pushed into the subconscious, and will be replaced in the conscious mind by some arational imperative symbol, such as 'ought not'. Once the rule has been internalised in this way, there is usually no need for the actual threat of force. The idea of the prohibited act will come to the mind, if at all, already imprinted with a disapprobative symbol. Olivecrona suggests that this is the way in which most of our so called 'moral' standards were created – that is, he reverses the common assumption about the historical relationship between morality and law. In the education of children, internalised rules will be directly transmitted in the typical form of idea plus ought-symbol; and the community may well attach the psychologically-loaded term 'moral' as well as the term 'legal' to them. But the special advantage of the psychological hold which 'legal' has over our minds is that it enables the powerholders in society to introduce new standards – employing the psychologically-loaded legislative formalities – which will gain some ascendancy over our personalities even without actual threat of force. Force is necessary if the internalisation process is to be maintained; but most of the time it can be kept in the background. Law and force are thus associated in two ways. First, law gains its initial psychological hold, and from time to time strengthens the hold it has, by the application of sanctions. Secondly, the content of legal provisions determine exclusively the circumstances in which the exercise of force is thought proper.

One of the chief criticisms of Olivecrona is that he reaches empirical generalisations through armchair theorising rather than through empirical research. He concludes that what underlies the law *must* be such and such psychological cause-and-effect relations because only if we assume this can legal language be given any meaning. Study of words thus tells us something about the psychological life of man. Many have questioned whether law creates morals in the way he says it does. Why is it, for example, that murder has always been regarded as more heinous than theft even though for centuries capital punishment was meted out for both? Is it not mere guesswork to insist that the existence of an 'ought' idea in a person's mind is evidence that he, or his forbears, must have repressed the temptation to perform an act so as to be free of the fear of sanctions? Empirical studies, based on questionnaires directed to popular knowledge and opinion about law, have become more common in recent years – see the discussion of 'living law' in chapter 18, below. It can be argued that we should base our psychological generalisations on them rather than on speculation about concepts. On the other hand, conclusions based on such researches are unlikely to give a total picture (an interpretative model) of the functions of law in society. Research demonstrating ignorance of positive law is of great value for those concerned with education about law, but can hardly tell us what effect law has on those who are not ignorant of it. Olivecrona's principle thesis would be falsified if it could be shown that, not-withstanding regular and well-publicised enforcement of a legal provision, automatic reactions of rightness or wrongness do not emerge. In so far as any thesis can be said to have been confirmed by modern research it is that normative views do not coincide with the law, and that they vary between age bands and social groups.

Another criticism of Scandinavian realism relates to the operation of law on the intellectual level. Even if it is true that legal rules achieve effects through internalisation, surely textwriters, practitioners and judges who describe 'the law' are not purporting to discuss the psychological lives of citizens? Surely, too, when lawyers perform logical operations on the law – such as deducing a particular prescription from a more general one – they are not making con-tentions about ways in which people 'feel bound'? If I work out the complexities of the schedules to various Finance Acts, using a calcu-lator to do the sums where necessary, and conclude that my client is liable now to pay so much tax, I would not expect to be told that I thereby committed myself to the view that he or some official had already (or would ever have) any particular sensations of compulsion in regard to the matter.

Alf Ross modified the principal tenets of Scandinavian realism to meet just these kinds of objection. 'Law in action', he says, is just what Olivecrona described; but when legal science speaks of 'law' it does not refer, directly, to the psychological lives of the citizenry. The 'directives' which it describes constitute a 'scheme of interpretation' which enables one to predict the behaviour of officials. The ought-ideas in the law, as they pass from the mind of law teacher to student, are 'ought' moulds with no stimulating effect; but armed with them, the student can tell what judges will do for he knows that, in the judicial mind, they will set off sensations of compulsion. To assert that such and such provision is valid law means no more than this; if the provision in question were to be cited to a judge, it would influence his decision. Ross coupled with the 'realism' he inherited from the Hagerstrom tradition a view of epistemology inherited from that movement of the 1920s and 30s known as 'logical positivism'. According to the high priests of logical positivism, sentences which were not mere tautologies could only be meaningful if the propositions they expressed were capable of verification. Ross believed that his view of legal science met this criterion. If when one says that there is a valid rule one intends to say that some entity independent of the world of time and space 'exists' and has some non-natural quality of 'bindingness', one is talking meaningless metaphysics as the realists had shown. But if (argues Ross) one means that a particular psychological phenomenon will, predictably, occur in the spiritual lives of judges, then one's assertion is one about this world and, consistently with logical positivism, it can be tested by experiment in the courts.

It will be seen that, at least in his discussion of legal science, Ross, like the American realists but unlike other Scandinavian realists, is specifically court-centred. Consequently, the same complaints of circularity have been raised against him: how can a judge's view of the law be interpreted as a prediction of what the judge will himself decide? But Ross differs from the American realists precisely by insisting that decisions which concur with pre-existing rules do show that the rules effectively control decisions: if they did not, then the verification he insists on would not be supplied. Ross and Frank agree that it is my lawyer's business to predict what courts will do; but Frank says that they are to beware of rules as grounds for prediction, whilst Ross says rules 'exist' just because they are good grounds for prediction. Neither appears to explain what happens when a judge announces: 'The law on this point is clearly as follows ... and therefore, alas, I must find for the defendant.' Such a judge, when he states what the law is, is not, on the face of it, making any kind of prediction.

Bibliography

American legal realism

Frank J.	*Law and the Modern Mind* (2nd edn, 1963)
	Courts on Trial (1949)
Fuller L. L.	'American Legal Realism' (1934) 82 U Pa L Rev 429
Garlan E. N.	*Legal Realism and Justice* (1944)
Grant G.	'Legal Realism: its Cause and Cure' (1961) 70 Yale LJ 1037

Gray J. C.   *The Nature and Sources of the Law* (2nd edn, 1963)

Hart H. L. A.   *The Concept of Law* (1961) ch 7

Holmes O. W.   'The Path of the Law' (1897) 10 Harv L Rev 457

Hunt A.   *The Sociological Movement in Law* (1978) ch 2

Llewellyn K. N.   'A Realistic Jurisprudence; the Next Step' (1930) 30 Colum L Rev 431
                         'Some Realism about Realism' (1931) 44 Harv L Rev 1222
                         'The Normative, the Legal and the Law Jobs: the Problem of Juristic Method' (1940) 49 Yale LJ 1355
                         The Bramble Bush (revised edn, 1951)
                         The Common Law Tradition (1960)
                         Jurisprudence: Realism in Theory and Practice (1962)

Llewellyn K. N.,
Adler M. J.,
Cook W. W.   'Law and the Modern Mind (a Symposium)' (1931) 31 Colum L Rev 82

Lloyd D.   *Introduction to Jurisprudence* (4th edn, 1979) ch 7

McDougall M. S.   'Fuller versus the American Legal Realists: an Intervention' (1941) 50 Yale LJ 827

Moore W. U.   'The Rational Basis of Legal Institutions' (1923) 23 Colum L Rev 609

Pound R.   'The Call for a Realist Jurisprudence' (1931) 44 Harv L Rev 697

Rumble W. E.   *American Legal Realism* (1968)

Rodell F.   *Woe Unto You Lawyers* (1957)

Schubert G.   'Behavioral Jurisprudence' (1968) 2 LS Rev 407

Taylor E. H.   'H. L. A. Hart's Concept of Law in the Perspective of American Legal Realism' (1972) 35 MLR 606

Twining W.   *Karl Llewellyn and the Realist Movement* (1973)

Yntema H.   'American Legal Realism in Retrospect' (1960) 9 Vand L Rev 317

Scandinavian legal realism

Castberg F.   *Problems of Legal Philosophy* (2nd edn, 1957) pp. 27–37

Hagerstrom A.	*Inquiries into the Nature of Law and Morals* (Olivecrona (ed), Broad trans, 1953)
Harris J. W.	*Law and Legal Science* (1979) ss. 6, 17
Hart H. L. A.	'Scandinavian Realism' (1959) 17 CLJ 233
Lewis J. U.	'Karl Olivecrona: "Factual Realism" and Reasons for Obeying a Law' (1970) 5 U Br Col L Rev 281
Lloyd D.	*Introduction to Jurisprudence* (4th edn, 1979) ch 8
Lundstedt A. V.	*Legal Thinking Revised* (1956)
MacCormack G.	'Scandinavian Realism' (1970) Jur Rev 33
	'Hagerstom on Rights and Duties' (1971) Jur Rev 59
Merrills J. G.	'Law, Morals and the Psychological Nexus' (1969) 19 U Tor LJ 46
Olivecrona K.	*Law As Fact* (1939)
	Law As Fact (2nd edn, 1971)
	'Legal Language and Reality' in Newman (ed) *Essays in Honor of Roscoe Pound* (1962)
	'The Imperative Element in Law' (1964) 18 Rut L Rev 794
Pasmore J.	'Axel Hagerstrom and his Disciples' in Sawer (ed) *Studies in the Sociology of Law* (1961)
Ross A.	*Towards a Realistic Jurisprudence* (1946)
	On Law and Justice (1958) chs 1–4
	Directive and Norms (1968) ch 4
Simmonds N. E.	'The Legal Philosophy of Axel Hagerstrom' (1976) Jur Rev 210

9   Hart's concept of law

'Notwithstanding its concern with analysis the book may also be regarded as an essay in descriptive sociology; for the suggestion that inquiries into the meanings of words merely throw light on words is false.'[1]

We saw in chapter 7, above that Professor Hart rejected theory raised 'on the back of definition'. The way to analyse legal concepts was to explore the ways in which terms standing for those concepts were used inside and outside the law. Not only would this method avoid the unnecessary puzzles to which other methods of analysis had led; it would also draw attention to important features of social life. Linguistic practices were good sociological evidence. From what has been called 'the method of ordinary language analysis' we are to expect both conceptual and sociological information. This chapter considers how far Hart's book (*The Concept of Law*) succeeds in these respects, as regards legal rules and legal systems.

1   Legal rules as social rules

Hart says that when a social group is said to have a 'rule', two things are true. First, the members generally perform certain actions. That is the 'external aspect' of the rule. If that were all, what would be present would be merely a 'habit'. There must, secondly, be an 'internal aspect', that is, a 'critical reflective attitude' shared by most members of the group towards the conduct in question. This internal aspect is manifested by criticisms made by members of the group against those who deviate or threaten to deviate from standard behaviour, by demands for conformity, and by acknowledgments that the line of conduct in question is indeed proper. Language exhibits the manifestation of this internal attitude by the use of a special kind of 'normative' vocabulary – you ought to do this, you must do that, such and such is right (or wrong). What emerges from this analysis is

1 H. L. A. Hart *The Concept of Law* p. vii.

an explanation of the concept of a rule in terms of a particular kind of social situation. So analysed, a rule is what I have called (in *Law and Legal Science*) a 'rule-situation', or what most commentators on Hart's analysis have called a 'social rule'.

There are, says Hart, many kinds of such rules, relating to etiquette, games, morals and so on. An important category are those rules which are 'conceived and spoken of' as imposing obligations. We find that people use a special type of normative term – 'duty' or 'obligation' – when 'the general demand for conformity is insistent and the social pressure brought to bear upon those who deviate or threaten to deviate is great'.[2] Obligation rules differ from other rules in two further respects: they are associated with some prized feature of social life, and it is generally recognised that what they require may conflict with a person's interests.

Obligation rules are divisible into sub-categories. If the social pressure brought to bear upon those who deviate includes physical sanctions, they represent a (possibly primitive) kind of law. But if the strong social pressure does not go that far, then they are rules forming part of the morality of the group. In a 'pre-legal' society, there may be no more by way of legal rules than obligation rules of the coercive type. Inevitably, there must be some such obligation rules in any society. For society to survive, there must be legal obligation rules restricting violence, theft and deception. Men always find such rules NB necessary because of man's nature as a partly selfish but partly cooperative creature, his typical wish to survive, and the limited resources of the world. As we saw in chapter 2, above, Hart describes these necessary rules as 'the minimum content of natural law'.

If a society has no more than obligation rules it will not be able, Hart says, to cope satisfactorily with the need to change rules from time to time, with the need to decide on disputed questions, and with the need for criteria to determine which rules are rightly regarded as obligation rules and which not. These needs can only be satisfied by the introduction of rules of change, adjudication and recognition. Their introduction represents a step from the pre-legal to a legal world. A 'legal system' comprises both legal obligation rules ('primary legal rules'), and 'secondary legal rules' – like the rules of change, adjudication and recognition. Secondary rules do not impose duties. They are 'power-conferring' rules. They are 'parasitic on' primary rules.

A wealth of critical literature has been devoted to this picture of law. Some of it has concerned alleged obscurities, and some of it has rejected all or part of the picture. Some critics have objected to the

2 *The Concept of Law* p. 84.

whole analysis of rules in terms of social rules. How can all rules be understood as combinations of patterns of behaviour and attitudes? Surely personal moral rules at least must be some other kind of rule. If a strict vegetarian tells you that he subscribes to a rule according to which eating animal products is wrong, he is not committing himself to any statement about the practices of any particular group. But then Hart, as a moral philosopher, must have been aware of this. So perhaps his analysis of rules as social rules was not meant to represent a complete explication of the concept of a rule. Perhaps his thesis was merely that legal rules are a species of social rule, not that all rules are social rules. But then we can easily think of legal rules as to which there is no matching social behaviour or social attitudes. Hart himself says that, in a developed legal system, a primary rule will be 'valid', and in that sense 'exist', provided only that it meets the criteria of recognition laid down by a rule of recognition. Should we stretch the concept of social rule to meet the case of a newly enacted statute by saying that the external aspect consists, not in what people do now, but in what they predictably will do under threat of sanctions, and the internal aspect consists, not in attitudes people now have, but in attitudes they will develop? So stretched, is the concept very different from Austin's command model, or from the American realist predictive model, both of which Hart rejects? Hart stresses that power-conferring rules do not comply with the command model, since they do not require people to do things. But he does not make clear whether they are to be regarded as social rules, and (if so) how their external aspect is manifested.

If legal rules need not be social rules, how does analysis of social rules enlighten us about the law? Perhaps the concepts deployed in social rules are similar to those used by the law. Central to Hart's analysis are the concepts of 'duty' and 'obligation' (treated by him as synonymous). Some critics have suggested that the words 'duty' and 'obligation' may not be used by members of a group even when there is strong social pressure and insistent demands for conformity. But supposing that there is the coincidence between language and social actions claimed by Hart, does it help us to analyse the concept of legal duty? Not if we accept that legal rules may impose 'duties' where the requisite social pressure is absent. J. C. Smith suggests that, using Hart's own method (analysis by investigation of ordinary language), a different conception of duty may be reached which (unlike Hart's conception) is appropriate for the concept of legal duty. His suggestion is that people only use the words 'duty' or 'obligation' about rules which they think are binding on them; and similarly, in legal contexts, people distinguish between legal rules which are binding and those which are not in the terminology of 'duty'. To accept this view, one would have to regard someone as misusing the English language were he to say: 'I have a legal obligation to do x, it is true; but the law is so unjust that I am not bound to comply.' Ordinary language philosophers tend to exhibit an extraordinary confidence about what ordinary usage is.

Perhaps the foregoing types of criticism miss Hart's point. It may be that he was not trying to define legal rules as a sub-species of social rules, nor trying to show that particular concepts (like that of duty) were related in their legal to their non-legal usage. Perhaps the object was to show, through examination of whole groups of linguistic usages, that rules of all kinds have typical functions and we would understand law better if we paid attention to its functional similarities and dissimilarities with other kinds of rule-practices. Thus, typically, when there is a rule rather than a mere habit, people make criticisms, demands and acknowledgments by reference to the rule as a standard. That is true of rules of games, moral rules and legal rules. This functional similarity is captured by his concept of 'the internal point of view'.

But how similar are these functions? How illuminating is the concept of internal point of view? There is some obscurity as to what the concept stands for. Hart indicates that it is not a psychological concept, not a mere 'feeling of being bound'. He rejects the internalisation-of-rules analysis made by the Scandinavian realists (see chapter 8, above). Nor does the internal point of view consist in approval of the rule, for, he says, people may accept rules out of fear, self-interest or habit. It may be that the so-called 'internal' aspect of rules consists exclusively of the criticisms, demands and acknowledgments which people make, that is, of speech acts. The point of the concept would then be, not to suggest that rule-governed practices require psychological internalisation of rules or convergence of group approval, but to make a functional generalisation about linguistic usage. Whenever you have rules, there will be expressions whose function is to draw attention to the rules or to apply them – 'off-side', 'out', 'wrong', 'unlawful', 'guilty'. Against this understanding of his concept stands the fact that Hart speaks of the internal attitude as 'critical' and 'reflective'.

Austin explained rules like those relating to the formation of contracts and wills in terms of conditional commands backed by the sanction of nullity (see chapter 3, above). Hart maintains that this distorts their social functions. Power-conferring rules have a function different from that of duty-imposing rules. They enable, not require, us to do things. It has been argued that Hart's own category of secondary rules distorts social functions by bracketing together rules with very different functions – for example, rules conferring capacities

or defining rights with rules of legislation, adjudication and ↓ NB.
administration. Can it be said that all secondary rules confer powers?
What about the rule of recognition? Are not judges bound to accept
that 'whatever the Queen in Parliament enacts is law'? And is it an
oversimplification to describe all secondary rules as 'about' or
'parasitic' on primary rules? Surely, rules governing legislation
enable secondary, power-conferring rules relating to contracts and
wills to be changed?

The functions of law are manifold. Clearly Hart did not suppose
that there were only two, for he indicated that three types of rule
(those of change, adjudication and recognition) met different needs.
The term 'power-conferring' may be no more than a misleading
catalogue label. In any case, should one try to categorise different
types of rules by reference to distinguishable social functions? As we
shall see in chapter 18, below, it is far from easy to give an objective
account of the functions of law. It is even more difficult to pair each
function with a particular kind of legal rule. It may be that some legal
rules perform more than one function, or that a single function
requires a cluster of different kinds of rules. When we speak of a rule's
'function', we may mean that which it was historically introduced to
achieve, or the use made of it in contemporary society. Clearly, when
the Statute of Frauds (1677) was enacted and certain formalities
stipulated for will-making, the object was not to enable people to do
something (make wills) which they could not do before. As to the uses
made today of these formality provisions, our characterisation
depends on evidence and evaluation. Maybe they do enable people to
make secure provision for their families, or maybe they inhibit people
from making informal 'wills'.

2 The union of primary and secondary rules

Hart offers no definition of a legal system, but he tells us that the
'union of primary and secondary rules' is at its heart. It may not
answer peripheral questions – like whether primitive systems or
public international law should, without qualification, be described
as 'law'. But it will explain much that has puzzled both the jurist and
the political theorist. On the analytic plane, it explains the use of
concepts such as 'validity'. Common to positivist writers in general is   NB
the thesis that there are in legal systems criteria by reference to which
'laws' can be distinguished from other things. Hart's version states
that rules are members of a legal system if, but only if, they meet the
criteria laid down by the rule of recognition. Some confusion has been
caused by Hart's use of the expression 'rule of recognition' sometimes

in the singular and sometimes in the plural. So far as the positivist thesis is concerned, it seems that it is one rule for each legal system. It performs the first of the two functions of Kelsen's basic norm distinguished in chapter 6, above. It enables lawyers to describe the products of legislation as a system. Hart does not suggest that we need the rule of recognition in order to distinguish a gangster's order from a taxman's demands – the second function of Kelsen's basic norm. He does explicitly point to one difference between his rule of recognition and Kelsen's basic norm; the former exists 'as a social practice', and is not a mere 'presupposition'. A further difference is that, whilst Kelsen formulates his basic norm either in terms of some historical date at which a constitution was promulgated or in terms of custom, Hart formulates his rule of recognition in terms of listed criteria. He does not spell out the rule for any system. He indicates that the rule of recognition in the United Kingdom is 'Whatever the Queen in Parliament enacts is law'. But elsewhere he states that precedents would be further criteria listed by the rule, albeit the rule would indicate that statutes prevail over them. Thus it is implicit that the rule of recognition will contain a full list of all criteria – statute, precedent, custom and so on – with an indication of their mutual ranking.

The analytic function of the concept of the union of primary and secondary rules is rejected by some anti-positivists. If it is not possible to articulate all the criteria by reference to which rules are identified as legal, then 'validity' cannot be merely a concept which relates a particular rule to a master rule. As we shall see in chapter 14, below, Dworkin mounts such an attack focusing on the concept of judicial discretion. Hart states that, in the penumbral area of uncertainty left by valid rules, a judge may have to reach beyond the law for reasons to justify his decision. Dworkin denies this, arguing that there are principles based on community morality which, collectively, provide the right answer in 'hard cases'. Such principles are applied because, as well as being moral, they are also legal. Therefore, no test of 'pedigree', such as the rule of recognition, can serve to distinguish law from morality or to draw lines around the legal system.

Others have objected, not to the possibility of a positivist test of validity, but to Hart's version of it. How is one to discover a rule of recognition existing 'as a social practice'? As we have seen, Hart tells us that we can find out whether there is a social rule about some behaviour by seeing whether members of a group criticise their own and others' conduct by reference to some standard. Do we find that those who administer the legal system make criticisms by reference to a single, all-embracing standard, a rule which sets out all the criteria for legal validity in a ranked order?

Even more attention has been paid to the non-analytic uses of Hart's concept of the 'union of primary and secondary rules' – that is, to its contribution to 'descriptive sociology' as compared with the light it throws on the use of terms. Like Austin's concept of 'habitual obedience' and Kelsen's concept of 'by and large effectiveness', the union of primary and secondary rules incorporates what may be called an 'existence thesis' about legal systems.

NB.

> 'There are therefore two minimum conditions necessary and sufficient for the existence of a legal system. On the one hand those rules of behaviour which are valid according to the system's ultimate criteria of validity must be generally observed, and, on the other hand, its rules of recognition specifying the criteria of legal validity and its rules of change and adjudication must be effectively accepted as common public standards of official behaviour by its officials.'[3]

The significance of this existence thesis is not altogether clear. Some have treated it as a developmental thesis. As we have seen, Hart envisages a pre-legal society (one without secondary rules) in which defects of three kinds emerge: uncertainty about which rules are members of the system, rigidity through lack of any recognised means of changing the rules, and diffuseness of social pressure when disputes arise about the application of rules. These three defects are matched by the introduction of rules of recognition, change and adjudication respectively. Hart cites anthropological works in the notes to this discussion, which might suggest that he is presenting a picture of historical developments. If so, it can be criticised by showing that 'primitive systems' do not lack secondary rules of the three kinds he mentions, or on the grounds that their introduction was not the result of observed 'defects'. But perhaps Hart's existence thesis is not developmental, and he postulates only an imaginary situation in which secondary rules do not exist in order to point up their functions.

Hart's existence thesis can be treated as heuristic or diagnostic – that is, it enables one to recognise legal systems when one finds them, and it enables one to express a diagnosis about a marginal case of 'legal system'. If we want to know whether a society has yet attained a legal system, Hart has provided a test. If a country is in a state of turmoil and the political scientist is trying to assess whether it has that social grace commonly known as 'law', wheel in the patient and apply this two-pronged stethoscope – 'Are your primary rules generally observed?' 'Do your officials accept your secondary rules?' It is questionable whether Hart himself had this sort of application of his

3 *The Concept of Law* p. 113.

existence thesis in mind. He indicates that social arrangements may more or less approximate the standard arrangements, and that there may be little point in drawing a sharp line between 'legal system' and 'non-legal system'.

So perhaps the existence thesis is merely informative. It provides us with information, in large-scale terms, about what happens in political societies. We might apply the same 'sociology for Martians' critique that we used in chapter 2, above, in connection with Hart's minimum content of natural law. Picture a Martian coming to earth and, astounded by the prevalence of normative utterances and co-ercive institutions, asking: 'What's all this law about?' We will get across the heart of the matter if we explain the nature of rules as social rules, secondly, distinguish primary from secondary rules, and finally, tell him that a legal system exists when the primary rules are generally observed and the secondary rules accepted by officials. Of course, there are no Martians; but there are students of institutions interested in distinguishing the central features of legal systems from peripheral ones, without going exhaustively into the detail of particular provisions.

Are general observance of primary rules and official acceptance of secondary rules the most important features of legal systems? To some extent, this must be a matter of evaluation. No attempt to extrude the universally significant from among a welter of social detail can be otherwise. Lawyers concentrate on rules. Other social scientists may see careers, role-structures and institutional frameworks. Hart's picture should be compared with that of other social theorists, such as those discussed in chapter 19, below.

The aspect of Hart's existence thesis which has caused most difficulties of interpretation is the significance of 'acceptance' by officials in the second condition. This might mean that officials have to 'approve' secondary rules – that such approval is important to the functioning of the legal system. Then it may be questioned whether a legal system might not function efficiently even if its officials did not approve its secondary rules, but merely applied them through motives of fear or career self-interest. Does the acceptance have to be shared, in the sense that the officials have a common ideology, or may they approve the rules on incompatible grounds?

It seems more likely that, as indicated in our discussion of the 'internal point of view', 'acceptance' does not imply approval. The second condition would then be satisfied so long as officials apply the secondary rules in the public arena, and in that sense 'effectively accept' them as 'common public standards'. In that case, just the converse of the afore-mentioned criticisms may be advanced. Law will not be able to perform its typical functions of inducing stability of expectations and organising physical and economic security unless the officials do indeed share a common ideology, approving the constitutional set-up which they operate. Critics taking this line may object to the first existence condition. For a legal system to be sustained over time it is not enough (it may be urged) that the citizens merely observe the primary rules; they, too, must have an internal attitude towards the secondary rules.

What cannot be denied is that Hart's concept of the union of primary and secondary rules has been thought-provoking. No one else has offered a substitute which, with equal brevity, sets out the crucial features of legal systems. It may be that they are too complicated to be capable of depiction in terms of a few concepts without serious distortion. Perhaps they are not the sort of entity of which any model can be an accurate one.

Bibliography

Cohen L. J.   'H. L. A. Hart: *The Concept of Law*' (1962) 71 Mind 395

Dworkin R. M.   *Taking Rights Seriously* (revised edn, 1978) chs 2–3

Fuller L. L.   *The Morality of Law* (revised edn, 1969) pp. 133–45

Hacker P. M. S.   'Hart's Philosophy of Law' in Hacker and Raz (eds) *Law, Morality, and Society* (1977)

Harris J. W.   *Law and Legal Science* (1979) s. 7

Hart H. L. A.   *The Concept of Law* (1961)

Hill R. E.   'Legal Validity and Legal Obligation' (1970) 80 Yale LJ 47

Hughes G. B. J.   'Rules, Policy and Decision Making' (1967–68) 77 Yale LJ 411

Kanowicz L.   'The Place of Sanctions in Professor Hart's Concept of Law' (1966–67) Duc U L Rev 1

King B. E.   'The Basic Concept of Professor Hart's Jurisprudence: the Norm out of the Bottle' (1963) 21 CLJ 270

McBride W. L.   'The Acceptance of a Legal System' (1965) 49 Monist 377

MacCormick D. N.   *Legal Reasoning and Legal Theory* (1978) appendix

Morris C.   'The Concept of Law' (1962) 75 Harv L Rev 452

Munzer S. R.   *Legal Validity* (1972) pp. 25–29, 50–56

Raz J.	*The Concept of a Legal System* (1970) pp. 121–202
	Practical Reason and Norms (1975) pp. 49–58
Samek R. A.	*The Legal Point of View* (1974) chs 8–9
Sartorius R. E.	'Hart's Concept of Law' in Summers (ed) *More Essays in Legal Philosophy* (1971)
Singer P.	'Hart's Concept of Law' (1963) 60 J Phil 197
Smith J. C.	*Legal Obligation* (1976) ch 2
Summers R. S.	'Professor H. L. A. Hart's Concept of Law' (1963) Duke LJ 629
Tapper C. F. H.	'Powers and Secondary Rules of Change' in Simpson (ed) *Oxford Essays in Jurisprudence* (2nd series, 1973)
Warnock G. J.	*The Object of Morality* (1971) ch 4
Woozley A. D.	'The Existence of Rules' (1967) 1 Nous 63

10 Freedom and the enforcement of morals

We all think that freedom is a value, and public debate about law often mentions it. Sometimes, people say that freedom is something the law can promote. Often this is done in the context of recommended constitutional restraints on state power. More generally, it is claimed that the law is needed to secure one man's freedom from his neighbour's invasion; or that community institutions, including law, are necessary to secure freedom from want. On the other hand, law may be seen as the enemy of freedom, as a set of prescriptions which necessarily detract from natural liberty. From this stance, any restraint on liberty to do what one likes is seen as something requiring justification. If the legislature wishes to make the wearing of seat-belts or crash-helmets compulsory, or to restrict the free sale of drugs or pornographic literature, it had better have a good reason.

Political rhetoric appeals to 'freedom' in many contexts, and the rhetoric may become embodied in legal principle. The movement towards decolonisation and national self-determination – the demand that men should only be ruled, for good or ill, by their co-culturals – appeals to freedom; and international charters have made the principle of self-determination a principle of international law. The liberal heritage of western democracies lays great stress on freedoms of expression – of speech, assembly and criticism – regarding them as both goods in themselves and as necessary means to arriving at policies best suited to the public good. Such freedoms are often embodied in written constitutions, or, as with the European Convention on Human Rights and Fundamental Freedoms, in the basic documents of supra-national institutions.

Discussions of freedom, on the level of moral or political philosophy, revolve around such questions as: Why do we value freedom? What is its relation to other values – pre-eminent or subordinate? Are there different kinds of freedom, some of which deserve our allegiance more than others? Most of us have heard the cynical jibe about the poor man who, in a free society, is 'free' to dine at the Ritz (there being no law to prevent him). On the philosophical plane, this jibe is resolved into some such abstract question as: Is freedom subordinate to equality in the sense that, without an equal or

115

at any rate 'just' distribution of resources, the mere absence of restraint is of little value to the majority? Politicians sometimes draw a distinction between 'freedoms to' or 'freedoms of', on the one hand (freedoms to criticise, freedom of speech etc.), and 'freedoms from', on the other (freedom from hunger, freedom from want etc.). Sir Isaiah Berlin has suggested that political philosophy should draw a distinction between negative and positive liberty. The former regards absence of constraint on human desires as an intrinsic value; the latter has the truly free man as an ideal, the realisation of which justifies coercion. He rejects positive liberty, on the ground that there is no such coherent ideal as the truly free man. The eighteenth-century philosopher, Rousseau, on the other hand, held that men could be 'forced to be free'; and Marxists believe that, only after the alienating effects of capitalism have been forcibly removed, can there be any true freedom. Many reject a sharp dichotomy between freedom, in the sense of absence of constraint, and freedom, in the sense of coerced self-realisation. Is not lack of education, for example, a form of coercion, so that people must be compelled to achieve that degree of self-realisation which education provides in order to be negatively free from the constraints which being uneducated entails? In this respect, liberals commonly amalgamate 'human rights' and 'fundamental freedoms', as the European Convention does: the moral status of the human individual entails that he ought to be afforded certain goods (sometimes, even against his will), and that constraints of some kinds ought not to be applied to him.

A conclusion about what it means (if anything) to be 'truly free' would, no doubt, affect one's attitudes to law as to the rest of life. To make the topic of freedom manageable for jurisprudential purposes, however, I shall postpone consideration of the relative value of freedom and other goods until the discussion of theories of justice in chapter 20, below; and deal here with the narrower question of what justifies legal restraints on negative liberty. If unmerited suffering is an evil, and if laws have some deterrent effect, it is not difficult to defend laws which prohibit murder, rape, assault, theft or fraud. But should the law restrict a man's liberty in respect of actions which harm no one else, either on the ground that he is too foolish to be the judge of his own interests, or on the ground that the action is intrinsically immoral? A negative answer to this question has been associated since the middle of the nineteenth century with the famous 'harm principle' of John Stuart Mill. In his *Essay on Liberty*, first published in 1859, Mill wrote:

'The object of this Essay is to assert one very simple principle, as entitled to govern absolutely the dealings of society with the individual in the way of compulsion and control, whether the means used be physical force in the form of legal penalties, or the moral coercion of public opinion. That principle is, that the sole end for which mankind are warranted, individually or collectively, in interfering with the liberty of action of any of their number, is self-protection. That the only purpose for which power can be rightfully exercised over any member of a civilised community, against his will, is to prevent harm to others. His own good, either physical or moral, is not a sufficient warrant.'[1]

Mill was an avowed utilitarian. For him, therefore, legislation and other institutional constraints could be justified only if they on balance promoted general happiness. He, like many other liberal utilitarians, never made clear the relationship of the value of liberty to the overall utilitarian principle which is supposed to be the test of all value. Is freedom merely instrumental, good because its exercise will in fact promote general welfare? Or does the harm principle provide an extra-utilitarian basis for valuation, to be assumed before a utilitarian calculation of pleasures and pains is to be made? If the former is correct, it is open to other utilitarians to take issue on the facts – doing what I like won't make me and others happy. If the latter is correct, my free choice of action has a special plus value, and the pain associated with others' mere disapproval of what I do (as distinct from proven harm to them) has a nil value. But then these special valuations do not come from the utilitarian happiness principle itself.

Another famous Victorian utilitarian, Sir James FitzJames Stephen, wrote an attack on Mill, *Liberty, Equality, Fraternity*, first published in 1873. Stephen denied that there were good utilitarian grounds for defending liberty as such – it all depended on what a person was at liberty to do. Further, no clear line could be drawn between acts which harmed others and acts which harmed only oneself. The punishment of 'the grosser forms of vice' was a proper object of legislation, as it would not be felt as a restraint by the vast majority, but would, on the contrary, satisfy feelings of hatred towards the vicious and provide proper substitutes for disorganised revenge.

The citation of Mill's harm principle given above shows that he was opposed to sanctions on self-regarding actions, whether emanating from the law or from other social institutions and arrangements – if what you do harms no one but yourself, not only should you not be subject to legal restraint, but you ought not to lose your place in an institution of higher education or your job. He can thus be seen as the apostle of what came to be known in the 1960s as 'the permissive society'. Whether he would actually have liked it is largely a matter of

1 *On Liberty* in *Utilitarianism, Liberty and Representative Government* pp. 72–73.

biographical speculation. Certainly, some advocates of permissiveness would reject two exceptions which Mill admitted to his principle. He thought that restraints, going beyond protection of others, were justified in the case of children, and in the case of primitive peoples. Today, much legislation in the area of sexual behaviour is seen by its critics as enforcing 'middle class' or 'bourgeois' or 'religious' morality on people who do not share it. But for any Victorian, there may not have seemed to be much incompatibility between such legislation and the harm principle. Those who promoted legislation raising the age of consent in 1875, or making incest for the first time criminal in 1907, believed that these measures were desirable to protect people, and it would probably have astonished them to be told that they were enemies of liberty.

'Permissive society' is, of course, a misleading label for what has emerged in Britain over the past two decades. In fact, more and more legal restrictions have been placed on what people are allowed to do. Breathalyser laws, laws prohibiting incitement to racial hatred, laws prohibiting the dumping of dangerous waste, all restrict people's freedom of action. The laws which supporters or critics of the 'permissive society' seem to have in mind are laws about homosexuality, obscenity, pornography, abortion, and so on. And some would bring within the same compass proposed changes in the law relating to voluntary euthanasia and the destruction of deformed infants.

The precise bearing of Mill's harm principle on all such laws is controversial. But a more fundamental controversy concerns the issue of the enforcement of morality. If society is entitled to use the law to uphold conventional moral standards, then Mill's principle is at least partially false; for then the enforcement of morality can be seen as a distinct warrant for punishment. Interest in this question received an enormous boost in 1957 from the Report of the Committee On Homosexual Offences and Prostitution, under the chairmanship of Sir John Wolfenden. The report includes some general observations which look Mill-like, and were undoubtedly influenced by the Mill libertarian tradition.

> '[The function of the criminal law] is to preserve public order and decency, to protect the citizen from what is offensive and injurious, and to provide sufficient safeguards against exploitation and corruption of others, particularly those who are specially vulnerable because they are young, weak in body or mind, inexperienced, or in a state of special physical, official or economic dependence.' (Para. 13.)

> 'Unless a deliberate attempt is to be made by society, acting through the agency of the law, to equate the sphere of crime with

that of sin, there must remain a realm of private morality and
immorality which is, in brief and crude terms, not the law's
business.' (Para. 61.)

The opposite view, that the law should prohibit conduct simply
because it is immoral, has an ancient pedigree. Plato in his *Laws*
stated that the lawgiver 'shall lay down what things are evil and bad,
and what things are noble and good'. The *Book of Common Prayer* calls
for 'the punishment of wickedness and vice'.

The Wolfenden Committee made two recommendations which
were eventually embodied in legislation. The first was that, while
prostitution itself should not be punishable, soliciting on the streets
by prostitutes should be punished more effectively than hitherto.
Substituting discreet call-girls in expensive flats for the old public
display of sexual wares – what the cynical press described as
'sweeping the dirt under the carpet' – was justified by the harm
principle. Soliciting caused 'offence' and so should be rigorously dealt
with. Prostitution in private harmed no one apart from the participants. The second recommendation was that homosexual acts
between consenting adults in private should no longer be a criminal
offence. The harm principle, as understood by the committee,
warrants punishing actions which involve 'corruption' or 'exploitation'. Hence, homosexual acts with persons under twenty-one, and
living off the earnings of prostitutes, were to continue to be offences.
The harm principle has also influenced the definition of obscenity in
the Obscene Publications Act of 1959, as pertaining to publications
liable to corrupt persons into whose hands they may fall. There may
be conventional moral standards according to which certain things
just are 'obscene', but (consistently with the harm principle) legal
prohibition requires one to prove that someone or other is likely to be
damaged – and, as critics of the law have pointed out, it is ticklish
business to produce witnesses who will say: 'Whereas I was pure,
since reading this I've become corrupted and depraved.'

The Wolfenden Committee's contention, that conflict with
morality is not enough to warrant legal prohibition, was challenged in
1959 by Lord Devlin. In his Hamlyn lecture on 'The Enforcement of
Morals', he put forward the view that society has a right to punish any
kind of act which, in the opinion of the man in the jury-box ('the
right-minded man'), is grossly immoral; there is no need for proof that
the act in question harms assignable individuals or groups. First, he
mounts an attack on the Wolfenden Committee Report in particular,
and the harm principle in general; and, secondly, he advances an
argument, in terms of social cohesion, why it is justifiable to enforce
society's morality by law. On both counts, he has been strongly

criticised by a number of writers, especially H. L. A. Hart; and the Devlin/Hart controversy has become a standard jurisprudential topic.

Devlin argues that what is 'indecent' or 'offensive', or what amounts to 'exploitation' or 'corruption', in Wolfenden terms, can, in many contexts, only be understood if we use the measure of society's morality. Further, he challenges those who advocate the harm principle to say why the following offences should (if they should) stay on the books: bigamy, bestiality, incest, living off immoral earnings; and to deal with the law's refusal to allow consent as a defence to homicide or serious assault. Many writers have answered Devlin but none, so far as I know, have taken the heroic stance of calling for all the following reforms: incest and bigamy should forthwith be removed from the criminal calendar; bestiality should be punishable only if it hurts the animal; soliciting in a courteous manner should be no more punishable than inviting someone to answer a political questionnaire; brothel-keeping should be subject to proper standards of public health, safety and security of employment but, beyond that, should not be interfered with; euthanasia and duelling should be allowed, provided consent is genuine; sexual acts with minors or mental defectives should be punishable only if that sort of thing can be shown to do actual physical or psychological harm – no more 'moral danger'!

Instead, the harm principle has been refined, restated and qualified so that change need be called for only in some of those areas of law associated with 'public morals'. Mill believed that minors could be required to refrain from certain actions for their own good. It has been argued that the proper development of the human personality requires that children should not be incited to become homosexuals, or promiscuous heterosexuals, not because these things are immoral, but because they are serious matters as to which a person can form no view of his own before attaining maturity. On this view, teaching children to play cricket is acceptable, while teaching them to be sexually promiscuous is unacceptable, not because the former is morally neutral while the latter is immoral, but because cricket is trivial while sexual behaviour is serious. Does this distinction provide a suitably amoral basis for the notions of 'corruption' and 'exploitation' which underlie the present criminal law relating to sexual acts with minors? Might it not prove too much, in the sense that it would justify penalising the biassing of children's minds over other 'serious' aspects of behaviour, for instance in the political sphere? At any rate, it would seem to follow that if, as some argue, homosexuality is a condition with which people are born, homosexual acts with consenting minors ought not to be prohibited, since the child is not taught to be something which he would not be in any event.

Hart's reply to Devlin produces two important qualifications on the harm principle. First, he disagrees with Mill that an adult's self-inflicted harm is no warrant for legal intervention. Hart is opposed to 'legal moralism', to the view that general agreement amongst the members of society that conduct is immoral is a ground for legal prohibition. But he favours 'paternalism', the view that society may prevent people from doing themselves physical harm. Paternalism justifies the criminal law in refusing the defence of consent to homicide and assault. Whereas Mill believed that a man's own good, physical or moral, did not warrant interference, Hart believes that his physical good does. It is not clear how far paternalism of this sort is to be taken. Does it justify legislation restricting the taking by adults of excessive drink, harmful drugs, or driving without seat-belts? Some would argue that restrictions of this sort can be supported by reference to the harm principle without any need to resort to paternalism. If I get myself injured in a duel, or through drink or drugs or driving without a seat-belt, do I not harm others in that I impose costs on society's medical services and perhaps deprive my dependants of support and the taxman of revenue? 'No man is an island', as John Donne told us. But, on that basis, might not the law prohibit dangerous sports, like potholing or mountaineering? If Mill is wrong, and a man's physical well-being is a ground on which society may restrict his liberty – either for Hartian paternalist reasons or on the no-man-an-island argument – no doubt libertarians would insist that the harm must be great in relation to the restriction on liberty involved before interference is justified. Is it practical or desirable to disregard, in this equation, whether the physical harm is self-inflicted in morally neutral or immoral ways?

Hart's second qualification to the harm principle concerns the definition of 'harm' itself, and imports a distinction between offence through public spectacle and offence through knowledge. Hart says that punishment of bigamy can be justified on the ground that, as a public act, it causes offence to religious sentiments: but that, in deciding whether any act inflicts 'harm', we must disregard the distress suffered by X through knowing that Y is doing what X regards as immoral. This is an exclusion to be made as a prior step to any utilitarian balancing. It is justified, seemingly, on distinct libertarian grounds, and is not derived from the principle of utility itself.

> '[A] right to be protected from the distress which is inseparable from the bare knowledge that others are acting in ways you think wrong, cannot be acknowledged by anyone who recognises individual liberty as a value ... If distress incident to the belief that

others are doing wrong is harm, so also is the distress incident to the belief that others are doing what you do not want them to do. To punish people for causing this form of distress would be tantamount to punishing them simply because others object to what they do: and the only liberty which could coexist with this extension of the utilitarian principle is liberty to do those things to which no-one seriously objects.'[2]

Offence-through-knowledge is not a ground for restricting liberty, but offence-through-witnessing is. This distinction would suggest, for example, that displays of pornographic literature in the public part of shops can legitimately be banned, whilst there is no ground for interfering with the private display or circulation of 'hard porn'. This is the conclusion of the Williams Committee, whose recent report embodies a rigorous allegiance to Mill's harm principle. Some argue that Hart's offence-through-witnessing concession in reality allows for the enforcement of morals, for otherwise it would justify penalising much that is now outside the criminal law. Feminists may be offended by certain kinds of advertisement which show women in a degrading light; teetotalers may be offended by seeing people drink; and many with strong political convictions are offended by processions of their opponents. If only some kinds of outrage to people's feelings are to be prohibited by the criminal law on the ground that they infringe 'decency', is not that a legal buttress for the moral opinions of the majority rather than an objective weighing of harms?

Mill advanced the harm principle as a banner of individual liberty, but it appears to leave many questions unanswered: What is to count as harm? How is harm to be proved? In what circumstances is society in a paternalist relationship to the individual so that he may rightly be protected from himself? It cannot deal with fundamental issues such as who is to count as a person capable of suffering relevant harm. If the foetus or the deformed infant counts as a person, then depriving him of life involves the same kind of harm as does painless homicide to any other human being, and consequently abortion and infanticide should be prohibited. If they do not count as persons, their destruction is no 'harm' to them; but we still have to decide whether distress to fathers, as well as mothers, is a relevant harm. If it is not, abortion on demand and humane infanticide (on the mother's sole say-so) appear not to infringe the harm principle.

Is there any other basis on which someone who values individual liberty can draw the limits which such a belief ought to impose upon legal intervention? In his essay on 'The Enforcement of Morals',

2 *Law, Liberty and Morality* pp. 46–47.

Devlin advances what Professor Mitchell has called the 'social cohesion' argument. Devlin argues that one of the essential elements of a society is a shared morality. Different societies have different moralities, and there is no way in which the legislature can or need choose between them. As it happens, he says, our own society's shared morality is derived from Christianity, even if Christian belief as such is no longer prevalent. If a society's shared morality is weakened, this has a tendency to lead to the destruction of the society itself. Even if an act which is wrong by the society's morality is committed in private and harms no one in the way of offence-to-decency, corruption or exploitation, its very practice weakens the shared morality and so may lead to a weakening of society. Individual freedom of choice is an important value, but it is outweighed by the overriding right of society to survive. No society can be expected to make provision for its own dissolution. Just as treason is punishable because it threatens society's existence, irrespective of the private moral opinions of the traitor; so, Devlin argues, society is entitled to punish any act which, according to popular opinion, is grossly immoral.

Devlin's view is that our society's morality is historically derived from Christianity; but he does not suggest that the way to discover whether any act is immoral is to consult Christian opinion. Indeed, it would be difficult for anyone engaged in rebutting Wolfenden-type programmes to make any such suggestion, since there has been no consensus among leading church figures about the morality or immorality of such matters as homosexuality or obscenity. Devlin himself seems highly suspicious of intellectuals as having any special right to speak on moral issues, whether they are churchmen or not. The Christian nature of society's morality is now beside the point. It should be enforced now, not because it is or was Christian, but because it is the shared morality of the majority and without it society, as we know it, cannot exist. Hence, the person whose moral opinion is to be consulted is the man in the jury-box. In this respect, Devlin's views march in line with those of many other English judges. Since 1962, the courts have recognised an offence of 'conspiring to corrupt public morals', which gives an important role to jury moral opinion;[3] and, more recently, the courts have held that the concept of 'honesty', incorporated by statute into the definition of theft and cognate offences, is not a legal term of art but something which the jury is to test by its own moral standards.[4]

3 Shaw v Director of Public Prosecutions [1962] AC 20; Knuller (Publishing, Printing and Promotions) Ltd v Director of Public Prosecutions [1973] AC 435.
4 R v Feely [1973] QB 530; R v Lewis (1975) 62 Cr App Rep 206; Boggeln v Williams [1978] 2 All ER 1061.

'[T]he moral judgment of society must be something about which any twelve men or women drawn at random might after discussion be expected to be unanimous ... No society can do without intolerance, indignation and disgust; they are the forces behind the moral law, and indeed it can be argued that if they or something like them are not present, the feelings of society cannot be weighty enough to deprive the individual of freedom of choice.'[5]

Devlin does not suggest that all popular morality is to be enforced. An act must be sufficiently grave as to be likely to cause a jury intolerance, indignation and disgust. Even then there may be grounds which make legal intervention undesirable. The law should be concerned with the minimum necessary for the preservation of society – there must always be a gap between the criminal and the moral law. The practical difficulty of enforcing any law must be taken into account and, as far as possible, privacy is to be respected. Despite the apparent drift of his original lecture, Devlin has since indicated that he is not in favour of punishing homosexual acts between consenting adults in private.

Hart's criticism of Devlin's social cohesion argument is twofold. First, he denies that a society need have a shared morality in Devlin's sense. Hart believes that there is a morality which every society must have and indeed must embody in law. This is his 'minimum content of natural law' discussed in chapter 2, above. Every society must have rules restricting violence, theft and deception. This morality is common to all societies, although its detailed implementation varies. Apart from this minimum, a society need have no shared morality peculiar to itself. Our own society is pluralistic, especially in relation to sexual morality. Secondly, Hart argues, even supposing a society does have a shared morality peculiar to itself, there is no good reason to believe that its preservation is necessary to the survival of the society. The fact that people differ from the majority of their fellow citizens on matters of personal morality does not in any way indicate that they are likely to be less loyal citizens. Furthermore, moral experiment – the permitting of activities which the majority now regard as immoral – is positively beneficial. It is always possible that the majority may be wrong, and they will be able to make more informed judgments if they can see other people behaving in 'deviant' ways.

The debate raises some issues of fact; and also some issues about our perception of social bonding, which involve a subtle interplay between the facts we know and the conceptions of society we have. Is

5   *The Enforcement of Morals* pp. 15,17.

it the case that our society has a shared morality about certain kinds of acts which traditional Christianity considered immoral? Do most people regard homosexuality, or incest, or bestiality, as morally wrong? If the answer is no, then Hart seems to be right in his contention that not *every* society need have its own distinctive shared morality. Presumably, Hart would not deny that *some* societies have distinctive moralities of this sort, that some Muslim societies, for example, have a distinctive morality about the consumption of alcohol, and some Hindoo societies a distinctive morality about killing cows.

If a society does have a shared and distinctive morality, does allowing deviant behaviour, as compared with repressing it by law, tend to the society's 'dissolution'? One can see that it might lead to a social change, in that one will have a society which is seen to be more diversified than would be one in which deviations were suppressed; and this would make changes in social behaviour possible in an open way. Those Arab countries which imprison European visitors who flout the local laws against drink could cite Devlin in support of what they do. The distinctively Muslim nature of their societies would be threatened if they tolerated such activities on the part of non-believers. Hart's answer would be that, if you define 'society' in terms of all its current morality, of course there is a 'change' if you tolerate deviation and the deviants persuade the majority. But that is not necessarily bad. It is not the same thing as a breakdown in society, a destruction or dissolution of it, so that Devlin's analogy with treason is inapposite. In the name of freedom, the western drinkers should be tolerated.

The crux of the disagreement about social cohesion turns on whether one believes in social contamination from laxness in one kind of standard to laxness in others. Does not enforcing conventional morals tend to laxness about paying taxes, to more shop-lifting, to a general disregard for the claims which society makes upon us? It is common enough to hear complaints in our society about 'the decay in standards', in which all these things are bracketed together. No doubt, an apologist for prohibition laws in a Muslim state, or an apologist for restrictive legislation about sexual behaviour in a communist state, would agree with this bracketing together, when he deplores 'western decadence'. Hart says that it is implicit in Devlin's social cohesion argument that we 'swallow our morality whole' – relax part of it, and the rest is weakened. Whereas, he says, morality is not a 'seamless web'; we can reject part of it and adhere just as strongly to the rest. This is no more than an unproven assertion about human psychology and social bonding; and Devlin's view is an unproven counter-assertion. The disagreement is paralleled by one kind of disagreement about a duty to obey the law – between those who say that the moral man is free to decide in the case of each legal obligation whether it morally binds him, and those who say that, if we allow freedom to pick and choose, wrong choices will be made as well as good (see chapter 16, below).

Faced with such disagreements, one can only rely on such experience as one has, and on imaginative guesses about the nature of man and of societies. Imagine two neighbouring states, in both of which the overwhelming majority agree that eating pork is morally wrong, in both of which theft is punishable under the criminal law, but, whereas in Millhart land, eating pork is visited with no sanction, in Devlin land it is subject to a criminal fine. Says the Millhart parent, or schoolteacher, or university professor: 'Both eating pork and shop-lifting are wrong, but we don't punish the former because it does no one (other than the actor) any harm. Harm is what matters when it comes to punishment. That is so because we believe in freedom.' Says his Devlin land equivalent: 'We punish all serious transgressions of morality, pork-eating and shop-lifting included. Once allow people to think they have a right to choose, save where harm is involved, and who is to say that someone might not take the view that shop-lifting does no "harm"? Freedom is very well, but standards must be upheld.' Who is right?

Bibliography

Bayles M. D.	'Criminal Paternalism' in Pennock and Chapman (eds) *The Limits of Law* (1974)
Berlin I.	'Two Concepts of Liberty' in Quinton (ed) *Political Philosophy* (1967)
Devlin P.	*The Enforcement of Morals* (1965)
Dworkin G.	'Paternalism' in Laslett and Fishkin (eds) *Philosophy, Politics and Society* (5th series, 1979)
Dworkin R. M.	*Taking Rights Seriously* (revised edn, 1978) ch 10
Hart H. L. A.	*Law, Liberty and Morality* (1963)
Henkin L.	'Morals and the Constitution: the Sin of Obscenity' (1963) 63 Colum L Rev 393
Hughes G. B. J.	'Morals and the Criminal Law' in Summers (ed) *Essays in Legal Philosophy* (1968)
MacCallum G. C.	'Negative and Positive Freedom' in Laslett, Runciman and Skinner (eds) *Philosophy, Politics and Society* (4th series, 1972)
Mill J. S.	*On Liberty* (1960)

Mitchell B.	*Law, Morality, and Religion in a Secular Society* (1967)
Regan D. B.	'Justifications for Paternalism' in Pennock and Chapman (eds) *The Limits of Law* (1974)
Rostow E.	'The Enforcement of Morals' (1960) CLJ 174
Samek R. A.	'The Enforcement of Morals: a Basic Re-examination in its Historical Setting' (1971) 49 Can Bar Rev 188
Sartorius R. E.	'The Enforcement of Morality' (1972) 81 Yale LJ 891
Stephen J. F.	*Liberty, Equality, Fraternity* (2nd edn, 1874)
Summers R. S.	Summers and Howard—*Law: its Nature, Functions, and Limits* (2nd edn, 1972) ch 9
Taylor C.	'What's Wrong with Negative Liberty?' in Ryan (ed) *The Idea of Freedom* (1979)
Williams Committee	Report of the Committee on Obscenity and Film Censorship (Cmnd. 7772 (1979))
Wolfenden Committee	Report of the Committee on Homosexual Offences and Prostitution (Cmnd. 247 (1957))

11   The morality of law and the rule of law

'Legality' and 'the rule of law' are parts of the currency of political debate. To say of a country that its officials observe legality, or that the rule of law is maintained, are expressions of approval. The mere word 'law' has an honorific ring. How is that to be squared with the positivist contention that law is one thing, good law another? Positivists like Hart, Kelsen and Austin tell us that a legal system exists if rules (norms, general commands) are effectively enforced. By that reckoning, there seems to be 'law' and 'legality' in racist and tyrannical regimes. Yet, at the end of chapter 6, above, we noted the distress produced amongst commentators on the Rhodesian rebellion when Kelsen's theory seemed to lead to the conclusion that it had introduced a new legal system. Some people deny that there is legality or the rule of law in South Africa, pointing to provisions which allow for detention without trial and alleging that no legal restraints are applied to the police. Others make the same accusation against the Soviet Union, instancing sham political trials in which constitutional safeguards are ignored, and the abuse of psychiatric medicine for the purpose of detaining political opponents. In the United Kingdom, governmental measures are from time to time criticised in the name of 'the rule of law' – such as retrospective legislation in the field of taxation and immigration control, and selective withdrawal of subsidies by a government seeking to enforce pay policy.

Where an official acts contrary to some formally valid legal rule, a positivist account enables us to say that he is acting illegally. Nothing in positivist definitions commits us to saying that his action is morally wrong. Whether there is a moral duty to obey the law is controversial (see chapter 16, below). The question here is whether we can give some non-positivist account of law which will make sense of political criticisms not based on breach of formally valid provisions, but which yet appeal to 'legality' or 'the rule of law'. Such an account would show how 'law' itself has some necessary moral qualities.

One way of attacking positivism is to deny that law is just a system of rules, by fastening attention on 'hard cases'. This is Dworkin's approach, as we shall see in chapter 14, below. But that will not yield conclusions like: 'Nazi law was not "law" at all.' Another way is to adopt the higher-law view of natural law, that any rule which contradicts natural law is a nullity (see chapter 2, above). This was the approach adopted in some of the post-war trials of Nazi supporters by German courts. But it requires a belief in higher law which not all share. Professor Fuller (1902–1978) has suggested a third method of attacking positivism. He accepts that law is a system of rules and he does not ask us to believe in higher law. His strategy is to fasten on the concept of 'purpose'. He uses it in three ways. First, we cannot know what any rule is unless we know what it was intended to achieve.

> 'We must in other words be sufficiently capable of putting ourselves in the position of those who drafted a rule to know what they thought "ought to be". It is in the light of this "ought" that we must decide what the rule "is".'[1]

Secondly, we cannot understand what a system of rules is if we try to comprehend it as a brute social fact. Instead, we must view it as a purposive enterprise: 'The enterprise of subjecting human conduct to the governance of rules.'[2] So conceived, we will appreciate that it cannot exist unless it has certain moral qualities.

Thirdly, it should be recognised that the definition of law is itself purposive. Positivists have usually purported to define merely to clarify terms. Often, however, there are concealed definitional purposes, such as promoting the ideals of peace and good order. Legal philosophy should, Fuller argues, deliberately define law so as to assist good legal enterprises.

> 'No one more than [the legal philosopher] runs the risk of forgetting what he is trying to do ... Though there are no doubt many permissible ways of defining the function of legal philosophy, I think the most useful is that which conceives of it as attempting to give a profitable and satisfying direction to the application of human energies in the law.'[3]

This third use of the concept of purpose raises the most fundamental of the questions in the positivist/non-positivist debate. Should we strive for two pictures, one of what law is, another of what law ought to be? Or do we want one picture only, in which moral colours can be shaded in? That depends on what one makes of all the theories and issues discussed in this book.

1 (1958) 71 Harv L Rev 630 at 666.
2 *The Morality of Law* pp. 53,74,91,106.
3 *The Law in Quest of Itself* p. 2

The first use of the concept of purpose raises issues about the nature of legal reasoning. Fuller accuses Hart of a 'pointer theory of meaning', since he seems to suggest that there are cases where rules (conceived as the meaning of words) clearly apply. The truth, argues Fuller, is that we can never apply a rule without attention to its purpose. Whether deductive reasoning is ever possible, and (when it is not) whether it is 'purpose' or some other criterion which guides decisions, are matters discussed in chapter 15, below. Even supposing Fuller is right, however, and that no rule can be understood or applied without reference to its purpose, it is not clear that this bridges the is/ought gulf in any way a positivist would wish to deny. The positivist view is that what the law ought to be, all things considered, is a different question from what the law is. We may have no doubt what the purpose of a rule is, whilst maintaining that the law ought to contain no such rule.

Fuller's most important contribution to jurisprudence turns on the second use of the concept of purpose. It is his claim that law, as a purposive enterprise, necessarily fulfils certain moral requirements. He lists eight principles of what he terms 'the inner morality of law', or 'principles of legality', or 'procedural natural law'. These are the requirements of generality, promulgation, non-retroactivity, clarity, non-contradiction, possibility of compliance, constancy through time, and congruence between official action and declared rule.

These requirements are contingently necessary if law is to work, given the definition of law as an 'enterprise of subjecting human conduct to the governance of rules'. First, some generality is essential because there must be rules. Second, the enterprise could not be forwarded without promulgation. Third, retroactivity would normally be pointless, especially in the sphere of criminal law, because of the brutal absurdity of today commanding someone to do something yesterday. Fuller denies, however, that laws imposing taxes on gains made at an earlier date are objectionable on the score of retroactivity, since their object is to raise revenue, to command payment now, not to control past conduct. He concedes also that the judge-made retroactive law can be justified. All legal systems seek to govern conduct. Some also have a side-purpose of settling disputes and hence employ courts. In the latter, it may be necessary to allow courts retroactively to change rules. Here, the dispute-settlement function prevails over the conduct-governance function. Fourth, rules, to achieve their object, must be clear — although they may incorporate standards whose content can be determined by reference to community and commercial mores (such as 'good faith', 'due care' or 'fairness'). Fifth, the requirement of non-contradiction has, Fuller says, nothing to do with the principles of logic. There is nothing contrary to logic in making a man do something and then punishing him for it. Non-contradiction, as a requirement of the law enterprise, outlaws incompatible provisions which, in the context of governing conduct by rules, could not together 'make sense'. Sixth, commanding the impossible is clearly inconsistent with the enterprise. This does not mean, however, that strict liability is never justified; for it can be viewed either as a tax on conduct, or as a way of directing people to adopt even higher standards of care than ordinary negligence rules require. Seventh, very frequent changes in the law must diminish the effectiveness of the enterprise. Eighth, 'congruence between official action and declared rule' is a requirement upon which Fuller lays much stress, but which he does not define very clearly. It seems to mean two things: first, officials must themselves comply with rules which impose duties on them – so that lawlessness by the police is an infringement of the requirement; secondly, law officers must require of citizens only that they (the citizens) observe rules imposing duties on them – so that the requirement is infringed when rules are misinterpreted.

Fuller demonstrates, by means of a parable about an incompetent king, that a system which failed totally by reference to any one of these criteria would not be 'law' at all. On the other hand, all legal systems fail by some of the criteria to some extent. They are not – except perhaps the publicity requirement – the subject of 'the morality of duty', but of 'the morality of aspiration'. That is, these principles of legality set ideals of excellence. They may, indeed, conflict. Fuller says that retroactivity may sometimes be justified in order to correct other failings – for instance, where a law was not properly publicised or could not in practice have been obeyed. Total failure would mean that no law exists. Gross failure means that law exists only in a rudimentary form. This was the case in Nazi Germany, owing to the enactment of retrospective legislation to legalise government out-rages, and the frequent reliance on secret legislation. To the extent that a governmental apparatus does not observe the internal morality of law, it is not true law.

Some of Fuller's critics take issue with him for making the existence of law a matter of degree, arguing that it does not make sense to say that a legal system relatively exists. If Fuller's criteria are applied, this issue might be thought to be merely verbal: does it matter whether we say that, by these criteria, a legal system is partially in operation, or that the legal system in operation is partially defective? On the other hand, there do appear to be contexts in which it is important to give a yes/no answer to the question: Is there (or was there) a legal system in existence? Day-to-day descriptive legal science may have to presuppose an answer to it – for example, when a lawyer is giving advice about 'the law' now in force in a territory, or when a comparative lawyer is seeking to show how bad the laws of country X are compared to those of country Y. The needs of descriptive legal science are, of course, the basis of positivist definitions of law. Even in the context of law-politics, we may need a yes/no answer – although we might use non-positivist criteria. Fuller himself wished to deny that, in the context of an evil system, we have to choose between a duty to obey the law and other moral claims, and he was anxious to support the German courts who refused to recognise immoral Nazi laws. Would it not have been better, then, if he had stipulated, not relative existence, but a cut-off point? He could have said that a sufficiently gross departure from the principles of the internal morality of law means that no legal system exists, so that the usual moral claims of 'law' disappear, and courts passing judgment after the event can act on the basis that there was no 'legality'.

A more important criticism levelled at Fuller is that his criteria are not 'moral' at all. Granted that some compliance with them is necessary for law to work, no amount of compliance guarantees that the system has moral worth. Evil laws would be no less evil merely because they were general, well publicised, prospective, clear, consistent, capable of performance, permanent, and strictly upheld. Conversely, no failing by reference to Fuller's criteria is, his critics claim, in itself morally wrong. Fuller gives as an example of laws not meeting the clarity requirement those South African laws which discriminate against non-whites by reference to imprecise notions of racial classification. What about American laws which discriminate in favour of blacks? Those who consider the South African discrimination laws to be bad and the American reverse discrimination laws to be good do so by reference to moral considerations unconnected with any lack of clarity – which, if it exists, is the same for both. All that Fuller has done is to set out criteria which must be met for a legal system to be effective. You might as well speak, argues Hart, of criteria for successful poisoning as the 'morality of poisoning'.[4]

Two issues must be distinguished. First, in so far as Fuller's eight 'principles of legality' are instrumental, are they necessarily an instrument of something good? Secondly, do they represent non-instrumental values? So far as the first question is concerned, Fuller argues, by reference to evidence of practices in tyrannical regimes, that bad aims are not achieved through the use of his principles. Tyrants do not find it expedient to make public their evil aims through the medium of promulgated general rules which are then consistently enforced; good rules are left on the books, but ignored by officials. His critics reply that, although this may often be true, there

4 (1965) 78 Harv L Rev 1281.

is no necessary connection. In South Africa, there are racist laws *pt.* which are public and generally adhered to by officials; and they are no less objectionable for that. A lot here turns on what one makes of 'necessary' connection. Fuller has not established any logical, *NB* instrumental connection between his principles and substantive moral criteria; but if one's survey of the world's regimes suggests that evil aims are generally better advanced where principles of legality *I agree* are infringed, one may conclude that insisting on these principles has a tendency towards achieving good.   *Raz's pt.*

NB   The second issue raises the question of the inherent, as distinct from instrumental, value of the principles of legality; and that depends on the political value one ascribes to the rule-of-law ideal. In the revised edition of *The Morality of Law*, Fuller adds a new chapter in which he replies to his critics. Drawing on interactional social theory, he claims that they have misunderstood the nature of law, in that they have confused it with 'managerial direction'. Positivists, he says, think of law as a 'one-way projection of authority'. An interactional view of law, on the other hand, reveals that it is a cooperative enterprise between legislator and citizen, each with reciprocal expectations, each with a role conceived in terms of 'the rule of law'. The confusion between law and managerial direction occurs because analogues of five of the principles of legality are relevant to efficient managerial control. A managerial authority must promulgate his wishes to his subordinates, and they must be reasonably clear, free from contradiction, possible of execution, and not changed so often as to frustrate the efforts of the subordinate to act on them. The requirements of generality and official congruence, however, are not essential to managerial control, and the issue of non-retroactivity will not arise. There is no need for a managerial authority to limit his own actions by reference to general rules, whereas the specific morality of their role does impose this limitation on lawful governments. It is this role-limitation which explains why retrospective legislation is sometimes resorted to; it provides a means of making what the government has already done conform to general rules. We may have more or less effective systems of managerial direction. Such systems approach more or less to 'legality' depending on how much they observe the inner morality of law, including the two crucial rule-of-law requirements, that prescriptions should be general, and that official action itself conforms to general prescriptions.

'[T]he existence of a relatively stable reciprocity of expectations between lawgiver and subject is part of the very idea of a functioning legal order ... Though the principles of legality are in large measure interdependent, in distinguishing law from managerial direction the key principle is that I have described as "congruence between official action and declared rule".

Surely the very essence of the Rule of Law is that in acting upon the citizen ... a government will faithfully apply rules previously declared as those to be followed by the citizen and as being determinative of his rights and duties. If the Rule of Law does not mean this, it means nothing. Applying rules faithfully implies, in turn, that rules will take the form of general declarations; ... law furnishes a base line for self-directed action, not a detailed set of instructions for accomplishing specific objectives.

The twin principles of generality and of faithful adherence by government to its own declared rules cannot be viewed as offering mere counsels of expediency.'[5]

Does this building in of the rule-of-law ideal into the definition of a legal system provide a satisfactory answer to our initial questions about some concept of law which would be serviceable in the language of political controversy? That depends, first, on whether one thinks that Fuller has provided an adequate characterisation of the rule of law; and, second, on how one sets this ideal alongside other political ideals. As to the first question, Fuller's list of principles does not include two things which some might think essential to the rule of law, namely, the need for independent courts, and the need for some monopolisation of force within a territory. Fuller indicates that the concept of a legal system is not to be so limited. He regards rules of non-state bodies, like schools and clubs, as legal systems. Such bodies plainly do not seek to monopolise force, and they need not employ courts. There is a common association between the ideas of 'the rule of law' or 'legality' and what in America is called 'due process' and in England 'the rules of natural justice'. Fuller says that where courts are used as a means for enforcing congruence between official action and declared rule, due process is a useful instrument. Others might claim that independent courts observing due process is of the essence of the rule of law.

What is the political value of the rule-of-law ideal? This stark question is one which Fuller does not confront. When not employed to condemn systems like the Nazis', Fuller's main use for his principles of legality is by way of recommending more sensitive legal craftsmanship. In *Anatomy of the Law*, he seeks to show that there are 'made' and 'implicit' elements (though in different degrees) in four forms of legal enterprise: enacted law, adjudicative law, law made by contracts, and customary law. All these forms of legal enterprise have

5 *The Morality of Law* pp. 209–210.

their place, and those who handle them will do so better if they are conscious of both made and implicit elements. The main function of ℕᴮ⋅ the principles of legality is to show what is implicit in enacted law.

The literature of political and social theory contains many answers to our stark question. I shall cite three, which cross the political spectrum from right to left. On your right, you have the views of Professor H. A. Hayek. He associates the rule-of-law ideal with an individualistic conception of liberty.

> 'Nothing distinguishes more clearly conditions in a free country from those in a country under arbitrary government than the observance in the former of the great principles known as the rule of law. Stripped of all technicalities this means that government in all its actions is bound by rules fixed and announced beforehand – rules which make it possible to foresee with fair certainty how the authority will use its coercive powers in given circumstances, and to plan one's individual affairs on the basis of this knowledge.'[6]

Hayek

Hayek draws a distinction, similar to Fuller's, between law proper and the rules of an organisation. Law proper consists of 'rules of just conduct' which first evolved as custom and later became articulated by judges. They are typically represented by what is called 'lawyers' law', or 'private law' (including criminal law). They impose negative restraints upon people, only so far as necessary to preserve each man's free domain of life, limb and property. The ideal method of articulating such rules is exemplified by common law judges in the eighteenth century, before everything began to be ruined by Benthamite legal positivism. Judges were then aware that rules of just conduct evolve to meet evolutionary needs of society, and that their job was to declare them. They employed proper criteria of consistency, and not fallacious notions of purposive social engineering. The rule-of-law ideal requires that legislatures too must only lay down rules modelled on those of private law, that is, general rules of just conduct. The legislature has authority to amend existing judge-declared rules where, owing to fossilisation or change of economic background, they no longer reflect community standards of corrective and distributive justice. But it has no authority to make selective redistributions of resources in the interests of particular groups. Overall social planning can be shown to be based on misconceptions of the nature of science and a failure to appreciate the inevitable limits on human knowledge. The idea that such planning could be achieved through the medium of 'law' is the fault of the legal positivists. They confused the rules of governmental organisations ('public law'), with

6 *The Road to Serfdom* p. 54.

the rules of just conduct, by calling both 'law'. They consequently failed to realise that true law grows and is not made; and they failed to appreciate that the rule of law requires that governmental managerial functions must not detract from the maintenance of general rules of just conduct.

> 'Thus it came about that governmental assemblies, whose chief activities were of the kind which ought to be limited by law, became able to command whatever they pleased simply by calling their commands "laws".'[7]

For an approach representing the political centre, we may turn to Professor, J. N. Shklar. She announces her commitment to liberal toleration, to a recognition that there is no consensus about morals and politics in society and to a belief that we ought not to try to produce one. She seeks to expose the preoccupation of lawyers with 'legalism', the view that ethical conduct is a matter of rule-following. She claims that 'justice', the policy of legalism, should be recognised for what it is: one particular 'ideology', that is, one kind of political preference. Lawyers, she believes, do not appreciate that governing conduct by rules is merely one kind of political policy. Legal rules are devices for compromising conflicts in society, and are to be compared with other political devices.

> 'Direct bargaining, splitting the difference, direct coercion, or propaganda not only compete with legalism, they also provide the conditions within which it exists socially.'[8]

She argues that, in some contexts (such as international relations), harm may be done by insisting on legalism. She seeks to show that, in the trials of war criminals at Nuremburg and Tokyo, there was a pretence of legalism which was mere sham, since there were no pre-existing rules. It would have been more frank to recognise these trials as the elimination of enemies, justified on political grounds. Nevertheless, although she begins by announcing that she is going to be controversial and to put legalism in its place, she seems to conclude that, from a liberal standpoint, legalism has a lot to be said for it.

> 'On the political level it is thus the manipulative state that is the real rival of the legalistic state, and the policy of inducement, whether by propaganda or by terror and related pressures, competes with the policy of legalism.'[9]

7 *Rules and Order* p. 130.
8 *Legalism* pp. 105–106.
9 *Legalism* p. 120.

On the left stands Professor R. M. Unger. For him the rule-of-law ideal is a failed attempt to legitimate domination. As we shall see in chapter 19, below, he claims that such an attempt is made necessary 'liberal' societies, because the consensus of customary law has broken down, and no single individual or group is accorded the right to impose its will through bureaucratic law. The attempt fails because domination persists and is perceived as illegitimate.

> 'Thus, the very assumptions of the rule of law ideal appear to be falsified by the reality of life in liberal society. But, curiously, the reasons for the failure of this attempt to ensure the impersonality of power are the same as those that inspired the effort in the first place: the existence of a relatively open, partial rank order, and the accompanying disintegration of a self-legitimating consensus. The factors that make the search necessary also make its success impossible. The state, a supposedly neutral overseer of social conflict, is forever caught up in the antagonism of private interests and made the tool of one faction or another. Thus, in seeking to discipline and to justify the exercise of power, men are condemned to pursue an objective they are forbidden to reach. And this repeated disappointment accentuates still further the gap between the vision of the ideal and the experience of actuality.'[10]

Unger makes Marxist assumptions about society being comprised of antagonistic groups rather than competing individuals and about the psychology of alienation and domination. But he does not share the Marxist-historicist view that any particular outcome from our present impasse is inevitable. What he thinks would be desirable is a spiralling back to a new form of customary law. If real inequalities were eliminated, we might regain spontaneous conceptions of the rules of group life, without loss of freedom or loss of the ability to criticise current practices.

Thus, according to Hayek, the welfare state stands condemned by reference to the rule-of-law ideal – or at least, all measures of social amelioration not formulated on the model of the rules of private law. According to Shklar, the ideal is merely a political device, to be considered along with others, for dealing with the permanent and desirable pluralism of a tolerant society; and it compares well with manipulative devices used in intolerant societies. For Unger, the ideal is a failed experiment; it masks, but can never hide, intolerable domination. Take your pick.

If one believes that some conception of the rule of law represents a political ideal worth pursuing, then one may praise or blame regimes

10 *Law in Modern Society* p. 181.

and measures in terms of their 'legality'. To avoid misunderstanding, however, some way must be found for distinguishing such legal-political critiques from employment of 'legality' in that other sense stressed by positivists, where it signifies merely that conduct accords with some formally valid rule. Which sense of 'legality' should we have in mind when we define law?

The answer may be that there is no single definition of 'law' or 'legal system' which will meet all our needs. The practising lawyer who merely provides information about 'the law' may mean no more than the rules in force at the time, and may use the words 'legal' and 'legality' solely with this conception in mind. But the political assessor who attributes 'legality' or 'the rule of law' to a system of law may presuppose a system which consists, not of rules, but of a complex of institutions. If that is right, Fuller's eight criteria are misleading in so far as they suggest that the inner morality of law is an attribute of rules. It is an attribute of institutions. Legislatures and courts fail to comply with the rule of law *if they operate with* rules which are not general, well publicised, prospective, clear, consistent, possible of performance, permanent, and strictly upheld. Reading the contents of a country's legal rules will often not help very much if we are asked to decide whether the rule of law flourishes there. Such a perusal cannot tell us whether the rules are strictly upheld; and information about institutional practices may convince us that the generality, clarity etc. of the rules is mere window-dressing. Perhaps then positivists and Fuller passed each other in the dark without really colliding; for the former were concerned with law as the subject matter of descriptive legal science, and Fuller with law as a complex of political institutions.

Bibliography

Dworkin R. M.	'Philosophy, Mortality and Law: Observations Prompted by Professor Fuller's Novel Claim' (1965) 113 U Pa L Rev 668
Friedmann W.	*Law in a Changing Society* (2nd edn, 1972) ch 15
Fuller L. L.	*The Law in Quest of Itself* (1940)
	'Positivism and Fidelity to Law – a Reply to Professor Hart' (1958) 71 Harv L Rev 593
	The Morality of Law (revised edn, 1969)
	Anatomy of the Law (1971)
Hailsham Lord	*The Dilemma of Democracy: Diagnosis and Pre-scription* (1978) chs 13, 16

Hart H. L. A.	'Positivism and the Separation of Law and Morals' (1958) 71 Harv L Rev 593
	'Fuller's *The Morality of Law*' (1965) 78 Harv L Rev 1281
Hayek F. A.	*The Road to Serfdom* (1946) ch 6
	The Constitution of Liberty (1960) Pt 2
	Law, Legislation and Liberty vol 1
	Rules and Order (1973) chs 4–6
Jones H. W.	'The Rule of Law and the Welfare State' (1958) 58 Colum L Rev 143
Marsh N. S.	'The Rule of Law as a Supra-national Concept' in Guest (ed) *Oxford Essays in Jurisprudence* (1961)
Murray J. E. et al	'The Morality of Law (a Symposium)' (1965) 10 Vill L Rev 631
Rawls J.	*A Theory of Justice* (1972) pp. 235–243
Raz J.	*The Authority of Law* (1979) ch 11
Samek R. A.	*The Legal Point of View* (1974) ch 10
Sartorius R. E.	*Individual Conduct and Social Norms* (1975) ch 9
Scarman L.	*English Law-the New Dimension* (1974) chs 6–7
Shklar J. N.	*Legalism* (1974)
Summers R. S.	'Professor Fuller on Morality and Law' in Summers (ed) *More Essays in Legal Philosophy* (1971)
	'Professor Fuller's Jurisprudence and America's Dominant Philosophy of Law' (1978) 92 Harv L Rev 433
Unger R. M.	*Law in Modern Society* (1976) pp. 66–68, 166–242

12 Statutory interpretation

The American jurist, J. C. Gray, was very fond of quoting the following words of Bishop Benjamin Hoadly, contained in a sermon delivered before the King in 1717:

'Nay, whoever hath an *absolute authority* to *interpret* any written or spoken laws, it is *he* who is truly the *Law-giver* to all intents and purposes, and not the person who first wrote or spoke them.'[1]

But that cannot be right, can it? Surely the judges are limited in their decisions by statutes, else why do we bother with parliaments and elections?

How should statutes be interpreted? This question has often been posed, but there has been no agreement about what sort of question it is. Is it a question of positive law? If so, one would expect to find the answer in one of the usual sources – a written constitution, a statute, or case law; and one would expect the answer to differ from one legal system to another. In some ways, this is true. English principles of statutory interpretation are often contrasted with those in the United States or in continental countries. On the other hand, there seems to be something about rules of interpretation which makes them not like other legal rules. For one thing they have to be formulated in terms of concepts which cannot be elucidated like other legal concepts. One comes across intractable notions like 'meaning', 'purpose' and 'legislative intent'. Such concepts might have a universal sense, the same for all legal systems. On the assumption that they do, juristic writers have treated statutory interpretation as a trans-systemic topic. But then again, critics call for reform in methods of statutory interpretation, suggesting that the needs which the law is supposed to serve could be better served by improved techniques or, more fundamentally, that our polity would be improved if our approach to interpretation embodied a rather different match between legislative and judicial power. Thus, the subject of statutory interpretation has something to do with particular canons, which differ from one system to another; something to do with universal concepts, which indicate

1 *The Nature and Sources of the Law* pp. 125,172.

that these canons have a special status different from that of ordinary legal rules; and something to do with improvable techniques, or alterable constitutional arrangements. I shall try to pick out some of the issues which have been raised under these three heads in the context of the English legal system. The first and third of these topics – what canons do we have, and how (if at all) should they be changed – are questions about English law. Only the second – what sort of animal is a canon of interpretation – is strictly a jurisprudential question; it would arise in any system which had statutes and generalised prescriptions for their interpretation. But, as mentioned in chapter 1, above, no strict division should be attempted between questions of particular jurisprudence and questions of positive law; and, in any case, the process of unpacking the simple question – how should statutes be interpreted – is itself a jurisprudential exercise; as is any attempt to elucidate some general question about law or legal institutions.

1 English canons of statutory interpretation

The English canons of interpretation are to be found in the decisions of the courts and are therefore part of English common law. They are notoriously difficult to formulate, for two reasons. First, one does not find with them, as with other settled common law rules, a match between a rule and a *ratio decidendi* of a case or a series of *rationes decidendi*. For the most part, judicial formulations of these canons are *obiter dicta*. Secondly, the *dicta* are often obscure and sometimes conflicting. The best one can do is to postulate formulations supported by the greatest possible weight of *dicta*. The most elegant and persuasive of recent efforts in this direction is contained in Sir Rupert Cross's book, *Statutory Interpretation*. If his conclusions are disputed, this can only be done by suggesting that other formulations better capture the majority of judicial pronouncements.

The English canons make reference to the 'ordinary' or 'natural' meaning of words, to the 'absurd', 'inconvenient' or 'unreasonable' consequences of particular interpretations, and to the 'purpose', 'object' or 'underlying scheme' of legislation. The first controversial issue is: how do the canons interrelate these matters of meaning, consequences and purpose? The traditional view has been that there are three rules: the literal rule, the golden rule, and the mischief rule. Professor J. Willis argued that these were distinct rules so that a court invokes 'whichever of the rules produces a result which satisfies its sense of justice in the case before it'.[2] Similarly, Llewellyn argued that canons of statutory construction 'hunt in pairs'.[3]

2 (1938) 16 Can Bar Rev 1, 16.
3 (1950) 3 Vand L Rev 395.

There have been innumerable statements by English judges over
the past two centuries to the effect that, if the meaning of the words of
a statute is plain, their job is simply to give effect to that plain
meaning. One of the most frequently cited is that of Tindal CJ, when
advising the House of Lords on the *Sussex Peerage Claim*:

> 'My Lords, the only rule for the construction of Acts of Parliament
> is, that they should be construed according to the intent of the
> Parliament which passed the Act. If the words of the statute are in
> themselves precise and unambiguous, then no more can be
> necessary than to expound those words in their natural and
> ordinary sense. The words themselves alone do, in such a case, best
> declare the intention of the lawgiver.'[4]

This is a statement of the 'literal rule'. Other judicial pronouncements, however, indicate that even when words are clear, they should
not be given effect if this will produce a result so outrageous that the
legislature cannot have intended it. In the words of Lord Blackburn in
River Wright Commissioners v Adamson:

> 'I believe that it is not disputed that what Lord Wensleydale used
> to call the golden rule is right, viz., that we are to take the whole
> statute together, and construe it altogether, giving the words their
> ordinary signification, unless when so applied they produce an
> inconsistency, or an absurdity or inconvenience so great as to
> convince the court that the intention could not have been to use
> them in their ordinary signification, and to justify the court in
> putting on them some other signification, which, though less
> proper, is one which the court thinks the words will bear.'[5]

Both the literal and the golden rules emphasise fidelity to the
legislature's words, although the latter makes some allowance for
consequences. There was a time in English legal history when judges
were far less preoccupied with the words of enactments. In the
sixteenth century, 'purpose' was much more to the fore. The classic
formulation of the mischief rule appears in the resolutions of the
barons of the Exchequer in *Heydon*'s case:

> 'And it was resolved by them, that for the sure and true inter-
> pretation of all statutes in general (be they penal or beneficial,
> restrictive or enlarging of the common law), four things are to be
> discerned and considered –
>
> 1st: What was the common law before the making of the Act.

4 (1844) 11 Cl & Fin 85 at 143.
5 (1877) 2 App Cas 743 at 764–765.

2nd: What was the mischief and defect for which the common law did not provide.

3rd: What remedy the Parliament hath resolved and appointed to cure the disease of the Commonwealth. And

4th: The true reason of the remedy; and then the office of all the Judges is always to make such construction as shall suppress the mischief, and advance the remedy, and to suppress subtle inventions and evasions for continuance of the mischief, and *pro privato commodo*, and to add force and life to the cure and remedy, according to the true intent of the makers of the Act, *pro bono publico*.'[6]

Even in the nineteenth century, when fidelity to the written word was at its height, one comes across *dicta* which indicate that plain meaning falls, not merely before bad consequences, but also before achievement of legislative purpose. For example, Alderson B said in *A-G v Lockwood*:

'The rule of law, I take it, upon the construction of all statutes ... is, whether they be penal or remedial, to construe them according to the plain, literal, and grammatical meaning of the words in which they are expressed, unless that construction leads to a plain and clear contradiction of the apparent purpose of the act, or to some palpable and evident absurdity.'[7]

Can the stand which modern English judges take on the issues of meaning, purpose and consequences be accurately represented in terms of these three rules? Professor Cross contends that it cannot. He points to the stress which modern judges lay on 'context' in determining what the natural meaning of statutory language is. 'Context' includes the object of the legislation. Therefore, it is not a case of, first catch your plain meaning and then drop it in favour of consequences or purpose. Purpose and meaning are taken on board together in determining whether we have a plain case. If we do, we may still defer to consequences; provided we can find some secondary meaning. Cross recommends the following reformulations of the old rules:

'(1) The judge must give effect to the ordinary or, where appropriate, the technical meaning of words in the general context of the statute; he must also determine the extent of general words with reference to that context.

(2) If the judge considers that the application of the words in their ordinary sense would produce an absurd result which cannot

6 (1584) 3 Co Rep 7a.
7 (1842) 9 M and W 378 at 398.

reasonably be supposed to have been the intention of the legislature, he may apply them in any secondary meaning which they are capable of bearing.'[8]

Cross disagrees with the view advanced by E. A. Driedger who, in effect, argues that consequences are relevant only so far as they indicate the limits of legislative purpose. Driedger cites *dicta* which deny that the court itself decides whether consequences are absurd. The following statement by Lord Esher is an example:

'If the words of an Act are clear, you must follow them, even though they lead to a manifest absurdity. The Court has nothing to do with the question whether the legislature has committed an absurdity. In my opinion, the rule has always been this – if the words of an Act admit of two interpretations, then they are not clear and if one interpretation leads to an absurdity, and the other does not, the Court will conclude that the legislature did not intend to lead to an absurdity, and will adopt the other interpretation.'[9]

The issue is this. Is the displacing effect which foreseen bad consequences have over primary meaning due to an evidential connection between such consequences and legislative intention, or is it entirely independent of any such connection? Cross cites as 'conclusive support' for the latter view the decision of the House of Lords in *Richard Thomas and Baldwins Ltd v Cummings*. Legislation required fencing of dangerous parts of machines while they were 'in motion'. It was held that these words did not include a mere transitory manual turning, because such a conclusion would be so 'unreasonable'.[10] In this case, Cross argues, the House of Lords cannot be regarded as having rejected plain meaning in favour of legislative purpose, for the purpose was the protection of workmen and that would have been advanced by a contrary holding. So the House must be understood as rejecting plain meaning because they (the members of the House) thought that application of the words in their ordinary sense would have had bad consequences.

Taking the view he does, one may wonder why Cross did not exclude from the formulation of his second rule the words 'which cannot reasonably be supposed to have been the intention of the legislature'. He tells us that 'the intention of Parliament' is 'not so much a description as a linguistic convenience'.[11] If this means that, given a contextually-determined prima facie meaning, nothing then

8 *Statutory Interpretation* p. 43
9 *R v City of London Court Judge* [1892] 1 QB 273 at 290.
10 [1955] AC 21.
11 *Statutory Interpretation* p. 36.

turns on what the court thinks the legislators had in mind, but everything turns on the court's own view of consequences, omission of these words would make his second rule clearer. Whether it would be accurate will appear only after we have considered whether legislative intention can be dismissed as a mere 'linguistic convenience'.

The relationship which the English canons stipulate between meaning, purpose and consequences is controversial. There seems to be less doubt about the evidence the courts are confined to in examining these things. They may look at the whole of the enacting part of the statute in which the provision is contained. In construing it and other statutes 'in pari materia', they must apply the rules of grammar and, unless some contrary intention appears, they must give any word or phrase the meaning laid down in the Interpretation Act 1978. They may give weight to three maxims of linguistic convention. The _eiusdem generis_ rule indicates that a word of general scope following particular words standing for members of a class is to be construed as referring only to members of that class. The House of Lords has recently made it clear that the 'class' must contain at least two members.[12] The _noscitur a sociis_ maxim allows the meaning of any word to be known from words surrounding it. The maxim _expressio unius est exclusio alterius_ permits one to infer that, where one of a natural collectivity of items is expressly mentioned, the legislature must have intended not to include the rest. The courts may look at the rest of the law, and take judicial notice of any facts of common knowledge when the statute was enacted. To resolve an 'ambiguity', they may look at the statute's long title, the preamble (if any), and its cross-headings; but there is more doubt as to whether they may consider punctuation, short title and side-notes. What they must not look at, according to English rules, is the history of parliamentary debates – a rule recently reaffirmed by the House of Lords.[13] They may only look at reports of committees preceding the enactment in order to ascertain the mischief the statute was designed to remedy, not the meaning of the provisions enacted. The contrast here with other jurisdictions is marked. In the United States and in Europe, all aspects of legislative history are generally open to inspection in order to determine both why the law was passed and what the law was intended to achieve. The House of Lords has now laid down that, where an Act of Parliament incorporates an international treaty, English courts may look at the _travaux préparatoires_ which preceded it, provided that the material involved is public and accessible, and that it clearly and indisputably points to a definite legislative intention.[14]

NB.

12 _Quazi v Quazi_ [1979] 3 All ER 897.
13 _Davis v Johnson_ [1979] AC 264.
14 _Fothergill v Monarch Airlines Ltd_ [1980] 2 All ER 696.

There are as well various presumptions of legislative intent, although their scope and strength is often unclear. They include presumptions against wide construction of penal legislation, against the imposition of criminal liability without fault, against changes in fixed rights, against deprivation of property without compensation, and against the conferral on officials of arbitrary discretion. There is also sometimes said to be a presumption against change in the common law, though, in so far as this goes beyond the presumptions just mentioned, it may mean no more than that the courts will employ established common law and equitable doctrines as guides to determine all doubtful legal issues.

2 The status of the canons of statutory interpretation

Many of the canons just discussed are 'constitutional' principles in that they purport to delimit the respective spheres of the legislature and the judiciary. The presumptions of statutory intent may be thought of as a common law bill of rights. In our system, constitutional rules can be changed by legislation. But would it make sense for Parliament to enact, say: 'The judges, in construing statutes, shall take no account of the meaning of words, or of conjectures as to the purpose of the enactment, or of the consequences of different constructions'? It is not merely that such a prohibition would be undesirable. It would, having regard to the nature of the adjudication process, be impossible to obey. This suggests that there are unalterable (ideal) elements inherent in the notion of statutory interpretation, even though their mix and implementation varies from system to system. This is why the subject has been treated as one of general juristic speculation.

I can do no more here than point to some of the issues raised by analysis of the leading concepts of 'meaning', 'purpose' and 'consequences'. Legislation in any society would be pointless if it were not the case that some assignable meaning can be given to statutory words by those to whom the legislation is directed. Yet, as we saw in the last chapter, Fuller argues that the meaning of words is always dependent on how their author intends them to be understood. On this view, it is misleading to speak of the 'natural', 'ordinary' or 'plain' meaning of statutory words. On the other hand, your average motorist need engage in no speculation as to author's intention in order to know that the common or garden directive addressed to 'drivers of motor vehicles' applies to him.

The semantic theory presupposed by the English courts contains (I would suggest) three propositions. First, some words have a natural meaning 'in context'. Second, some words have both a primary and a secondary meaning – the latter being the proper meaning to adopt in certain circumstances. Third, all statutory words have an outer perimeter of possible meanings, beyond which one must not go.

> 'It is a cardinal principle applicable to all kinds of statutes that you may not for any reason attach to a statutory provision a meaning which the words of that provision cannot reasonably bear. If they are capable of more than one meaning, then you can choose between those meanings, but beyond that you must not go.'[15]

Despite the frequency of judicial pronouncements like that of Lord Reid just cited, it may be questioned whether the third proposition is universally adhered to. Professor Cross cites cases of obvious draftsman's error where courts have substituted new words for statutory words (such as 'and' for 'or'), or have deleted statutory words, or even written in words. To account for these, he formulates a third rule of statutory interpretation:

> 'The judge may read in words which he considers to be necessarily implied by words which are already in the statute and he has a limited power to add to, alter or ignore statutory words in order to prevent a provision from being unintelligible or absurd or totally unreasonable, unworkable or totally irreconcilable with the rest of the statute.'[16]

The first of the above propositions of judicial semantic theory is in special need of clarification. 'Context' may refer to the fact that the statute is of such a type that no legislature enacting it could have intended the word to mean other than X – no legislature enacting a speed limit for 'motor vehicles' could have intended it to apply to aircraft. In that case, speculations as to the purpose of this particular legislature are unnecessary. Alternatively, 'context' may denote that, given common knowledge about the reasons prompting the enactment, this particular legislature must have intended the word to have meaning X. In both cases 'purpose' enters into 'meaning'; but in the first, only negatively to exclude fanciful suggestions; in the second, positively to give semantic colour to the words. It is because 'natural meaning in context' is used in this second sense that we find, commonly enough, that judges disagree as to the natural meaning of statutory words.

Thus sometimes even when judges conclude that the meaning of words is plain, they have in mind a conjecture about what the

15 *Jones v Director of Public Prosecutions* [962] AC 635 at 662 per Lord Reid.
16 *Statutory Interpretation* p. 43.

enacters of the measure were seeking to achieve; and the mischief rule indicates that they should always do this where the meaning is not plain, for example, where general words have a fringe of uncertain application. This raises the vexed question of what is meant by 'legislative intention'. It has frequently been argued that a body of persons cannot have a common intention; or, at any rate, a body like a legislature never does, because a minority may have voted against the measure and a fluctuating majority are unlikely to have been of one mind as to its exact scope and intended effect. In England, it would be of no relevance to prove to a court – if one could prove it – that every member of Parliament had such and such in mind when he voted. Professor Cross concludes that it is pointless to try to identify the intention of Parliament with the intention of any individuals, and that the expression is 'a linguistic convenience'.

If the 'intention of Parliament' never refers to the intentions of actual individuals, any proposal for changing English law on the admissibility of parliamentary history appears to be ruled out *in limine*. This is the view of the Law Commission. In its paper on Statutory Interpretation, the Law Commission distinguished three questions: Would such evidence be 'relevant' to the interpretative task? Would it be 'reliable'? Would it be readily 'available'? As to the first, it approved the view that:

> 'If [legislative intent] is looked upon as a common agreement on the purposes of an enactment and a general understanding of the kind of situation at which it is aimed, to deny the existence of a legislative intention is to deny the existence of a legislative function.'[17]

The Commission went on to conclude that, in the context of the United Kingdom, parliamentary proceedings should not generally be admissible, on the grounds of reliability and availability.

If the 'intention of Parliament' within the English system, has no connection with the intention of particular individuals in the legislative process, then it is illogical even to suggest that courts might be better informed of the intention of Parliament if they could look at what those individuals said or wrote. It would also follow that other systems, in which evidence of legislative history is admissible, have a different conception of what legislative intention is; and that when practices changed in the direction of admission in the United States, there was an unobserved change in the American conception of legislative intention.

To maintain that legislative intent is a function of the intent of individuals, it is not necessary to assume that the intention of a body

17 Law Com. No. 21, para. 55.

of persons is the same sort of thing as the intention of a single person. One can adopt either a majoritarian or an agency model of corporate intention. Consistently with the first, one could say that Parliament intends that which one has reason to believe that the majority of its members actually had in mind. Two recent decisions of the House of Lords illustrate this process. The issue was whether, under the Trade Union and Labour Relations Act 1974 (as amended), the immunity conferred on trade unions in respect of acts done 'in furtherance of a trade dispute' covered interference with the activities of third parties when union leaders believed that such interference would strengthen their industrial action. The Court of Appeal took the view that Parliament could not have intended the immunity to be so wide. The House of Lords reversed the Court of Appeal, holding that the Parliament which passed the 1974 Act and amending Acts – that is, the Labour party majority of that Parliament – might well have taken the view that trade unions could be relied on not to abuse their immunity.[18]

In accordance with the agency model of corporate intention, one could say that Parliament intends what one has reason to believe that some agent of it (the draftsman, or a committee) had in mind.

'It is the duty of a court so to interpret an Act of Parliament as to give effect to its intention. The court sometimes asks itself what the draftsman must have intended. This is reasonable enough: the draftsman knows what is the intention of the legislative initiator (nowadays almost always an organ of the executive); he knows what canons of construction the courts will apply; and he will express himself in such a way as accordingly to give effect to the legislative intention. Parliament, of course, in enacting legislation assumes responsibility for the language of the draftsman. But the reality is that only a minority of legislators will attend the debates on the legislation.'[19]

One might take the distinction made by the Law Commission between 'particular intent' as to the meaning of words, and 'general intent' as to the purpose the legislature sought to achieve, and argue that there is a different intention-agent in each of these cases, or that an agency model of intention is appropriate for the former and a majoritarian model for the latter. It may well be that, as between these competing conceptions, English practice gives no sure guide. Some *dicta* refer to draftsmen, some to the promoters of the bill; but

18 *Express Newspapers Ltd v MacShane* [1980] 1 All ER 65; *Duport Steels Ltd v Sirs* [1980] 1 All ER 529.
19 *Ealing London Borough v Race Relations Board* [1972] AC 342 at 360 per Lord Simon of Glaisdale.

⌊most speak only of 'Parliament'. One can find many *dicta* which⌉ specifically deny that 'intention of Parliament' takes us outside the four corners of the statute. In assessing the latter, one must bear in mind the distinction between the thing that intention is (or is supposed to be) and the admissible evidence for ascertaining it. The⌉ overwhelming judicial opinion has been that Parliament's words are the best evidence of its intention; but from that it does not follow that⌊ what the words are supposed to be evidence of is not the intention of specific individuals engaged in the legislative process. When in *Assam Railways and Trading Co Ltd v Commissioners of Inland Revenue*, Lord Wright ruled out legislative history as admissible evidence of Parliament's intention, it was not because it was irrelevant but because it was unreliable:

> 'It is clear that the language of a Minister of the Crown in proposing in Parliament a measure which eventually becomes law is inadmissible and the Report of Commissioners is even more removed from value as evidence of intention, because it does not follow that their recommendations were accepted.'[20]

If, in a particular case, the courts do have a clear conception of meaning and purpose, we have seen that it is a controversial question whether the English canons permit the court to disregard what was meant and intended in the light of its own assessment of consequences. It may be that this is an unreal issue, since if the courts are quite clear that the consequences of a particular construction are disastrous, they will not be persuaded by any evidence that nonetheless that outcome was what the legislature wished. However this may be, there are many circumstances in which meaning and purpose still leave room for doubt, and here the court may be guided by its view of what would be 'an absurdity' (or else by some received legal doctrine, such as one of the presumptions of statutory intent). It is common to speak of such cases as instances of 'intersticial judicial legislation'. As we shall see in chapters 14 and 15, below, this characterisation of such a situation, and the general problem of the significance of consequentialist reasoning, is highly controversial.

3   Should English canons of statutory interpretation be reformed?

It seems clear that the answer to this question depends, in part, on one's view of issues raised under the last heading. To the extent that⌉NB

20 [1935] AC 445 at 458.

statutory interpretation is a process which necessarily involves the
application of linguistic conventions in the ascertainment of meaning,
considerations of legislative purpose and consequentialist reasoning,
there are limits to the changes in the process that one can bring about
by legislation. It is therefore not surprising that some have drawn the
conclusion of Lord Wilberforce that statutory interpretation 'is what
is nowadays popularly called a non-subject. I do not think that law
reform can really grapple with it. It is a matter for educating the
judges and practitioners and hoping that the work is better done.'[1]

The rules for admissible evidence of the legislators' purpose –
granted that such a thing is relevant – could, of course, be changed. At
present, the predominant view is that there should be no wholesale
change, at least in the absence of modified parliamentary practices –
such as the provision of authoritative reports of parliamentary
committees. The Law Commission rejected any move to introduce
the whole of parliamentary history as admissible evidence, bearing in
mind such problems as the deliberate manufacture of legislative
history by interested groups, the difficulty of assessing whether what
is said at the early stage of a bill really represents the final view of the
majority, and the practical difficulties of time and effort involved if
Hansard had always to be searched before one could be sure how to
interpret a statute. It did, however, take the view that there was a case
for admitting explanatory statements (approved by Parliament) to be
published with statutes and used as guides to interpretation, as well
as reports issued by royal commissions and similar bodies, and
relevant international treaties. The Renton Committee Report on the
Preparation of Legislation (1975) disagreed with these proposals,
except so far as they relate to the admissibility of treaties. The view is
there taken that any advantage gained from admitting explanatory
statements and commission reports would be outweighed by the extra
time consumed by courts and practitioners who would have to consult
such documents.

Apart from questions of legislative reform of admissible evidence,
can the judges change their ways to advantage including altering by
judicial decision the common law rules about natural meaning,
statutory objectives and 'absurdity'? Should they be more 'purposive'
in their approach, like the continentals, and less 'mechanical' or
'legalistic'? Some see the issue as one of improved technique; some see
it as constitutional. The latter are split between those who call for
more 'judicial activism', on the pattern of the bold, progressive judges
in the American Supreme Court, and those who are suspicious of a
change which would give judges more freedom of manoeuvre.

1 277 HL Official Report (5th series) col. 1254.

How the same question – should judges stick to the letter or should they carry out the objectives of the enacters – can be seen either as an issue of technique, or as an issue of constitutional propriety, is well illustrated by the disagreement about gap-filling between Lord Denning and Lord Simmonds in *Magor and St Mellons Rural District Council v Newport Corporation*. In the Court of Appeal Denning LJ said:

'We sit here to find out the intention of Parliament and of Ministers and carry it out, and we do this better by filling in the gaps and making sense of the enactment than by opening it up to destructive analysis.'[2]

This proposition was repudiated by Lord Simmonds in the House of Lords:

'The duty of the court is to interpret the words that the legislature has used; those words may be ambiguous, but, even if they are, the power and duty of the court to travel outside them on a voyage of discovery are strictly limited.'[3]

He spoke of filling in gaps in a statute as a 'naked usurpation of the legislative function under the thin disguise of interpretation.'[4]

Lord Denning has recently reiterated his view about gap-filling, and has again been snubbed (though this time silently) by the House of Lords. In *Nothman v London Borough of Barnet*, the issue was whether a woman schoolteacher had any right to sue for unfair dismissal once she had reached the normal retiring age of sixty (within the relevant provisions of the Trade Union and Labour Relations Act 1974), it being clear that a man retained that right until he reached the age of sixty-five. The industrial tribunal had held that, although it was a gross anomaly, the statute left no alternative but to conclude that she had not. To this Lord Denning MR rejoined:

'[I]t sounds to me like a voice from the past. I heard many such words 25 years ago. It is the voice of the strict constructionist... [Presumably, he meant Lord Simmonds' voice.] Faced with glaring injustice, the judges are, it is said, impotent, incapable and sterile. Not so with us in this court. The literal method is now completely out-of-date ... Whenever the strict interpretation of a statute gives rise to an absurd and unjust situation, the judges can and should use their good sense to remedy it – by reading words in, if necessary – so as to do what Parliament would have done had they had the situation in mind.'[5]

2 [1950] 2 All ER 1226 at 1236.
3 [1952] AC 189 at 191.
4 Ibid at 191.
5 [1978] 1 All ER 1243 at 1246.

The other members of the Court of Appeal did not concur in these sentiments, although they, and a three-to-two majority of the House of Lords, agreed that Miss Rothman's appeal should be allowed. All the members of the House of Lords, majority and minority alike, purported to give effect to the natural meaning of the words, pointedly disclaiming any power to fill in gaps.[6]

The same mixture of technical and constitutional issues appears in *Black-Clawson International Ltd v Papierwerke Waldhorf-Aschaffenburg AG*,[7] where the House of Lords, by a bare majority of three to two, upheld the rule that reports of committees are admissible only as evidence of the mischief prompting an enactment and not as evidence of the meaning Parliament intended to attach to its words. The majority took this view, even though the report contained a draft bill identical in all material respects with the terms of the Act. They saw practical objections to admitting the commentary on the draft bill contained in the committee's report, since that would mean construing two documents instead of one, and would open the door to the admission of other aspects of parliamentary history. There was also a constitutional objection, expressed by Lord Wilberforce in the following terms:

> 'Legislation in England is passed by Parliament, and put in the form of written words. This legislation is given legal effect upon subjects by virtue of judicial decision, and it is the function of courts to say what the application of the words used to particular cases or individuals is to be. This power which has been devolved upon the judges from the earliest times is an essential part of the constitutional process by which subjects are brought under the rule of law – as distinct from the rule of the King or the rule of Parliament; and it would be a degradation of that process if the courts were to be merely a reflecting mirror of what some other interpretation agency might say.'[8]

This is a continuing debate. It involves issues of technique and more fundamental questions about the separation of powers and the rule of law. It also raises conceptual problems, about the extent to which interpretation is possible at all without conjectures as to legislative purpose, and about how, on the other hand, one can know that one is carrying out the purposes of the legislature rather than making the law one thinks to be in the public interest.

6 [1979] 1 All ER 142.
7 [1975] AC 591.
8 Ibid at 629.

Technical and constitutional issues also form part of the current debate about whether the United Kingdom should adopt a bill of rights. The more modest proposal is that a bill of rights should provide guidance to the courts in interpreting statutes, but could always be overridden expressly in any statute – it would not limit Parliament's ultimate sovereignty. The effect would be to codify and bring up to date those presumptions which the courts already employ in interpreting statutes. This codification would, so its advocates claim, facilitate dissemination of crucial features in statutory interpretation; and the discussions leading to the formulation of the bill of rights would encourage democratic participation. Those opposed to the measure insist that the provisions of such a bill would inevitably be vague, so that they would both diminish predictability and increase the power of the judges. On the latter ground, they object even more strongly to the more far-reaching proposal, that a bill of rights should derogate from Parliament's sovereignty, by enabling judges to declare statutes unconstitutional. Such technical and constitutional issues are, of course, only part of the ground covered by this particular debate. It also raises fundamental conceptual and normative questions about the nature of rights and of justice. For example, if Dworkin is right (see chapter 14, below) in contending that rights are, by their nature, interests of individuals which override community goals and that judges are peculiarly fitted to determine what rights we have; and if Rawls is right (see chapter 20, below) in contending that a just society is one in which basic liberties always have priority over other aspects of distributive justice; then we must adopt the more far-reaching proposal, whatever we think about problems of drafting and predictability and the doctrine of the separation of powers.

Bibliography

Cross R.	*Statutory Interpretation* (1976)
Curtis C. P.	'A Better Theory of Legal Interpretation' in New York Bar Association *Jurisprudence in Action* (1953)
Denning Lord	*The Discipline of Law* (1979) Pt 1, ch 2
Dias R. W. M.	*Jurisprudence* (4th edn, 1976) ch 7
Dickerson F. R.	'Statutory Interpretation: Core Meaning and Marginal Uncertainty' (1964) 29 Miss L Rev 1
Driedger E. A.	*The Construction of Statutes* (1974)
Fitzgerald P. J.	*Salmond on Jurisprudence* (12th edn, 1966) ch 4

Frankfurter F.	'Some Reflections on the Reading of Statutes' (1947) 47 Colum L Rev 527
Friedmann W.	'Statute Law and its Interpretation in the Modern State' (1948) 26 Can Bar Rev 1277
Gottlieb G.	*The Logic of Choice* (1968) ch 7
Landis J.	'A Note on "Statutory Interpretation"' (1930) 43 Harv L Rev 886
Law Commission	The Interpretation of Statutes (Law Com. No. 21 (1969))
Llewellyn K. N.	'Remarks on the Theory of Appellate Decision' (1950) 3 Vand L Rev 395
MacCullum G. C.	'Legislative Intent' in Summers (ed) *Essays in Legal Philosophy* (1968)
MacCormick D. N.	*Legal Reasoning and Legal Theory* (1978) pp. 203–213
Marsh N. S.	'The Interpretation of Statutes' (1967) 9 JSPTL (ns) 416
Paton G. W.	*A Textbook of Jurisprudence* (4th edn, 1972) ch 9
Payne J. J.	'The Intention of the Legislature in the Interpretation of Statutes' (1956) CLP 96
Radin M.	'Statutory Interpretation' (1930) 43 Harv L Rev 863
Renton Committee	Report of the Committee on the Preparation of Legislation (Cmnd. 6953 (1975))
Twining W. and Myers D.	*How to do Things with Rules* (1976) ch 10
Willis J.	'Statutory Interpretation in a Nutshell' (1938) 16 Can Bar Rev 1

13 Precedent

When I was on holiday in Greece in the summer of 1966, I was confronted one morning with a report in *The Times* that the judges in the House of Lords had issued a new practice direction. They would no longer consider themselves absolutely bound by their own decisions. What next! Would the senior judges get together some day and announce that they were no longer going to observe the absolute sovereignty of Parliament? In my undergraduate days, it had been a commonplace that the rule which required the House never to over-rule a previous decision of its own was a bad rule, leading to excessive inflexibility and over-subtle distinguishing of bad precedents. Every-one agreed that the rule should be changed. It was a matter of controversy whether this could be done by a decision of the House announced in some future case where overruling would be crucial to the decision, or whether it could only be done by statute. No one, so far as I recall, suggested that the change could be effected by a mere 'practice statement'.

I shall deal with issues involved in the 'doctrine of precedent' under similar headings to those used in the discussion of statutory inter-pretation in the last chapter: What special rules exist in England? What is the status of these rules? What reforms, if any, are desirable?

1 The English rules of precedent

The English rules of precedent may be divided into those whose operation depends on the distinction between *ratio decidendi* and *obiter dicta*, and more general practice rules not dependent on this distinc-tion. The former answer the question: which courts bind which, within the English hierarchy? They can be stated with much greater precision than the canons of statutory interpretation, although their merits are controversial and their permanency cannot be assumed. The House of Lords is not bound by its own decisions, though it will not depart from them merely because they are 'wrong'. The Court of Appeal and all inferior courts and tribunals are bound by decisions of the House of Lords. The Court of Appeal, in exercising the civil side of its jurisdiction, is bound by its own decisions, with certain exceptions mentioned below. In exercising its criminal jurisdiction, it is not bound by its own decisions. All inferior courts and tribunals are bound by decisions of the Court of Appeal. Divisional courts are bound by their own decisions, with the same exceptions as those applicable to the Court of Appeal; and inferior courts and tribunals are bound by decisions of divisional courts. Judges of the High Court are not bound by each other's decisions. It seems that their decisions do bind county court judges and magistrates. In relation to all these rules, 'decisions' refers to the *ratio decidendi* of a case, the 'reason' or 'ground' of the court's decision, as opposed to mere *obiter dicta* – that is, any statement about the law made by the court which was not necessary to the decision. Where there is more than one *ratio decidendi*, each is binding.

The practice statement of the House of Lords, read by Lord Gardiner LC on 26 July 1966, runs:

> 'Their lordships regard the use of precedent as an indispensable foundation upon which to decide what is the law and its application to individual cases. It provides at least some degree of certainty upon which individuals can rely in the conduct of their affairs, as well as a basis for orderly development of legal rules.
>
> Their lordships nevertheless recognise that too rigid adherence to precedent may lead to injustice in a particular case and also unduly restrict the proper development of the law. They propose therefore to modify their present practice and, while treating former decisions of this House as normally binding, to depart from a previous decision when it appears right to do so.
>
> In this connection they will bear in mind the danger of disturbing retrospectively the basis on which contracts, settlements of property and fiscal arrangements have been entered into and also the especial need for certainty as to the criminal law.
>
> This announcement is not intended to affect the use of precedent elsewhere than in this House.'[1]

In *Fitzleet Estates Ltd v Cherry (Inspector of Taxes)*, the issue was whether a company was liable to account to the revenue for tax deducted from interest on a loan, where that interest had been capitalised by being debited to the cost of land in the company's balance sheet – it being the case that, the company having taxed profits equal to the interest in question, there would be no liability to account had the interest not been capitalised. In an eleven-year-old

1 [1966] 3 All ER 77.

decision (conceded to be indistinguishable) the House had held by a majority of three to two that there was an obligation to account in these circumstances. It was argued on behalf of the company that the House should now depart from that earlier decision on the ground that it was wrong. This invitation was unanimously rejected. Lord Wilberforce said:

> 'My Lords, two points are clear. (1) Although counsel for the taxpayer developed his argument with freshness and vigour, it became clear that there was no contention advanced or which could be advanced by him which was not before this House in 1966 ... (2) There has been no change of circumstance such as some of their Lordships found to exist in *Miliangos v George Frank (Textiles) Ltd* such as would call for or justify a review of the 1966 decision ...
>
> There is therefore nothing left to the taxpayer but to contend, as it frankly does, that the 1966 decision is wrong. This contention means, when interpreted, that three or more of your Lordships ought to take the view which appealed then to the minority.
>
> My Lords, in my firm opinion, the 1966 Practice Statement was never intended to allow and should not be considered to allow such a course. Nothing could be more undesirable, in fact, than to permit litigants, after a decision has been given by this House with all appearance of finality, to return to this House in the hope that a differently constituted committee might be persuaded to take the view which its predecessors rejected. True that the earlier decision was by a majority: I say nothing as to its correctness or as to the validity of the reasoning by which it was supported. That there were two eminently possible views is shown by the support for each by at any rate two members of the House. But doubtful issues have to be resolved and the law knows no better way of resolving them than by the considered majority opinion of the ultimate tribunal. It requires much more than doubts as to the correctness of such opinion to justify departing from it.'[2]

'Change of circumstance' seems to be the most likely ground on which the House will depart from earlier decisions, although Lord Wilberforce's speech suggests that the fact that all relevant contentions were not put forward in the earlier case could be another. In *Miliangos v George Frank (Textiles) Ltd*,[3] the House of Lords, by a majority of four to one, overruled a previous unanimous decision of its own given fifteen years earlier. The previous decision had affirmed the rule that judgments in English courts could only be given in

2 [1977] 3 All ER 996 at 999.
3 [1976] AC 443.

sterling, even where the defendant had broken a contractual obligation to make payment in some foreign currency; and the damages would be assessed by taking the sterling equivalent of the foreign currency at the time when the contract was broken. Abrogation of this rule was held to be justified by reference to the two considerations mentioned in the 1966 statement. Because of the changed circumstance of rapidly inflating exchange rates, it would be unjust if a creditor who has contracted to be paid Swiss francs on a certain date were only to receive the sterling equivalent obtaining at that date when judgment was given or enforced much later. Secondly, abrogating the old rule would facilitate the development of the law, for it was possible to formulate a better rule – namely, that where the proper law of the contract was not English law and the money of account was some other currency than sterling, judgment should be entered for payment in that foreign currency or in its sterling equivalent at the time when the judgment was enforced. In the four other cases in which some or all of the members of the House of Lords have been prepared to overrule ('depart from') earlier decisions, the 'change in circumstance' has related, not so much to events which *could not* have been foreseen, as to effects of the rule which *were not* foreseen but which experience has brought to light.[4]

In two decisions of the House of Lords, the unqualified obligation of the Court of Appeal (as of all other United Kingdom courts) to follow decisions of the House has been reaffirmed. In *Cassell and Co Ltd v Broome*,[5] the House rejected the view that the Court of Appeal could depart from a decision of the House if, in the view of the Court of Appeal, the decision of the House was made *per incuriam* – that is, by an oversight of some established rule of law. In the *Miliangos* case, the House rejected the view that the Court of Appeal could depart from a decision of the House on the much wider ground that it was abrogated by virtue of the maxim *cessante ratione cessat ipsa lex* – that is, where the reason for a law has gone, so has the law itself. Nothing, it seems, can justify any inferior court in not applying the *ratio decidendi* of a decision of the House of Lords.

In *Miliangos*, Lord Simon reaffirmed the unqualified duty of judges to follow decisions of the Court of Appeal, and stated that the rule applied even where the Court of Appeal had itself erred in performing its duty to follow decisions of the House of Lords. If the House renders a decision on a date (t/1), and on a subsequent date (t/2) the Court of

---

4   *Conway v Rimmer* [1968] AC 910; *British Railways Board v Herrington* [1972] AC 879; *The Johanna Oldendorff* [1974] AC 479; *Vestey v Inland Revenue Commissioners (Nos. 1 and 2)* [1979] 3 All ER 976.
5   [1972] AC 1038.

Appeal wrongly fails to follow that decision, a judge at first instance rendering a decision on a date (t/3) must follow the decision of the Court of Appeal given at (t/2), because it is not for him to conclude that the Court of Appeal's view of the House of Lords' decision was wrong.

It was laid down in a decision of a full Court of Appeal (consisting of six rather than the usual three judges) in _Young v Bristol Aeroplane Co Ltd_,[6] that the court of Appeal is bound by its own decisions, with three exceptions: first, where there are two conflicting decisions of the Court of Appeal; second, where a decision of the Court of Appeal cannot stand with a decision of the House of Lords; third, where a decision of the Court of Appeal was made _per incuriam_. Since then, Lord Denning has expressed the view on several occasions that this practice should be changed and that the Court of Appeal should have the same freedom to depart from its decisions as does the House from its. In _Davis v Johnson_, a majority of three to two in a full Court of Appeal held that the exceptions should at least be expanded. This view was rejected when the case went to the House of Lords.[7] The three exceptions therefore remain, at present, the only exceptions. Their exact scope is not clear. In particular, does the second exception relate only to a decision of the House of Lords which was made after the impugned decision of the Court of Appeal? If it does, could a decision of the Court of Appeal nonetheless be departed from on the ground that it conflicted with an earlier decision of the House of Lords under the third (_per incuriam_) exception, at any rate if that decision of the House was not cited in the impugned case?

It is much more difficult to formulate those rules belonging to the English doctrine of precedent which do not depend, for their direct operation, upon the distinction between _ratio decidendi_ and _obiter dicta_. They all have to do with the notion of the common law, as an evolving set of rules, principles and classification, built up by statements of judges in individual cases. This concept is frequently contrasted with continental views of precedent, where evolving law is seen partly in lines of court decisions and partly in the writings of jurists. The contrast is not complete. In common law jurisdictions, the works of certain classic authors – such as Coke, Hale and Blackstone – are accepted as authoritative statements of what the common law was when they wrote; and English courts do to-day sometimes refer to modern textwriters as at least prima facie guides. Nevertheless, the primary method for arriving at the case law on any issue, not covered

6 [1944] KB 718.
7 [1979] AC 264.

by a binding *ratio decidendi*, is to read as many relevant statements of individual judges as one can find.

What rules about precedents does this common law method imply? They have never been authoritatively and definitively enunciated, and they may vary in scope and importance from one common law jurisdiction to another. They may be thought of as governing three questions. First, what is a judge bound to regard as relevant authority? Second, what weight must he give to different parts of relevant authority? Third, when, if at all, are precedents so firmly established that it would be unconstitutional for any court to change the law they lay down?

If counsel advancing contentions before an English court says: 'I wish to refer your Lordship to what was said by (judge X) in (an English case)', it would – would it not? – be inconsistent with his office if the judge were to say: 'I don't wish to know that, kindly shut the book'? He could do that if counsel were referring to a political pamphlet, or even a draft bill. There is then a negative obligation not to dismiss as irrelevant *in limine* anything contained in English law reports. How far does this negative obligation extend? Courts frequently listen, and give weight, to judicial statements made in other common law jurisdictions, and in jurisdictions which have accepted parts of the common law, such as South Africa and Scotland. Must they at least listen to all such citations?

What weight the court should give to judicial statements (not being binding *rationes decidendi*) is said to depend on many factors: the position in the judicial hierarchy of the judge whose statement it is; the individual reputation of the judge; the number of judges who concurred with what was said, if the court was an appellate court; whether the point was properly argued; how relevant it was to the issue upon which the case turned – that is, how far it fell short of being *ratio*; whether it was in line with other judicial statements in other cases. The circumstances vary from *dicta* unanimously approved, after elaborate argument, in the House of Lords (which because of some peculiarity of the litigation were not strictly necessary to the decision), to an off-the-cuff and totally *obiter* observation of a judge at first instance. It is difficult – and some would say undesirable – to be more precise than this.

When is case law so settled that not even the House of Lords can (or, at any rate, should) alter it? It is generally assumed that there are such areas, but notoriously difficult to formulate criteria for recognising them. Three factors may be taken into account: the longevity of a particular rule, principle or classification; its interconnection with other parts of the law, particularly statute law; and possible limitations on the ability of judges, as distinct from the legislature, to consider all the issues involved in changing the law. In the *Miliangos* case, Lord Wilberforce expressed the view that much more weight should be given to the second and third factors than to the first:

'I cannot accept the suggestion that because a rule is long established only legislation can change it – that may be so when the rule is so deeply entrenched that it has infected the whole legal system, or the choice of a new rule involves more far-reaching research than courts can carry out.'[8]

The *Miliangos* decision abrogated a common law rule said to be 350 years old. Nevertheless, longevity may be regarded as decisive against change where people have relied on the old rule in entering into transactions. In *Re Compton*[9] Lord Greene MR indicated that he would have held trusts for poor relations non-charitable if the issue had come up for the first time; but it was impossible now to overrule cases holding that they are charitable, because people would have relied upon them.

As to the second factor, whole slices of the common law now interconnected with statute law could not be swept away by the courts. For example, the courts could not now decide that all restrictions on contracts made by minors should be removed – having regard to the Infants Relief Act 1874. Is it so clear, however, that what were thought of at one time as fundamental elements of the common law could never be altered by judicial evolution, once they have produced classifications adopted in statutes? What about the supposedly exhaustive distinction of contractual terms into conditions and warranties, reflected in the Sale of Goods Act 1893, and subsequent legislation? On the other hand, legislation altering one aspect of the common law may be held to authorise reconsideration of other areas which otherwise were rock solid. In *Hyam v Director of Public Prosecutions*, Lord Diplock said that the abolition of constructive malice aforethought by the Homicide Act 1957 made it now 'constitutional' for the courts to reconsider the merits of the long-established distinction between actual and implied malice.[10]

The third of the factors mentioned above raises the issue of 'justiciability'. Are there questions of policy which judges are not equipped to settle? Some House of Lords' decisions suggest that there are. In *Morgans v Launchbury*,[11] the House refused to reconstruct common law rules relating to vicarious liability of the owners of motor

8 [1976] AC 443 at 469.
9 [1945] Ch 123.
10 [1975] AC 55 at 87.
11 [1973] AC 127.

vehicles in the light of information about insurance practices. It was said that the courts should not make law where matters of social policy were involved which are more suited for resolution by the collective wisdom of Parliament. In *Lim Poh Choo v Camden and Islington Area Health Authority*[12] the House rejected the view of the Court of Appeal that the principles upon which damages for personal injuries are assessed should be changed. They held that, whilst a radical reappraisal of this area of the law is needed, it calls for social, financial, economic and administrative decisions which can be taken only by the legislature and not by judges.

There is more disagreement among senior English judges about the justiciability of calls for reform of well-established features of the common law in the area of criminal law. In *Director of Public Prosecutions for Northern Ireland v Lynch*,[13] the majority of the House of Lords held that the defence of duress could be extended to the crime of murder in the second degree, notwithstanding a long common law tradition excluding murder from the scope of that defence. The minority contended that such a change in the common law involved social considerations fit only for Parliament. In the following year in *Abbott v R*,[14] the majority of the Privy Council (hearing an appeal from Trinidad and Tobago) refused to extend the defence of duress to murder in the first degree. They held that so entrenched a part of the common law could not be altered by judicial decision; and that, even if it had been altered in England by the decision of the House of Lords in *Lynch*'s case, it had not been altered so far as Trinidad and Tobago were concerned. The minority of the Privy Council maintained that, as the common law develops with changing circumstances, there is nothing improper in its 'alteration' by judicial decision; and that, furthermore, the common law is one and indivisible. The minority's view, that the common law cannot differ from one jurisdiction to another, contradicts the weight of authority;[15] but they were surely right in arguing that it 'develops'. The very imprecision of the factors governing the propriety of judicial innovations has attractions for admirers of the common law.

2 The status of precedent rules

Rules governing the authority of precedents are not contained in statutes and, in common law jurisdictions with written constitutions,

12 [1979] 2 All ER 910.
13 [1975] AC 653.
14 [1977] AC 755.
15 *Australian Consolidated Press Ltd v Uren* [1969] 1 AC 590, PC; *De Lasala v De Lasala* [1979] 2 All ER 1146, PC.

they are not generally set out in the constitution. In one sense, therefore, they are rules of the common law. On the other hand, they do not deal directly with the rights and obligations of citizens, but with the law-declaring or law-creating powers of judges. In that sense, they are constitutional rules. They have evolved, and are evolving, as judicial practices change. So they are also rules of judicial practice or judicial custom. Which label one gives to them may affect one's view as to whether, and by what means, they can be changed. In his dissenting speech in the *Miliangos* case, Lord Simon of Glaisdale stated that, it being 'clear law' that the Court of Appeal was bound by its own decisions, 'any change in this respect would require legislation'.[16] But he referred to the Lords' practice statement of 1966 as a 'constitutional convention having the force of law'.[17] In the United Kingdom, many of the most important provisions of our constitution are the result of 'convention' rather than 'law' – that is, they have not been enacted in statutes or promulgated as *ratio decidendi* of court decisions. This being so, it is easier to change the rules of precedent if they are called 'constitutional convention' than if they are called 'common law'. The judges can do it by getting together and issuing a practice statement. In countries with written constitutions, the reverse would be the case. Their superior courts can change case law rules, and generally feel freer to do so than does the House of Lords. But changes to the constitution require a special, non-judicial procedure.

Questions have been raised about the logical and constitutional propriety of the House of Lords' 1966 Practice Statement, as they used to be about the decision in *London Street Tramways v London County Council*,[18] which laid down the rule that the House must never depart from its earlier decisions. It used to be argued that the House of Lords in 1898 could not, logically, have introduced this rule. One could not say that the rule that the House was always bound by its decisions was established by the *London Tramways* case, without assuming that the rule already existed to confer unchallengeable authority on that case. The House of Lords could not have hoisted itself to unchallenge-ability by its own boot-straps. Further, what right had it to alter the constitutional limits of the power of its successors? Similar arguments have been advanced since 1966. Mr R. Stone suggested that the practice statement is self-contradictory, because so long as it is operative there is at least one decision of the House of Lords which cannot be departed from, namely, its decision not to be absolutely

16 [1976] AC 443 at 470–471.
17 Ibid at 472.
18 [1898] AC 375.

bound by its past decisions.[19] Professor J. Stone argued that the practice statement was a non-statement, because the House was acting neither in its legislative nor its judicial capacity; and it is a mystery how rules of precedent, being rules of law, could be amended by extra-curial *ipse dixit*.[20] Professor Cross met these objections by insisting that precedent rules, even when announced in cases, are not themselves subject to the distinction between *ratio decidendi* and *obiter dicta*, and by asserting of the 1966 Practice Statement: 'can there be any doubt that it owes its validity to the inherent power of any court to regulate its own practice?'[1]

If Cross is right and precedent rules are merely the practice rules of a particular court, it ought to follow that the Court of Appeal can lay down which rules it will follow. Yet, as we have seen, the House of Lords has assumed the right to dictate to the Court of Appeal, both on the question of whether the Court of Appeal is always bound by the House of Lords, and on the question whether the Court of Appeal is free to overrule its own decisions. It might be suggested that, whatever the merits of conceptual arguments about the status of precedent rules, the problem in the end is one of power. The House of Lords is the final appellate court and can therefore overturn any decision which presupposes precedent rules it does not approve; in consequence, it effectively has the power to specify precedent rules for all courts. However, as the litigation in the *Miliangos* case and in *Davis v Johnson* demonstrates, a decision may not be reversed merely because the House disagrees with the view taken below of the Court of Appeal's ability to depart from precedents. If (predictably) the House of Lords is going to agree on the desirability of overruling a certain decision, then the Court of Appeal can 'get away' with overruling it itself.

NB.

A more fundamental question concerns the problem of identifying *rationes decidendi*. Unless there is some procedure whereby the binding part of a decision can be isolated, what is the point of having rules about which courts bind which? Much of the difficulty stems from the interrelation of the words in the judge's opinion and the facts of the case as criteria for identifying the *ratio*. It is frequently asserted that the judge's words are not the rule of the case. A judgment is not to be treated like a statute. It is permissible for a later judge – one who is notionally 'bound' by the decision of the earlier judge – to reformulate the rule for which the earlier case is authority in his (the later judge's) words. He will be justified in doing that if the formulation appearing

V·NB.

---

19 (1968) 26 CLJ 35.
20 (1969) 69 Colum L Rev 1163.
 1 Hacker and Raz *Law, Morality and Society* p. 157.

in the earlier judgment was not based on the facts of the case. This is an inherent limitation on any doctrine of *stare decisis*. No precedential system could contemplate that a judge, however elevated in the court hierarchy, could say: 'I conclude this issue of labour law as follows ... and while I'm at it, I lay down the following general rule for the law of wills ...'. On the other hand, there would be no point in having precedent rules which required courts to follow earlier cases only when the facts are identical to those of the present case. The facts are never literally 'the same'. Apart from this tension between judicial words and reported facts, many other difficulties have been noted. How does one identify the *ratio decidendi* of an appellate court when judges who concur in the result differ as to their reasons? How does one account for the practice of seeking the *ratio decidendi* of a particular case, in the light of prior and subsequent cases? Should one elucidate what the judge was saying by reference to other evidence one has about that particular judge's views? Does it matter if the judge's statement was not strictly necessary to his decision, in the sense that there are grounds for thinking the same order would have been made without it?

Problems such as these were among the considerations which influenced the American realists in their sceptical approach towards legal rules in general (see chapter 8, above). However, against all these difficulties must be set the fact that judges frequently announce themselves to be bound by previous decisions, sometimes with regret. Are these all instances of self-delusion?

The literature on this topic is enormous. I mention the views of two writers which illustrate what may be called a 'stick to the facts' approach, on the one hand, and a 'stick to the reasons' approach on the other. Whether their conclusions turn out to be all that different remains to be seen.

Dr. A. L. Goodhart suggests that the *ratio decidendi* of a case is to be found by adding the facts which the judge treated as material to the conclusion he drew – where material facts A, B and C obtain, a defendant is liable. This provides a rule which a later judge can apply and, given a lower status in the judicial hierarchy, is bound to apply in any case in which the same material facts, and no other material facts, occur. Goodhart says that the facts of person, time, place, kind and amount are, on their face, 'immaterial'. This suggests that his 'material facts' are different in kind from brute facts, being generalisations from them – like the 'fact' that the defendant could have foreseen damage to the plaintiff. Being this sort of generalisation, they can recur. Further, Goodhart states that potentially material facts are not to be treated as such by the later judge if the earlier judge regarded them as immaterial. In finding the *ratio decidendi*, he is to have regard only to those facts which the earlier judge expressly or impliedly treated as material. In the event of a decision comprising several judgments the *ratio decidendi* is given by adding all the facts treated as material in all the majority judgments to the conclusion.

Sir Rupert Cross offers the following definition:

> 'The *ratio decidendi* of a case is any rule of law expressly or impliedly treated by the judge as a necessary step in reaching his conclusion, having regard to the line of reasoning adopted by him, or a necessary part of his direction to the jury.'[2]

Cross's definition is not apt to meet those cases where no reasons are given or can be implied (which are few), nor those appellate cases where there is no majority agreement on reasons (which are all too frequent). On the other hand, Goodhart's test may be thought inappropriate in those appellate cases where all concur in the result, a majority concur in reasons, but a minority give different reasons; why should we then, as his test requires, add up all the facts which majority and minority treated as material in order to get our rule? More importantly, Goodhart's test may be difficult to apply even to a single judgment when the 'facts' treated by the judge as material can be characterised in different ways – for example, at different levels of generality. If we say the facts are to be characterised just as the judge described them, are we not back to citing his reasons as *ratio*? How do we know that the fact treated as material in *Donoghue v Stevenson*[3] was not a decomposed snail in a ginger beer bottle, rather than a potentially harmful product, unless we look at the underlying reasoning of the decision?

The general objection to both these approaches to the identification of *rationes decidendi* is that they do not adequately deal with the time-honoured common law technique of 'distinguishing'. A judge may say of an earlier decision, binding within the hierarchy, that what was said there does not bind him since the case is distinguishable on its facts. By this he may mean either that the true *ratio* of the earlier case is narrower than the earlier judge's statement; or, where the statement imposed some limiting condition which the present judge wishes to discard, that the true *ratio* is wider than the earlier statement. Since all agree that the words of the earlier judge are not to be treated like the words of a legislature, this distinguishing process appears to be unstoppable by any definition of *ratio decidendi*. The later judge can always say that, notwithstanding his language, the earlier

2 *Precedent in English Law* p. 76.
3 [1932] AC 562.

judge did not really intend certain facts to be treated as material; or that the reasons which the judge really treated as a necessary step in reaching his conclusion are not properly expressed in the language he chose to employ.

If judges can always distinguish, should we regard the so-called 'rules of precedent' as not normative at all, but mere descriptions of practices in which judges purport to follow decisions? Or should we say that the obligations which the rules impose are real, but not quite what they appear to be on their surface? Perhaps what a judge has to do in regard to a binding decision is to find some rule for which the case is authority and, having found it, see whether it applies to his case – an obligation, that is, to follow or distinguish. If that is right, then there is only a difference of degree between what judges, under a system of strict *stare decisis*, are required to do in relation to decisions above them in the hierarchy, and what the doctrine of precedent requires common law judges to do in relation to all court decisions. In both cases, the judge must listen to what the earlier judge said; in both, he must give some weight, which may include working out why the earlier judge said what he did. But under strict *stare decisis*, he must go further and formulate some rule for which the earlier case is authority. That rule may be based on the case in isolation, or it may take into account treatment of the case in subsequent decisions. It is of no consequence whether we use the expression *ratio decidendi* to stand for the rule attributed to a case read on its own, or the rule for which, given subsequent legal development, the case is now authority.

If, however, the obligation is merely to formulate some rule (follow or distinguish), how does that account for judges being bound *malgré soi*? Perhaps there are limits to the plausibly acceptable rules for which a case can be said to stand; and when a judge follows reluctantly, what he means is that, although a certain rule-formulation is (all things considered) undesirable, he cannot think of any better rule for which the binding case could be said to stand.

3 Should our precedent rules be changed?

As with statutory interpretation, arguments about changing precedent rules tend to mix technical with constitutional considerations: certainty versus flexibility; judicial freedom to alter the law versus judicial restraint. Would it lead to an improvement in judicial technique if appellate courts were to deliver a single judgment so that the *ratio decidendi* could be more easily identified, or would that sacrifice too much the flexibility which a plurality of judgments gives to later courts? Would the law be more satisfactorily adaptable if the House of

Lords could overrule its own decisions merely on the ground that they were 'wrong', or would that undermine the certainty of the law? Would such a change assist the legislature by removing the burden of abrogating undesirable precedents, or would it be a usurpation of the power which, in a democracy, rightly belongs only to the legislature? If the Court of Appeal had greater freedom in regard to its own past decisions and decisions of the House of Lords, would that avoid the need for costly appeals to the House, or would it lead to more litigation, less certainty and a further increase in anti-democratic judicial power?

Apart from the unelected status of judges (which for some is an important reason for favouring strict precedent rules), there is another general objection to any reform which would make it easier for judges to alter the law. It concerns retroactivity. If when the judges overrule precedents they make new law – a controversial characterisation of what they do, as we shall see in the next chapter – then they make it with retroactive effect so far as the parties to the litigation are concerned. The decision may also have retroactive implications for all those who have entered into, but not yet completed, transactions on the faith of the overruled precedent. One suggested solution is for the courts (or at any rate the House of Lords) to assume a power of prospective overruling. The court would apply the old precedent in the instant case, but would announce that, for the future, a new rule is going to be followed. If precedent rules are mere 'practice rules', perhaps the law lords could issue a new practice statement introducing the device. If they are conceived of as 'common law' rules, then persuasive authority for adopting prospective overruling can be provided from another common law jurisdiction. In the United States, the technique has been employed in recent years, especially where a court has wanted to introduce a new rule nullifying exercises of administrative power without upsetting arrangements previously made by virtue of such power, or a new rule nullifying procedures in criminal prosecutions where it has not wished all past convictions obtained by such procedures to be upset.

The argument for introducing prospective overruling is that the courts would then be more free to make new law without deleterious effects on those who have relied on the old law. There are many arguments against. If the new rule was totally prospective, litigants would have no incentive to argue for it since it would not affect the outcome of their case. If the new rule were made partially prospective – for example, if it were applied to the present case but not to past transactions which were not the subject of the current litigation – where precisely is the cut-off point to be? Should the new rule apply to other litigation which has been commenced but not yet reached resolution? A more fundamental objection is one based on formal justice. If the court decides that such and such a rule is the correct rule, how can it be just to apply it to rights and duties of parties in the future but not to the present parties? Whether judges 'declare' or 'create' the law, like cases should be treated alike.

There are two aspects of the doctrine of precedent which can be cited in favour, not so much of a change in our precedent rules, but of overall codification of the common law. First, one of the unarticulated assumptions of common law jurisidictions is, as we have seen, that all precedents must be considered. The burden might be diminished if we made a fresh start with a code. Second, since *rationes decidendi* cannot be unambiguously identified, the law would be made more determinate if embodied in a code. These were among the considerations which led Bentham to condemn the common law and advocate codification, and they have been voiced again by enthusiastic supporters of the injunction laid upon the Law Commissions by section 3 of the Law Commissions Act 1965, to 'take and keep under review all the law with a view to its systematic development and reform, including in particular the codification of such law'. The opposite view is that, whilst particular reforms and even codifications of particular areas may be desirable, the common law as a whole is best left to evolutionary development, the doctrine of precedent providing the right balance between certainty and flexibility.

General questions about certainty, flexibility, judicial activism or restraint, and specific questions about the merits of prospective overruling and codification, require us to examine assumptions about the nature of legal reasoning in general, about the proper interaction between statutory interpretation and the evolution of case law, and whether or not there is an ideal model of what settling legal issues ought to be like. To these questions we turn in the next two chapters.

Bibliography

Cross R.	*Precedent in English Law* (3rd edn, 1977) 'The House of Lords and the Rules of Precedent' in Hacker and Raz (eds) *Law, Morality, and Society* (1977) 'The Ratio Decidendi and a Plurality of Speeches in the House of Lords' (1977) 93 LQR 378
Denning Lord	*The Discipline of Law* (1979) Pt 7
Dias R. W. M.	*Jurisprudence* (4th edn, 1976) ch 6
Douglas W. O.	'Stare Decisis' (1949) 49 Colum L Rev 735
Fitzgerald P. J.	*Salmond on Jurisprudence* (12th edn, 1966) ch 5
Freeman M. D. A.	'Standards of Adjudication, Judicial Law-making and Prospective Overruling' (1973)

26 CLP 166

Fuller L. L.   *Anatomy of the Law* (1971) pp. 120–156

Goldstein L.   'Four Alleged Paradoxes in Legal Reasoning'
                     (1979) 38 CLJ 373

Goodhart A. L.   'Determining the Ratio Decidendi of a Case'
                     in *Essays in Jurisprudence and the Common Law*
                     (1931)

Gottlieb G.   *The Logic of Choice* (1968) ch 6

Hahalo H. R.   'Here Lies the Common Law: Rest in Peace'
                     (1967) 30 MLR 241, 607
                     'Codifying the Common Law: Protracted
                     Gestation' (1975) 38 MLR 23

Hicks J. C.   'The Liar Paradox in Legal Reasoning' (1971)
                     29 CLJ 275

MacCormick D. N.   'Can Stare Decisis be Abolished?' (1966) Jur
                     Rev 196
                     Legal Reasoning and Legal Theory (1978)
                     pp. 213–228

Marshall G.   'Justiciability' in Guest (ed) *Oxford Essays in
                     Jurisprudence* (1961)

Nicol A. G. L.   'Prospective Overruling: a New Device for
                     English Courts' (1976) 39 MLR 542

Radin M.   'Case Law and Stare Decisis: Concerning
                     Prajudizienrecht in Amerika' (1933) 33
                     Colum L Rev 199

Raz J.   *The Authority of Law* (1979) ch 10

Rickett C. E. F.   'Precedent in the Court of Appeal' (1980) 43
                     MLR 136

Sartorius R. E.   'The Doctrine of Precedent and the Problem
                     of Relevance' (1967) 53 ARSP 343

Simpson A. W. B.   'The Ratio Decidendi of a Case and the
                     Doctrine of Binding Precedent' in Guest (ed)
                     Oxford Essays in Jurisprudence (1961)
                     'The Common Law and Legal Theory' in
                     Simpson (ed) *Oxford Essays in Jurisprudence*
                     (2nd series, 1973)

Stone J.   '1966 And All That: Loosing the Chains of
                     Precedent' (1969) 69 Colum L Rev 1162
                     'On the Liberation of Appellate Judges – How
                     Not to Do it' (1972) 35 MLR 449

Stone R. L.   'The Precedence of Precedents' (1968) 26 CLJ
                     35

Topping M. R. and   'Ibi Renanscit Ius Commune' (1970) 33 MLR
Vandenlinden J. P.   170

Twining W. and
Myers D.   *How to do Things with Rules* (1976) ch 8

14 Dworkin's rights thesis

We have seen that, according to positivist accounts of the nature of law, 'what the law is' is always potentially different from 'what the law ought to be'. The opposite contention of natural lawyers appeared easily dismissed by reference to professional practice. When lawyers give information about the law, or apply the law, they often complain about its contents; they show no readiness to trace its validity back to a moral basis. If asked to justify an assertion about the law, they cite authority, not reason; precedents and statutes, not treatises about justice or the good life.

On the other hand, listen to a professor of law being interviewed on radio or television about the law on some controversial aspect of industrial relations or racial discrimination. You may find it difficult to draw a line dividing those sentences in which he says what the law is, from those in which he says what it ought to be: 'The Act says ... and it's clear that Parliament must have intended ... after all, the reactions of the TUC make it plain how absurd it would be if any other view were taken ... so my answer to your question is, yes, the law does require that ....'

Furthermore, as we saw in the last chapter, precedents are regarded as authority for rules, yet no one has been able to devise a logically watertight procedure for deriving any rule from any case. Judges justify holding that a rule formulated in one way is the correct proposition for which an earlier case stands as authority, by reasons which look rather like arguments about what the law ought to be.'I cannot accept counsel's contention. It seems to me incredible to suppose that Doodle J had the sort of situation I am confronted with in mind when he said ... and that accordingly his language must be read in a narrower sense. To my mind, the law laid down in *Alph v Bloggs* is as follows: ...'

Controversial cases, then, and perhaps most cases turning on the interpretation of judge-made law, challenge the positivist claim about 'is' and 'ought' in law. On the other hand, it seems implausible to say that the law is always what it ought to be, that all law is good law; for are there not countless instances where what the law requires is only too clear to its vocal critics? Sometimes, what the law is has a clear

172

answer by reference to authority, and then many may claim that it is bad and ought to be changed. But sometimes the law is uncertain, and disputants will argue for what it is on the basis of what it ought to be.

One solution to the problem is the cynical solution of the realists, discussed in chapter 8, above. But as we saw, their kind of cynicism is ultimately stultifying of legal argument and legal reform. If the law is simply anything the judge cares to say it is, how is an advocate supposed to argue, and a judge justify, any decision? And what is the point of Parliament laying down new rules about anything, if they do not have a clear range of application?

So there is clear law and argued law, and neither is a sham. The clear law can be good or bad, but the argued law appears to be law only if its goodness is accepted. How are we to understand the relation between the two? Does the one deserve more political allegiance than the other? Do judges apply the one and choose the other? If judges do choose the law in controversial cases, is that something democrats can accept? If they do not choose the law in such cases, how do they find it?

Professor R. M. Dworkin has tried to provide an answer to questions like these by means of his rights thesis. The thesis has emerged from a series of essays, the most important of which are collected in his book *Taking Rights Seriously*. His examination of the logic of adjudication in 'hard cases' – that is, cases about which informed people can reasonably disagree – leads him to three important conclusions about the nature of law. First, law is not solely comprised of rules. Secondly, no line can be drawn between law and morality. Thirdly, judges do not legislate.

1 Rules are not enough

Dworkin does not challenge the conventional positivist assumptions about the decision of legal questions in clear cases by the application of valid rules. Rules are part of the law. But in hard cases, he argues, judges are guided to their decisions by standards which are not rules. Such standards include policies and principles. A policy is that kind of standard that sets out a community goal, generally an improvement in some economic, political or social feature of the community's life; for example, the policy that 'automobile accidents are to be decreased'. A principle is a standard to be observed because it is a requirement of justice or fairness or some other dimension of morality; for example, 'no man may profit by his own wrong'.[1]

1 *Taking Rights Seriously* p. 22.

Of course, questions about accidents or wrongful gains can be dealt with by rules. Non-rule standards do not differ from rules because of their content. The difference is a 'logical distinction'; that is, they ✳ differ by virtue of the part they play in controlling decisions. When a judge finds that a rule is applicable to a case, he concludes either that it is binding on him – in which event it determines the issue – or that it is not binding at all. Assuming that the rule really is applicable – that is, that the facts it specifies are present and that no exception is in point – validity is an all-or-nothing question. The rule is either part of the law or it is not.

Non-rule standards, however, have a dimension different from validity, namely, that of 'weight'. A judge may find that a principle is applicable without that finding being determinative of the issue. The principle or policy provides a reason for deciding in a certain way, but it may be outweighed by other considerations. If it is outweighed, that does not mean that it is not part of the law. Weight, unlike validity, is a relative concept.

For example, the legal maxim that 'no man may profit by his own wrong' does not operate as a rule. Dworkin cites the case of a murderer who was, on the face of the applicable inheritance law, entitled to the estate of his victim. Here the maxim was applied as a reason for finding an exception to the inheritance rule, so that the case was settled by a holding that the rule did not apply in favour of the murderer.[2] But in the context of the law of limitation, Dworkin argues, this maxim would be outweighed by other considerations. If one man is in adverse possession of another's land for the length of time specified in a limitation statute, the original owner would lose his right to claim back the land. The adverse possessor could be said to have profited from his own wrong (being a trespasser), but that would be outweighed by the important policy of not allowing the uncertainty that would ensue if long-established possession were always vulnerable to stale claims.

Dworkin attacks the 'model of rules' for its failure to take account of these non-rule standards. Any conception of law which regards it as merely a system of rules must be incomplete. It suggests that in hard cases a judge's investigation consists exclusively of a search for applicable rules. In fact, it consists of a weighing of many standards other than rules, either because there is no applicable rule, or because what makes the case a hard one is precisely the question whether what looks like an applicable rule is not subject to some relevant exception.

2 *Riggs v Palmer* 115 NY 506 (1889), 22 NE 188.

Dworkin's distinction between rules and other standards has been used in substantive academic analysis of case law – for example in the law of trusts and English criminal law.[3] The distinction has also been widely attacked. The essence of the criticism has been that his point of departure from the model of rules is an inadequate conception of 'rule'. Dworkin's analysis suggests that the significance of rules in legal arguments is limited to the questions of applicability and validity. If a rule applies and is valid, it settles the case. If it applies but is not valid, it has no significance. If it is debatable whether it applies or not, we drop the rule and look for principles. The latter, weighed together, will tell us whether the rule ought to apply, and on that basis we will decide whether or not it does apply.

Dworkin's critics reject this analysis of the functioning of rules. They argue that, when it is uncertain whether a rule applies to a case, we do not drop the rule and move over to other standards. Instead, we advert to the purpose or policy embedded in the rule. Reference to the purpose of inheritance rules will show that they do not apply in favour of murderers. There is no need to invoke standards other than rules, since what Dworkin calls principles and policies are either restatements (in summary form) of the purposes embodied in a number of rules, or are themselves large-scale, vaguely worded rules. Hard cases – those in which reasonable lawyers differ as to the outcome – are likely to be precisely those where it is not clear that some rule or rules apply. We may then find that the policy of one allegedly applicable rule conflicts with the purpose of another. But a judge who gives predominance to one of the two does not thereby impugn the validity (the status as 'legal') of the other. If we set out all the rules that are relevant to a dispute, and spell out all their policy implications, any further reference to non-rule standards will be redundant.

How are we to adjudicate between Dworkin and his critics on this issue? Neither side would appeal to actual use of the words 'rule' or 'principle' by judges and other lawyers. Dworkin would say that 'rules' of statutory interpretation are 'principles' in his sense, since they are weighed against one another rather than adjudged valid or invalid. On the other hand, the critics would claim that the 'principle' of 'respondeat superior' is a rule – a complex rule with many exceptions and policy implications – governing the liability of employers in contract and tort.

One assessment criterion relates to convenience of description. Which is the more convenient way to set out the law on a topic, such as the formalities requisite for *inter vivos* and *post mortem* dispositions of

3   J. H. Grey 'In Re Vandervell: the Jurisprudential Aspects' (1975) 21 McGill LJ 160; A. Dashwood 'Logic and the Lords in *Majewski*' [1977] Crim LR 532.

property? Should we state various statutory and judge-made rules, and then add as a separate piece of legal information: 'Many of the more specific rules have resulted from the application of an equitable maxim that "a statute shall not be used as an engine of fraud"; and this principle may always be used in the future to justify further exceptions'? Or would it be better to set out all the rules, mentioning that the application of many of them is limited by the fact that their purpose is the prevention of fraud, or else to say that 'you cannot use a statute as an engine of fraud' is just another, large-scale rule about formalities?

I think the balance of descriptive convenience, in instances such as this, is on Dworkin's side. But it does appear to be a matter of style only. If a judge finds that a rogue who has conned an old lady into transferring a house to him holds it on trust for her, notwithstanding that statute requires trusts relating to land to be evidenced in writing,[4] it will make no difference to our approval or disapproval of the decision whether we say that the judge gave effect to the purpose of the rule or that he interpreted the rule by reference to a principle.

A more important argument for Dworkin's distinction between rules and non-rule standards concerns system-membership, the ways in which the two sorts of standards are introduced into or taken out of the law. A statutory rule becomes law when it is enacted, and ceases to be law when it is expressly repealed or is superseded by some derogating rule. The origin of judge-made rules is more problematic because of their inherent fluidity – and sometimes because of the inadequacy of older case reports; but quite often their authority can be traced to a particular decision or line of decisions. The same is true of their demise. But there are standards whose title to be 'parts of the law' rests, not on authoritative creation and the absence of authoritative repeal, but on a developing and changing tradition. The common employment rule – that an employer is not liable for negligent damage inflicted on his employee by a fellow employee – was introduced into the law by the decision in *Priestley v Fowler*[5] and was repealed by the Law Reform (Personal Injuries) Act 1948. The policy of 'freedom of contract' was an important part of English law a hundred years ago, but today is withering on the vine. That is to say, in the nineteenth century a doubtful case might well be tilted by some such argument as: 'The courts do not mend men's bargains'; but today such an argument would carry much less weight. It would be difficult to find a case or series of cases in which the policy was

4 *Hodgson v Marks* [1971] Ch 892.
5 (1837) 3 M & W 1.

introduced; and it would be very odd if Parliament were to enact: 'There shall be no more freedom of contract.'

Thus, the distinction between rules and other standards can be justified on the ground that the former are parts of the law by virtue of specific authorities, whereas, the latter are so by virtue of a judicial tradition. Dworkin, however, advances a much more radical version of the above argument. Upon it he founds the second of his novel claims about the nature of law.

2 No line between law and morals

Dworkin identifies his attack on 'the model of rules' with an attack on 'positivism'. This is not simply because most positivists have represented law as exclusively comprised of rules. It is because, in Dworkin's view, once one accepts that law consists of other standards as well as rules, one cannot maintain a distinction between what the law is and what, morally speaking, the law ought to be. For the non-rule standards which judges employ in order to determine 'what the law is' in hard cases include principles embedded in the community's morality. The judge cannot discover them by reference to any amoral test. No master rule, such as Hart's rule of recognition, is available to distinguish legal from non-legal principles. A judge must decide whether a principle is part of the community's morality; and once he has decided that it is, he has already decided that it is law.

The foregoing might suggest that Dworkin is advocating a form of legal-moral conservatism − that the judge should consult what he believes to be the majority moral opinion on a contested issue and make his decision accordingly. Nothing could be further from Dworkin's aim. For the 'community's morality' is not a function of majority opinion. It is what judges ought to discover by applying a special technique of reasoning in terms of rights. Whenever Dworkin applies his 'rights thesis' to particular issues of American law, he is able to show that the technique results in 'liberal' perceptions of what the community's true morality is − that women have a right to abortion, that white students have no right to admission on equal terms with blacks to colleges which practice reverse discrimination, that political demonstrators have a right to break laws which is strong enough to make it wrong to punish them, and so on.

The community's true morality is not to be discovered by taking opinion polls about particular moral issues. It is to be discovered by asking what answer to a particular issue would fit consistently with abstract rights to which the community has already committed itself in its constitution and institutional practices – such as rights to liberty, dignity, equality and respect.

The rights thesis describes the appropriate technique for settling hard cases. It also, Dworkin argues, describes the underlying technique which judges actually do employ, although they may often get particular answers wrong. The thesis is both a normative and a descriptive theory of adjudication.

The crux of the thesis is his distinction between arguments of principle and arguments of policy.

> 'Arguments of policy justify a political decision by showing that the decision advances or protects some collective goal of the community as a whole. The argument in favor of a subsidy for aircraft manufacturers, that the subsidy will protect national defense, is an argument of policy. Arguments of principle justify a political decision by showing that the decision respects or secures some individual or group right. The argument in favor of anti-discrimination statutes, that a minority has a right to equal respect and concern, is an argument of principle.'[6]

Principles are propositions that describe rights. Policies are propositions that describe goals. A right differs from a community goal in several important respects. First, its specification calls for an opportunity or resource or liberty to be accorded to particular individuals. For example, Dworkin cites the case of *Spartan Steel and Alloys Ltd v Martin and Co*,[7] in which the court had to decide whether factory owners were entitled to compensation for the economic loss occasioned to them when the defendants' employees damaged an electricity cable causing the factory to be temporarily closed down.

> 'It might have proceeded to its decision by asking either whether a firm in the position of the plaintiff had a right to recovery, which is a matter of principle, or whether it would be economically wise to distribute liability for accidents in the way the plaintiff suggested, which is a matter of policy.'[8]

A second characteristic peculiar to a 'right' is that it must have a certain 'threshold weight' against collective goals in general. Dworkin contends that one would not be speaking consistently if one agreed that people have a right to free speech, but also took the view that any balance of community welfare would justify abrogating free speech.

6 *Taking Rights Seriously* p. 82.
7 [1973] 1 QB 27.
8 *Taking Rights Seriously* p. 84.

Thirdly, the doctrine of political responsibility requires, Dworkin argues, that rights be distributed consistently; whereas it does not prevent a community goal from being attained by unequal distribution of benefits and burdens. For example, the goal of boosting declining industries may be forwarded by subsidising some manufacturers and not others; whereas if they had a right to subsidy, political responsibility would require each to be accorded the same. In matters of principle, there is a requirement of 'articulate consistency', which does not have the same force in matters of policy.

On the basis of his distinction between arguments of principle and arguments of policy, Dworkin takes two giant strides in the realm of legal theory. First, judicial decisions in civil cases characteristically are and should be generated by principle not policy. Secondly, the determination of what legal rights people have must be made in the light of an overall political theory which recognises moral-political background rights as well as those concrete rights already demarcated by enactments.

It is the contention of the rights thesis that judicial reasoning takes place against a background of assumptions about rights. Whatever the legal question, the judge must finally decide whether the plaintiff has a concrete right to win, and that in turn depends on judgments about the moral and political background rights of the parties. If the judge is interpreting a statute, he will have to consider policy to the extent that he finds a policy in the legislation; but his interpretation will be guided by the assumption that, in pursuit of its policy, the legislature was conferring or taking away rights. In the context of the criminal law, the judge will ask himself whether the accused has or has not a right to be acquitted. He will not ask himself whether the state has a right to a conviction. (Why there should be this asymmetry of rights in the context of the criminal law is something Dworkin never explains.) In civil cases in which case law alone is applied, the judge will consider nothing but principles. He will decide which of the parties has the stronger right. In these cases, he will take no account of community goals.

Critics of Dworkin have urged that judicial decisions in hard cases are often dictated by policy considerations. In areas such as the law of nuisance, for example, courts take account of the benefit to the community of certain kinds of activities before ruling that they must not take place; and in the context of disclosure of documents in civil litigation, or of reasons for certain kinds of administrative decisions, courts listen to arguments of public policy against disclosure, and are sometimes swayed by them.

Had the primary thrust of the rights thesis been prescriptive – a call for a change in existing judicial practices – Dworkin might have urged

that these are instances where the courts do that which a proper
regard for rights should lead them not to do: they sacrifice the rights of
the individual in the interest of the community. But in fact Dworkin
insists that his thesis is not revolutionary in that way. In all the
instances mentioned by critics, he claims that there are no counter-
examples to the rights thesis. What the courts are really doing is
weighing the rights of some claimants against the rights of others. If
they go wrong, it is not because they take into account arguments of
policy rather than principles; it is because, in weighing the rights
described by various principles, they misunderstand or misbalance
particular rights.

If a judge's decision appears, on its face, to be based on
considerations of public policy, it ought really to be understood,
Dworkin argues, as an appeal to the rights of individual members of
the public. In support of this contention, he advances the conception
of the 'substitutability' of arguments of principle and arguments of
policy. If a judge refers to economic public policy or community
welfare, one can interpret what he says as statements about the
political rights of each and every individual member of the
community.

> 'If a judge appeals to public safety or the scarcity of some vital
> resource, for example, as a ground for limiting some abstract right,
> then his appeal might be understood as an appeal to the competing
> rights of those whose security will be sacrificed, or whose just share
> of that resource will be threatened if the abstract right is made
> concrete.'[9]

The argument between Dworkin and his critics, as to whether
judges decide hard cases by referring to individual rights rather than
community goals, cannot, then, be settled by looking at decided cases.
Any reference, by way of justification of the decision, to the
consequences of a holding can be 'understood' as a reason for finding
that the parties already have certain entitlements. Any mention of the
public can be understood as a reference to individual members of the
public. Dworkin does not ask judges to change the technique they
already employ. At most – so far as he has any message for the
judiciary – it is that they should better understand what they are
already doing; they might then make less mistakes. For the
argumentative force of a principle is, he says, less than that of the
equivalent argument of policy.

It seems, therefore, that if, when judges weigh an individual's right
against the community's good, they were to realise that they were

9 *Taking Rights Seriously* p. 100.

actually weighing the individual's right against the rights of others, the individual would have a better chance of winning. Thus, rights will be safer if it is appreciated that, in civil cases, they are measured against other rights and not community good.

For example, in a recent English case,[10] a baby suffered serious brain damage as the result of an 'error of judgment' on the part of the doctor who delivered it. The judge at first instance found that the doctor had been negligent and awarded substantial damages. The Court of Appeal, by a majority, reversed the judgment. In holding that medical negligence should be narrowly restricted, they appealed to certain issues of public policy. They adverted to the American experience of medical malpractice suits which had resulted in wasteful 'defensive medicine'. In the light of Dworkin's analysis one might argue as follows. If the court had realised that it was weighing the right of the plaintiff against the rights of particular individuals who would be adversely affected by defensive medicine, it might have come to a different conclusion.

If this were the only argument for understanding references to policies as references to rights, it seems to me that it would have little force. If 'public good' has a certain weight, I cannot understand how 'good to each and every member of the public' can have less. The contention that it does may conceal assumptions about the psychological force of certain kinds of expressions – that expressions like 'public interest' or 'welfare of the community' carry more psychological punch than they substantively deserve. No such assumptions are made explicit by Dworkin.

However this may be, the main thrust of Dworkin's substitution programme has nothing to do with changing judicial practices. His ground for insisting that we ought to understand reasoning in hard cases as reasoning about rights rather than reasoning about policy is one of political philosophy. If we do so understand it, it is then much easier to justify the settlement of controversies by non-elected judges.

One who supports a democratic theory, which calls for compromises between individual and group demands to be settled by elected representatives, has to face the problem that many important controversies are settled by adjudication. This problem is especially acute in the United States, where political issues of the greatest importance are determined by the Supreme Court. But in the United Kingdom also, highly contentious political questions are, at least temporarily, settled by the superior courts. Many of those opposed to the introduction of a bill of rights into this country express doubts about the justiciability of political questions. How can it be right that

10 *Whitehouse v Jordan* [1980] 1 All ER 650. Leave has been granted to appeal to the House of Lords (*Times* 22 February 1980).

a handful of non-elected men should impose their political judgments on the rest of us?

Dworkin's answer is that they don't. It may look as though they are deciding the sort of policy issues which political parties are at odds about, but really they are making determinations about existing individual rights.

One's assessment of Dworkin's contention (that arguments of principle underlie adjudication) must therefore be based, not on the evidence of decided cases, but on a judgment of political philosophy. Does looking at decisions in this light better justify the ways of the law to men than if one takes the alternative view that, in some cases, *faute de mieux*, judges do what normally we like political representatives to do? Does it carry conviction, or is it an elegant smokescreen?

Dworkin says that the supposed originality of judges in hard cases appears less objectionable if we regard them as deciding on principle, for two reasons. First, if they are considering the rights of individuals rather than the welfare of the community, then it does not matter so much that they lack the means of assessing the total impact on the community of decisions which politicians are supposed to have – no letters from pressure groups, constituency meetings, and so on. Secondly, if a judicial decision were thought of as based on public policy, then it would create a new duty imposed retrospectively, and therefore unfairly, on one of the parties to the litigation; whereas, if his decision is generated by principle, a judge discovers that the plaintiff already has a right against the defendant so that what is enforced is an existing corresponding duty of the defendant.

The first argument appears to have little force in the context of the substitutability programme. For if we are to understand references to public policy as references to all the rights of the individual members of the public, what difference does this make to the desirability of maximum information? Surely, mailbags and public meetings are just as useful for assessing public rights as for assessing public good? Of course, if the rights thesis were a critique and not a description of judicial practices, the argument might be thought to have some bite. It would demand of judges that they minimise, as far as possible, those excursions into public policy which they now make, since they are not equipped to determine such matters. But Dworkinian substitution means that in such cases judges are already deciding on principle.

As to the second argument, how can a decision in a hard case not create duties retrospectively? Because, says Dworkin, it is part of the responsibility incident to the office of a judge to make only such decisions as he can justify within a political theory that also justifies all the rest of the law. No enactment may cover the point in hand, but a consistent arrangement of all the moral and political assumptions which underlie other parts of the law will give the answer.

Now all lawyers are familiar with the judicial technique of reasoning by analogy, of getting more mileage out of a precedent than the prescriptive force of its *ratio decidendi*. This practice, Dworkin contends, is evidence of a general assumption about fairness. If the plaintiff had a right to win in that earlier, similar case, is there any reason in justice for denying a right in the present case? Like cases should be treated alike. Dworkin fills out this piecemeal sort of justification into a holistic theory of adjudication. He stresses two features which, he says, ideally underlie it. First, fairness requires the judge to look for analogies, not just to some case or cases which seem obviously in point, but to the whole of the law. Secondly, his office as judge requires him to develop an all-embracing philosophy of law and society.

Dworkin imagines a judge named Hercules, who is endowed with superhuman skill, learning and patience. Hercules has, in the highest measure, both the traditional legal skills associated with interpretation of statutes and precedents, and also the wisdom of the ages to be derived from political philosophy. He is Dworkin's ideal judge.

'The law may not be a seamless web; but the plaintiff is entitled to ask Hercules to treat it as if it were ... He must construct a scheme of abstract and concrete principles that provides a coherent justification for all common law precedents and, so far as these are to be justified on principle, constitutional and statutory provisions as well.'[11]

Thus, in order to discover whether the plaintiff has a background political right to claim the support of the community – which would justify the judge in awarding him a concrete right against the defendant – the judge must look at constitutional provisions, statutes and precedents bearing on the subject matter of the claim. But such researches may not be enough to settle the issue. There may be so many contradictions and so much vagueness in the relevant materials, that more than one reconstruction in terms of principles can be made to fit. This problem may be aggravated by the fact that much of the material is included in precedents which the judge is free to follow or not to follow as his understanding of the justice of the situation dictates.

This is where the second and crucially anti-positivistic step towards holism comes in. So far as the given legal materials permit more than one consistent reconstruction, which point in different

11 *Taking Rights Seriously* pp. 116–117.

directions on the question of the plaintiff's right, Hercules asks⤓ himself which sort of theory about law and justice best explains the kind of institutions his community supports, and measures the competing reconstructions against possible answers to that question.

'If a judge accepts the settled practices of his legal system – if he accepts, that is, the autonomy provided by its distinct constitutive and regulative rules – then he must, according to the doctrine of political responsibility, accept some general political theory that justifies these practices.'[12]

Dworkin draws an analogy between the position of a judge in a hard case, and the position of a referee in a chess tournament having to decide a novel issue which is not covered by any of the rules of chess or the rules of the particular competition. Supposing one of the players adopts behaviour tactics – such as putting on a peculiar smile – designed to distract his opponent's attention. The referee cannot decide whether this disqualifies him by looking at the rule book. He must reflect on what sort of game chess is. If it is a game of intellectual skill, does 'intellectual skill' include or exclude psychological intimidation of this kind?

Similarly, where the background right of a plaintiff cannot be determined even if one looks at the whole of the law and asks whether it would be consistent to give him a favourable decision, Hercules must reflect on the nature of law as an institution within his community. He must take into account professional opinion about what the law ought to be, and the moral convictions of his fellow citizens. But the final determinant depends on which theory about the nature of law provides the smoothest fit with the rest of the law and with all that his community claims to stand for.

'He must develop a theory of the constitution, in the shape of a complex set of principles and policies that justify that scheme of government, just as the chess referee is driven to develop a theory about the character of his game. He must develop that theory by referring alternately to political philosophy and institutional detail.'[13]
'Political rights are creatures of both history and morality: what an individual is entitled to have, in civil society, depends upon both the practice and the justice of its political institutions.'[14]

12 *Taking Rights Seriously* p. 105.
13 Page 107.
14 Page 87.

This is a powerful challenge to conventional ways of thinking about the judicial process. Various objections might spring to mind. First, no real judge could ever be a Hercules. Actual occupants of the bench are even less equipped to practice a Hercules' political philosophy than they are to investigate the ramifications of public policy. To this Dworkin may answer that the fact that questions about the true nature of justice are difficult is no reason why judges should not try; and do they not, in any case, from time to time refer to 'the spirit of our law', or 'the justice of our courts'?

Secondly, why should it be assumed that Hercules' answer to the question about the contested concept of law should incorporate the rights thesis? That is to say, why should he conclude that his society takes as fundamental – as Dworkin says it does – the right of every individual to equality of treatment and respect, and from there work down through a series of more or less abstract rights ending with a right (or the absence of a right) entitling (or disentitling) the plaintiff to judgment? Might he not conclude that his institutions are based on some other conception of justice? That question we must postpone until chapter 20, below.

Thirdly (and most important), may it not be that whatever political theory he adopts, that theory and the totality of legal materials, together still leave open the question of whether the plaintiff should be regarded as having a right to win? If there is no precedent in point, or if the existing precedents and statutes are crucially vague, is it plausible to assume that abstract statements about rights to equality and respect are going to provide unambiguous answers? If they do not, then will not the judge be forced back to making a choice, based on personal preference or on his own assessment of what is in the public interest?

This last question raises the spectre which Dworkin has consistently sought to exorcise: the notion that judges sometimes have discretion, or that they sometimes legislate.

3 Judges do not legislate

Blackstone took the view that judges merely declare the law, and was ridiculed by Bentham and Austin and by positivist writers ever since, for so holding. Is it not plain that much law has been judge-made? Bentham hoped that law-making by judges might be eliminated by adequate codification. Subsequent positivists, however, have contended that, in view of the inevitable imprecision of statutory language, judges are bound to legislate, at least 'intersticially'. This may have unfortunate implications for democratic political theory, but facts must be faced. Perhaps something can be done to mitigate the inevitable retroactivity of judicial legislation by instituting the practice of prospective overruling, discussed in the last chapter.

Dworkin contends that there is no clash with democratic theory in existing practices, and no retrospective judicial law-making to mitigate. This is so because, he says, judges do not legislate. Even in the most controversial cases, where lawyers disagree as to the proper verdict, the judge has no discretion. The answer may be difficult to find, and the judge may make a mistake; but there is always one right answer.

As we have seen, the way in which the judge finds the answer is by applying the rights thesis, by looking at the totality of the law in the light of the best political theory. But Dworkin's arguments for denying judicial legislation are not dependent on acceptance of his rights thesis. They are of two kinds. First, he denies that there comes a point in adjudication at which reasons have run out and the judge is left to his choice of a solution. Secondly, he says that the suggestion of 'no right answer' to a question of law would entail the following unacceptable assumption: that, between the contention that the law requires (p), and the contention that the law requires (not-p), there is some middle ground.

a Reasons never run out

Dworkin attacks the familiar assertion that, in some difficult cases, judges have discretion. He concedes that they have what might be called 'discretion' in two 'weak senses' of the word. First, it is true that their decisions, right or wrong, are generally determinative of the troublesome case. And secondly, in reaching their decisions they have to apply judgment. But they have no 'discretion' in the 'strong sense', of having a choice between a decision one way or the other.

In support of this contention, he draws analogies with moral and aesthetic judgments.

It would be strange, he says, to describe someone making a judgment in terms of community moral standards, or awarding an essay prize, as having 'discretion' in the sense of making an unreasoned choice. Similarly, a judge is expected to justify his decisions in terms of fundamental community justice. He is not supposed to say that all the available reasons leave the matter in balance, so that now he must simply report his own personal preference.[15]

He reminds us that, like legal principles, moral principles can be vague or incomplete; but that does not mean that, when someone is

15 (1963) 60 J Phil 624 at 634, 636–637.

deciding on a difficult question of morality (like whether he should keep a promise to X even though doing so will injure Y), he must choose by *fiat* or 'legislate' an answer.[16]

He imagines the participants in a conference of literary critics, debating an issue about certain details in the life of David Copperfield, to which there is no clear answer in Dickens' novel – such as, whether David had an affair with Steerforth. The disputants would advance reasons for their views, which they would find in terms of the plausibility of the truth or falsity of the assertion about the affair having a better fit with the rest of what Dickens tells us about David. They would assume that a right answer is to be sought in terms of reasons, even though there was no clear answer.[17]

Dworkin makes the following reply to those who argue that the fact that judges disagree about a question shows that they have no duty either way, and that therefore the matter is left to their discretion:

'The objection depends upon an assumption of moral philosophy. It assumes that duties cannot be controversial in principle. It assumes that if it is not plain what a judge's duty is, and not agreed what further evidence would decide the question, then he cannot have any duty, and we must only speak about what he ought to do. But that assumption is at least questionable. It does not square with the way we use the concept of duty in moral argument. The vegetarian need not accept that our duties are limited to what are uncontroversially or demonstrably our duties. It does not even square with how lawyers treat the issue of judicial duty. In the entrenchment clause dispute, for example, the one proposition that is common ground amongst the disputants is that the matter is not one in which judges are free to exercise discretion. Those who think that Parliament does have power to bind its successors believe that judges have no right to recognise a subsequent attempt at repeal. Those who believe that Parliament does not have this power believe that judges have a duty to recognise the subsequent repealer. It is true that some judges might be uncertain. But they are uncertain about their duties, not certain that they have none.'[18]

The point of these analogies is a strong one. If asked why he decided a question a certain way, the careful moral reasoner, the competition umpire and the literary critic, would none of them announce: 'In the absence of reasons, I tossed a mental coin.' Nor do judges in the hardest of cases announce to counsel: 'There is nothing to choose

16 (1965) 113 U Pa L Rev 668 at 686–688.
17 (1978) 53 NY U L Rev 1 at 19–20, 24–27, 29–30.
18 *Taking Rights Seriously* pp. 63–64.

between your excellent arguments, so I'll pick the solution I like best.' All these people give reasons which they say are sufficient for their conclusions.

However, the fact that reasons never run out does not entail that all possible reasons have been considered; and the fact that a judge believes his reasons are sufficient does not entail that they actually are. If a judge says: 'It seems to me that the plaintiff's argument is the stronger' – and if we could stop him there and ask 'Why?' – he would, no doubt, not answer: 'It's just a feeling I have.' He would give some second-order reason why the totality of the plaintiff's reasons out-weighed the defendant's. But if he had been forced to do that, it might have provoked some countervailing second-order reason from the defendant, seeking to show why all the plaintiff's reasons and the judge's balance-tilter were themselves outweighed by the defendant's reasons plus this new reason.

In an institutional decision-making process, the giving of reasons has to stop some time, and it may stop before all relevant reasons have been considered. In a hard case, the clinching reason may be one the judge himself has no opportunity to test against possible counter-vailing reasons – as evidenced by such expressions as: 'On the whole it seems to me that ...', 'To my mind this is a convincing reason for ...'.

It follows that Dworkin has made an important phenomenological point about the judicial role, which talk of 'discretion' might obscure: namely, that judges do not see themselves as free in hard cases to make choices based on personal preference rather than reasons. It does not follow that the community should not regard them as having discretion. Where the best legal advisers cannot be sure what is the right answer, citizens cannot be blamed if they look on the matter as follows. When the arguments on either side have been presented, a judge's personal morality, or his personal assessment of what is good for society, will dictate which of an open-ended set of possible second-order reasons he will give for saying that one side has the better case.

b No middle ground

Dworkin insists that there must be a right answer to virtually any question of law, because it would not make sense to say of a putative proposition of law (p) that it is false, and at the same time that its contrary proposition (not-p) is also false. There may be much dispute as to what the law is, but it must be one thing or the other. There is no middle ground.

He investigates two versions of the contention that there can be issues of law as to which there is no right answer. The first is one which might be advanced by empiricist sceptics. They would hold

that assertions about non-real entities can be neither true nor false –
for example, the assertion that the present King of France is bald. If
the law is an imaginary entity, then no proposition about it would, on
this view, be true or false either. We have already considered this kind
of scepticism in chapter 8, above. Even if the law is in some ultimate
sense not part of the furniture of the world, lawyers have to talk about
it as if it were. No solicitor, when asked about the law on a question by
a client, could say: 'Law, what sort of an animal is that?'

The second version of the 'no right answer' thesis, set out by
Dworkin, is more substantial. On this view, the judge has a discretion
because the law stipulates disjunctively: (p) if the judge so chooses,
or (not–p) if the judge so chooses.'

Dworkin meets this suggestion by an appeal to legal language.
Could it be that the law itself provides as to any question: 'Pending
the court's decision, it is neither true that the defendant is liable, nor
true that he is not liable'? Surely not, says Dworkin. That is not how
lawyers conceive of the law. The sort of practice which they engage in
denies the possibility of any middle ground. Consequently, although
it may be difficult to say whether a contract is valid or invalid, or
whether what X did was or was not a crime, the practice of the law
presupposes that there is a right answer; for it never happens that a
lawyer says that it was neither valid nor invalid, or that the accused
was neither culpable nor not culpable.

Dworkin admits that particular legal rules may require a judge to
decide an issue as to which there is no right answer, namely rules
which expressly confer a discretion. For example, a statute may fix a
maximum sentence of five years for an offence. Then, on the question
– should the prisoner go to gaol for one year? – there is no right
answer. What the law stipulates, as to this question, is an alternative:
the prisoner shall go to gaol for one year if the judge so decides, but not
if he fixes some other sentence. To hold that there is no right answer
on questions about the validity of contracts or tortious liability
amounts, Dworkin says, to this: the law stipulates that there is a
contract if the judge so chooses, or that there is liability if the judge
finds that there is – in other words, there is a discretion concealed in
what look like all-or-nothing concepts. But that cannot be right, he
argues, because validity or liability is given as a reason why the judge
should make his decision.

Dworkin's claim about the practices of lawyers may be open to
question. It all depends which stage of legal practice we have in mind.
It is perfectly true that no counsel will argue before a court: 'My Lord,
this is a contract if you think it ought to be'; whereas he would argue:
'Your Lordship may limit the sentence to one year, in view of the
pleaded mitigation.' The phenomenology of in-court argument is like
that of judges, in that it does not use the language of discretion.

But supposing a man takes a home-made will to his solicitor and tells him the following sad tale: 'You see that my aunt left everything to me; but her children are claiming that the will isn't valid. What's the answer?' The solicitor, after taking counsel's opinion, might say, as Dworkin insists he always does: 'It's certain that the will is either valid or invalid; but the matter is highly contestable, so we had better take out an originating summons in the court to get a definite ruling.' But perhaps he might say: 'I am afraid the law on this point is so uncertain, that whether or not the will is valid is up to the court to decide. It might go either way – there are plenty of arguments on either side. There's no right answer, because the law allows the court to choose between the arguments.'

The reader must bring to bear on phenomenological questions of this kind such experience and intuitions about legal practice as he has at his command. At the very least, Dworkin has shown how much is concealed by unreflective commonplaces about 'judicial legislation'. Even if his views are accepted in their entirety, there are at least two senses in which courts can be said to 'legislate'. If it is difficult to find the right answer to a question of law, it is the court which is authorised to make a binding determination. That is only to say that the court has 'discretion' in one of the weak senses of discretion which Dworkin distinguishes. Secondly, if by 'legislate' we mean 'add something new to the law', then Dworkin acknowledges that this does happen when the court makes a mistake. If the court correctly assesses the rights of the parties, it merely makes an existing institutional right concrete, and enforces an existing duty. But Dworkin recognises that a mistaken decision may become embedded in the law. If the decision is binding within a precedential hierarchy, other courts may be bound to apply it even though it wrongly assessed the parties' rights. A wrong decision may thus change existing rights. What Dworkin does deny is that courts 'legislate' in the way that parliaments 'legislate'. We do not have to accept his arguments about discretion and 'no right answer', in order to agree with that.

Even if Dworkin has not demonstrated that, from any standpoint outside the court, there is always a right answer and no discretion, at least he has focused attention on the fact that courts themselves act on the assumption that the right answer is always to be sought in terms of sufficient reasons. And the reasons they give are not typically the same as the kind of reasons advanced by promoters of parliamentary bills. Assumptions about political background rights may, in liberal jurisdictions, enter into arguments before courts more often than they do into arguments leading to legislative enactment. Perhaps such assumptions should cover the whole ground of contested legal issues, but can it be accepted that they already do? Lawyers sometimes

advance reasons which (in their view) so strongly indicate what the
law *ought to be* that they feel justified in claiming that that is what it
already is. Is Dworkin correct in saying that the explanation for such
claims is that they always have 'rights' in mind?

Bibliography

Amenard J.	'Dworkin's Rights Thesis' (1976) 74 Mich L Rev 1167
Bell R. S.	'Understanding the Model of Rules: Towards a Reconciliation of Dworkin and Positivism' (1971–72) 81 Yale LJ 912
Bodenheimer E.	'Hart, Dworkin and the Problem of Judicial Lawmaking Discretion' (1977) 11 Ga L Rev 1143
Cameron E.	'Are Dworkin's "Principles" Really Rules?' (1979) 96 SALJ 450 'Professor Dworkin's Views on Legal Positivism' (1979–80) 55 Ind LJ 209
Carrio G. R.	*Legal Principles and Legal Positivism* (1971)
Christie G. C.	'The Model of Principles' [1968] Duke LJ 649
Dworkin R. M.	'Judicial Discretion' (1963) 60 J Phil 624 'Philosophy, Morality and Law' (1965) 113 U Pa L Rev 668, 678 ff *Taking Rights Seriously* (revised edn, 1978) 'No Right Answer?' (1978) 53 NY U L Rev 1
Greenawalt K.	'Discretion in Judicial Decision: the Elusive Quest for the Fetters that Bind Judges' (1975) 75 Colum L Rev 359 'Policy, Rights, and Judicial Decision' (1977) 11 Ga L Rev 991
Gross H.	'Standards as Law' [1968–69] ASAL 575
Harris J. W.	*Law and Legal Science* (1979) s. 22
Hart H. L. A.	'American Jurisprudence Through English Eyes: the Nightmare and the Noble Dream' (1977) 11 Ga L Rev 969 'Between Utility and Rights' in Ryan (ed) *The Idea of Freedom* (1979)
Lyons D. B.	'Principles, Positivism, and Legal Theory' (1977) 87 Yale LJ 415
MacCallum G. C.	'Dworkin on Judicial Discretion' (1963) 60 J Phil 638
MacCormick D. N.	'Dworkin as Pre-Benthamite' (1978) 87 Phil Rev 585

192   Dworkin's rights thesis

Mackie J. L.	'The Third Theory of Law' (1977) 7 PPA 1
Marshall G.	'Positivism, Adjudication, and Democracy' in Hacker and Raz (eds) *Law, Morality, and Society* (1977)
Munzer S. R.	'Right Answers, Pre-existing Rights, and Fairness' (1977) 11 Ga L Rev 1055
✗ Pannick D.	'A Note on Dworkin and Precedent' (1980) 43 MLR 36
Raz J.	'Legal Principles and the Limits of Law' (1972) 81 Yale LJ 825
Smith J. C.	*Legal Obligation* (1976) ch 9
Soper E. P.	'Legal Theory and the Obligation of the Judge: the Hart/Dworkin Dispute' (1977) 75 Mich L Rev 473
Steiner J. M.	'Judicial Discretion and the Concept of Law' (1976) 35 CLJ 135
Tapper C. F. H.	'A Note on Principles' (1971) 34 MLR 628
Tur R.	'Positivism, Principles and Rules' in Attwooll (ed) *Perspectives in Jurisprudence* (1977)

15   Legal reasoning

'You're talking like a lawyer!' is sometimes a commendation, sometimes a sneer. Whichever it is, it does seem to be generally assumed that lawyers have a special way of talking and reasoning. Their professional preoccupation with statutes, regulations, precedents, court ways and (in some jurisdictions) constitutions leads them into thinking about problems in a peculiar way. Some critics call for change in legal styles of thought. Lawyers should be less 'mechanical', less conservative, more attuned to social needs. Both to understand what it is, and to decide whether it should be changed, we ought to see if we can pick out the crucial differentiating characteristics of this legal reasoning.

The first thing we might try to get clear is what is supposed to be the function of legal reasoning – what does it aim to achieve? That might be thought to vary depending on which sort of lawyer you are talking about. Books on legal reasoning in common law jurisdictions concentrate on judges, whose published opinions contain masses of reasoning. In civil law jurisdictions, they focus more on the writings of jurists; both because their works – 'la doctrine' – are regarded as important evidence of what the law is, and because court judgments are much less elaborate in their ratiocinations. But perhaps we should think about those lawyers who advise clients – solicitors and barristers. The function of their reasoning might be thought to be prediction – as the American realists claimed (see chapter 8, above). They give reasons for thinking that the other side is (or is not) likely to sue, defend or settle a claim; and reasons for thinking that a particular judge would (or would not) be likely to decide in your favour. Then there is the reasoning of advocates. They seek to persuade the court to make awards, render verdicts or issue orders. C. H. Perelman has argued that persuasion, rather than justification, is the overall function of legal reasoning. T. D. Perry contends that, in the legal as in the moral context, persuading an audience to accept your view is what 'justification' means. Most writers, however, have assumed that the object of legal reasoning is 'justification' in the more familiar sense of supporting the right answer. A lawyer gives his reasons for thinking that such and such a course of conduct or decision is legally justified – whatever its other merits.

Justification must be at least the ostensible purpose of judges' reasons. They are not in the business of predicting or persuading. Legal textwriters may go in for some prediction and persuasion, but do they not predominantly engage in giving reasons why something should be considered the 'correct', 'best', 'most justified' legal solution? They differ from advocates in that they are supposed to consider all sides of the question, whereas advocates 'submit' that the correct legal solution is the one which favours their clients. But in making such submissions, advocates marshall reasons which are of the same sort as those which judges and textwriters deploy by way of justification. Advisers, too, must have some regard to justificatory reasoning, at least if they take the view that what justifies a decision as legally sound has some effect upon the decisions judges are likely to render, and upon litigants' decisions to sue, defend or settle. In the succeeding discussion, I shall assume that justification is the primary function of legal reasoning, upon which the functions of prediction and persuasion are parasitic; but that view is certainly controversial.

NB

Having got that far, it is still a debatable question whether lawyers' justifying reasons differ from other people's. Theorists commonly draw an admittedly uncertain line between clear (easy) cases, and unclear (hard, penumbral) cases. With the former, of course lawyers give special reasons, for they point to some unambiguous authority. If a statute or regulation makes conduct illegal beyond any dispute, then a lawyer, who is practised in looking up the relevant text, tells you that it is unlawful. But in the unclear cases, where what is at issue is what the correct legal solution ought to be, are special sorts of argument available to legal reasoning? Or is it all a matter of 'politics'?

That it is 'politics' was Kelsen's view. He repudiated any attempt by legal science to produce solutions going beyond the reproduction of valid norms (see chapter 6, above). His view squares with the opinions of those who produce sociological evidence to show that, in any controversial case, what judges decide is no more than a reflection of their political opinions on the issue. A recent example is Professor J. A. G. Griffiths' *The Politics of the Judiciary*. Griffiths maintains that the conservative political views of English judges lead them to make decisions unfavourable to groups like trade unions and students. Such assessments are not uncommon on the radical left; and some critics draw the conclusion that the way forward is to appoint judges with politically acceptable opinions. Not so Professor Griffiths. He is pessimistic. Nothing, it seems, can be done to prevent those who attain judicial office from rendering politically conservative decisions, whose effect will be to support the dominant establishment, whether in capitalist or communist countries. The only ideal society would be one in which conflicts between different interest groups had been resolved, and then you wouldn't need judges at all.

What conclusions as to the nature of legal reasoning should we draw from this 'political' assessment of the judicial process? Should judges come clean? Should they drop all talk about various possible meanings of statutory words, the purpose underlying enactments, the persuasive weight of precedents and the logical implications of concepts, and, instead, give the same sorts of reasons as are put forward by those engaged in ordinary political debates? Should advocates frame their submissions directly in terms of the political attitudes they suspect the particular judge has? I was once told a story about a county court judge who was so prejudiced in favour of hirers under hire-purchase agreements – a freak, by Professor Griffiths' reckoning – that, if you were defending such a hirer, all you had to plead was: 'Your Honour, the plaintiff is a hire-purchase finance company.' But then that was a joke, I think.

What should textwriters do? 'Here is the law, and here are my politics. So far as the law is not cast iron clear, I will give nothing but political reasons as to the proper legal solution.' There would then be no difference between the sorts of reason advanced by a reformer who says that the clear law should be changed, and those advanced in arguing that a doubtful point should be decided in a certain way.

As things are, textwriters (including Professor Griffiths) make use of special legal justificatory arguments in doubtful cases – the purpose of the statute, consistency with other parts of the law, and so on. Just compare the different sorts of criticism in casenotes in legal journals with those in comments on new statutes. Counsel arguing before our judges – whatever their private suspicions – do not make use of the clincher: 'Hell, man, aren't you a conservative?' At the end of the day, perhaps we should dismiss legal reasoning as an illusion or a smoke-screen, but we had better first try to understand what sort of animal it is.

In recent years, English judges have not been shy in committing to print their own conceptions of the judicial process. We learn from these writings that they are generally aware of a tension between legal certainty and legal adaptability, between the requirement of fidelity to law and the value of judicial creativity. As to how this tension should be resolved, their views differ. As all lawyers and many laymen are aware, Lord Denning puts adaptability first. But even he concedes that the judge's business is to do 'justice according to law', rather than simply 'justice'. He views this task as a technical craft whereby the legal authorities, contained in statutes and law reports, may be interpreted so as not to impede the implementation of justice. For him then 'justice according to law' means not letting the law get in the way of justice; whereas for more orthodox judges, 'justice according to law' means doing justice within the limits laid down by the authorities. Our judges do not on the whole embark on speculations as to what 'justice' actually entails. Some of the different senses of the term are considered in chapter 20, below. They tend to deal with justificatory reasoning piecemeal: the way to treat authoritative materials, and the speculations to be made about wider social implications, vary from one kind of problem to another. They might perhaps regard a search for an overall view of legal reasoning as unnecessary.

It is far from easy to get a comprehensive view of the subject. Most writers who have discussed legal reasoning have either concentrated on the form as distinct from the substance of justificatory arguments, or else dealt with only part of the subject. Two forms of argument, the deductive and the inductive, have generally been considered inapposite characterisations of legal argument. Some take the view that deductive argument – from major and minor premises to a logically necessary conclusion – is inappropriate even in clear cases. This may be asserted on the general ground that deductive arguments only hold true of factual propositions not of norms; or on the more specific ground that even the clearest rule may be held not to apply to a case where that would frustrate the purpose of the law or produce absurd consequences, and the decision whether this is so or not cannot be dictated by logic. On the other hand, reasoning in clear cases seems very close to deductive reasoning – here is a speed-limit rule applying to all car drivers, I am a car driver, so it applies to me. Even in unclear cases, it can be contended that the form of the argument is deductive, since what is at issue is which of competing rulings should be adopted, granted that the winner will be applied deductively to justify the decision – although here our major concern will be with the substantive arguments which dictate choice amongst the rulings.

In view of what was said in chapter 13, above about judges being required at least to listen to all precedents, it might be argued that case law reasoning is inductive – arrival at propositions from survey of data. Such a view has been generally rejected. Judges may produce rulings which, they think, cover the majority of *dicta*, but they do not have to account for them all. It is not even bad legal reasoning to suggest that a few important authorities outweigh a mass of less important ones.

E. H. Levi tells us that the form is reasoning by example or analogical reasoning. The judge and other lawyers see how closely analogous the case in hand is to decided cases, or to the hypothetical example implicit in a statute. The only difference between the treatment of precedents and statutory interpretation is that, in the latter, the measuring rod for analogies cannot be changed; whereas in the development of the common law, concepts may be 'reworked'. Case by case analogical development may lead, for example, to the category of 'inherently dangerous products' being generalised and replaced by the category of 'foreseeably harmful conduct'. However, he does not tell us what reasons of substance justify choosing between competing analogies. G. Gottlieb depicts the form of reasoning employed in the law as one of using 'warrants' to be found in the corpus of legal material as guides to 'choice'. But we need to know how conflicting guidance from different such warrants is resolved, and, more especially, whether choices are ever 'justified' rather than merely 'guided'. Karl Llewellyn provided historical evidence for variations between a 'grand style' and a 'formal style' in legal reasoning. Benjamin Cardozo picks out four different procedures: the methods of philosophy, history, tradition and sociology. These are illuminating historical and classificatory descriptions of the surface features of judicial reasoning, but they do not give us any coherent theory of what, in the end, makes a particular conclusion legally sound. Julius Stone tells us that the existing restraints upon adjudication leave the judge 'leeways of choice', and he can only act within these leeways in the light of his own conception of justice. That may be true, but we can only decide that it is if no plausible theory is available of how a judge ought to decide.

R. A. Wasserstrom and D. H. Hodgson have debated the question of how, in principle, adjudication should proceed, but only in areas not covered by statute law, and primarily with reference to the respective merits of a rule-utilitarian and a precedential approach. Wasserstrom examines reasoning by reference to precedents, and finds it wanting. Given the quantity of precedents and the inexhaustible possibilities of distinguishing them, there can be no certainty about judicial decisions; and, in so far as judges can and do stick to precedents, their decisions are likely to be ill-adapted to social change. For the most part judges produce the decision which would (if universalised) have best consequences, so the best course would be to drop precedential reasoning and instead adopt a 'two-level decision procedure' analogous to rule-utilitarianism (see chapter 4, above). The judge should first ask himself what rule governing this sort of case would, if generally applied, have best consequences; and then make that rule the basis of his decision. Hodgson replies that the adoption of such a procedure would lead to greater uncertainty than we have with our present system of common law justification. There would be no certainty about judicial decisions because everyone would know that, although judge X had rendered a decision required by a rule which he (X) thought would have best consequences, future judges would not necessarily apply judge X's rule. They would, following the same two-level procedure ask again which rule would have best consequences. The result, Hodgson argues, is that the adoption of this rule-utilitarian approach, in substitution for reliance on precedents, would, paradoxically, have greater disutility than what we do now. He believes that existing common law justification means that the law is usually certain; but that there is some flexibility in that judges weigh precedents in the light of four factors: the authority of the precedential court; harmony with other rules; the length of time during which the precedential ruling has been relied on; and 'justice' or 'utility'. Both authors are expressly concerned with a hypothetical adjudicatory process, in which decisions are not pre-empted by legislation.

What we need is a view which synthesises form and substance, and comprehends all the varieties of argument regarded as relevant to settling a question of law. In my book, *Law and Legal Science*, I endeavoured to list the different sorts of substantive reason which, disregarding the form, were employed as justifications for legal decisions. I called these the 'will', 'natural meaning', 'doctrine' and 'utility' models of rationality. The former covers those situations in which genuine reference is made to what some agent in the legislative process, or some individual judge, actually had in mind when laying down a rule. The second covers those cases in which the fact that a word appearing in a rule has natural meaning X is a justifying reason. The third embraces all those situations in which some maxim – whether rule, principle, policy, classification or whatever comprised in a historic legal system is supposed to justify a decision. The fourth covers situations in which the perceived consequences of a decision are determinative. This listing of the models of rationality does distinguish legal reasoning from other kinds of justificatory reasoning, but does not set out a synthesis. Dworkin's 'rights thesis' does (see chapter 14, above). I suggested that Dworkin's view could profitably be contrasted with an (as yet) undeveloped theory which I called 'field utilitarianism'. It would see consequentialist arguments as determinative of legal decisions, but would take into account the fitting of a proposed ruling into the law as a whole and would show how the non-utilitarian models of rationality were to be slotted in. When my book was already with the printers, there was published just this sort of alternative comprehensive theory. It is Professor Neil MacCormick's *Legal Reasoning and Legal Theory*.

Like Dworkin, MacCormick sets out to provide a theory of legal reasoning which is both explanatory and normative. It both explains what reasons judges use in justification of their decisions – at any rate, English and Scottish judges – and contends that these are the reasons

they ought to use. He demonstrates at length how purely deductive⁊
reasoning is possible in justification of a judicial decision in law, using
as an example the decision of Lewis J in *Daniels and Daniels v R. White
and Sons and Tarbard*.[1] A publican (Mrs Tarbard), who sold to Mr
Daniels a bottle of R. White's lemonade which turned out to contain
carbolic acid, was held liable as a 'seller by description' of goods
which were not of 'merchantable quality', within the terms of section
14 (2) of the Sale of Goods Act 1893 (as authoritatively interpreted in
prior cases). In such cases, the major premise is an indisputable rule
of the legal system, the minor premise consists of proven facts, and the
conclusion is the holding; the decision is therefore justified purely by
deduction plus the normative assumptions which warrant acceptance
of the system's rule of recognition. In most cases where there is
litigation on a question of law, however, such deductive justification is
not possible. These MacCormick distributes under three heads: ✳
problems of 'relevancy', problems of 'interpretation', and problems of
'classification'. A problem of relevancy arises when it is open to
dispute what legal rule is relevant to the issue. The typical case is a
dispute arising in the area of case law, as in *Donoghue v Stevenson*[2] where
the majority of the House of Lords thought that there was, and the
minority thought there was not, a rule of law imposing a duty of care
on manufacturers vis-à-vis consumers. A problem of interpretation
arises when the words of a statute are ambiguous, and the court has to
choose between two interpretations. For example, in *Ealing London
Borough Council v Race Relations Board*,[3] the majority of the house of
Lords held that a statutory rule prohibiting discrimination on the
ground of 'national origin' did not apply to discrimination on the
ground of legal nationality, so that the council was not acting un-
lawfully when it limited its housing list to British subjects. A problem
of classification arises where the court has to decide whether the facts
admitted or proved do or do not come within a factual category
stipulated in a rule. For example, in *MacLennan v MacLennan*,[4] Lord
Wheatley held that artificial insemination was not classifiable as
'adultery'. MacCormick argues that problems of interpretation and ✳
of classification are, in truth, logically equivalent, since both involve
choice between two competing rulings. They are distinguished only
for institutional reasons, having to do with the distinction between
questions of law and questions of fact. A problem is treated as one of
classification rather than interpretation, and therefore a question of
fact rather than law, in situations where appeal to higher courts is

1 [1938] 4 All ER 258.
2 [1932] AC 562.
3 [1972] AC 342.
4 1958 SC 105.

limited to questions of law and it is felt that this particular question ought to be settled by the lower court; or where an issue is one as to which, it is felt, future cases should not be hampered by precedent – which they will not be if the issue is regarded as one of fact.

NB.

Reasoning in relation to these three sorts of problems is, MacCormick argues, limited as to form by the requirements of formal justice, and as to substance by the requirements of consistency and coherence. Within these limits, the reasoning is consequentialist; save that no ruling, however desirable its consequences, is legally permitted unless it is authorised by legal principle or is analogous to an existing legal rule.

The limitation of formal justice means that no decision may be given which cannot be universalised. As Kant and R. M. Hare argue for ethics, so MacCormick argues for law. It is formally irrational to say X is the right solution in circumstances Y, unless you accept that there is a class of Xs which will always be right for the class of Ys. That does not mean that rules can have no exceptions. Where there is an exception, there is something present besides Y. MacCormick makes it clear that what is formally essential is universalisability, not generalisation. So far as formal justice is concerned, one could support the holding in *Donoghue v Stevenson* by a universal rule to the effect that all manufacturers of ginger beer are liable to residents of Paisley who suffer foreseeable damage from decomposed snails in the manufacturers' bottles.

The requirement of consistency means that, in deciding whether a certain rule is legally relevant (that is, whether that particular rule-formulation can be said to be part of the law), or in choosing between two rules each of which is permitted by different interpretations of a statute or by different classifications of facts, no rule can be accepted which contradicts any other rule in the system. 'The system' here means all the rules valid by reference to criteria of recognition *at the time when the decision is made* – what I have called a 'momentary legal system'. I suggested in my book that legal science constructs 'the present law' of any jurisdiction by reference to four logical principles, those of exclusion, subsumption, derogation and non-contradiction. The first requires the law to be identified by reference to a finite set of sources. The second indicates that rules originating in an inferior source must be subsumed under rules originating in superior sources. The third stipulates a priority amongst rules depending on a ranking of sources. The fourth insists that any other contradiction must be eliminated. It should be stressed that the view for which I and MacCormick argue – that it is part of legal reasoning to eliminate logical conflicts between rules – is by no means universally admitted.[5]

5 See e.g. Kelsen 'Derogation' in *Essays in Legal and Moral Philosophy* and Raz (1972) Yale LJ 825 at 829–834.

MacCormick's requirement of coherence means that, even where there is no question of logical contradiction, the legal reasoner should not put forward a ruling which cannot be coherently sustained in conjunction with other rules in the system. Rules requiring different coloured cars to observe different speed limits would not be logically inconsistent, but would be incoherent since no set of evaluations could justify them. If a proposed ruling promotes value X, by indicating that a certain pattern of behaviour or a certain state of affairs is desirable, and it would not make sense to pursue value X whilst also pursuing values embodied in other rules of law, then it is irrational (MacCormick argues) to adopt the proposed ruling. The concept of coherence involves attributing rational purpose to the law, rather than regarding it as a wilderness of single instances. In *Donoghue v Stevenson*, Lord Atkin said: 'In English law there must be, and is, some general conception of relations giving rise to a duty of care of which the particular cases found in the books are but instances.' He then went on to formulate his famous 'neighbour principle' – the duty is owed to persons whom you can reasonably foresee would be likely to be injured by your careless acts or omissions.[6]

So long as a proposed ruling is consistent and coherent with the rest of the system, it is, according to MacCormick, legally permitted if authorised by principle or analogy, and legally justified if it would have better consequences than any other similarly authorised ruling. He rejects Dworkin's definition of principles as propositions describing rights. Principles are, he says, 'relatively general norms which are conceived of as "rationalizing" rules or sets of rules'.[7] A legal principle, in the view of the person putting it forward as a principle, explains and justifies existing legal rules. It authorises any new ruling which it would also explain and justify. As well as having this authorising function, a principle may, through regular explicit application by the courts, acquire great presumptive weight in its own right. But it never fully justifies a decision. Only consequences do that. For example, Lord Atkin's neighbour principle explained and justified rulings in earlier cases, and also the ruling about manufacturers' liability in *Donoghue v Stevenson* itself. It has since been used to authorise many other new rulings in the law of negligence. But it does not require them. Its persuasive force may be overriden by consequentialist arguments, as happened in *Rondel v Worsley*.[8] There the House of Lords held that there would be unacceptable consequences for the administration of justice if barristers were liable for the foreseeable harm resulting from negligent conduct of litigation.

6 [1932] AC 562 at 580.
7 *Legal Reasoning and Legal Theory* p. 232.
8 [1968] 1 AC 191.

A ruling is authorised by analogy, MacCormick says, if there is an existing legal rule or principle of the form: 'if P then Q', if the proposed ruling stipulates: 'if P/1 then Q', and if P/1 is similar to P. For example, the situation of a salvor putting himself in danger to save property is similar to that of a rescuer putting himself in danger to prevent injury; so if there already exists a legal rule entitling the rescuer to recover damages from the person responsible for the danger, the court is authorised (though not obliged) to announce a similar rule for salvors. The limits of analogical reasoning are set by the requirement that P, the operative facts of the rule or principle with which analogy is drawn, must be stated with reasonable specificity; otherwise one could find vaguely-worded pronouncements in the books, analogical application of which would justify anything.

MacCormick contends that, within the limits set by the requirements of formal justice, consistency and coherence, and within the range authorised by principle and analogy, legal reasoning is essentially consequentialist. In most problems of relevancy, interpretation and classification, more than one decision may be formally just (universalisable into a ruling), and more than one ruling consistent and coherent with the rest of the law and authorised by principle or analogy. When this is so, the perceived consequences of alternative rulings are what do (and what ought to) justify judicial decisions. In this sense, MacCormick says, his theory is a variety of ideal rule-utilitarianism (see chapter 4, above). But he prefers the label 'consequentialist' to 'utilitarian', because he is anxious to stress that there is no Benthamite objective scale for measuring good and bad consequences *inter se*. His view on this point should be contrasted with the theory of the economic analysis of law that, in common law contexts at least, the underlying logic of consequentialist reasoning is related to an objective scale (see chapter 4, above).

MacCormick distinguishes consequences of three sorts. First, there are considerations of corrective justice – 'for every wrong there ought to be a remedy'. Second, there are considerations of 'common sense' – a judicial expression which boils down (he says) to perceptions of community moral standards. Third, there are considerations of public policy. The latter include both direct public interest in bringing about changed behaviour, and also questions of convenience or expediency such as the desirability of having a clear rule or the floodgates argument – 'allow this claim, and the courts will be flooded out with litigation'. A particular decision may be shown to be irrational, if the foreseen consequences were premised upon incorrect facts. But there comes a point at which the consequences may be agreed and yet honest men still differ as to the rulings that are justified. At this stage, the choice is irreducibly subjective. For that reason, MacCormick disagrees with Dworkin's views on discretion. *also w/right answers*

It is with Professor Dworkin's 'rights thesis' that MacCormick's elegant theory of legal reasoning is primarily to be compared. Which of them is right about discretion, given Dworkin's 'reasons never run out' argument summarised in the last chapter? Should consequentialist arguments be understood (as Dworkin maintains) in terms of their distributive effects on individuals – that is, in terms of 'rights'? Does the fact that 'principles' enter into legal reasoning mean, as Dworkin urges, that no positivistic pedigree test of what counts as 'law' is possible, so that no line can be drawn between legal and moral argument? Or is MacCormick right in maintaining that legal principles are, indirectly, identifiable by reference to Hart's rule of recognition, in that they are always parasitic on the rules they underpin and justify? Supposing two lawyers contend for different principles, each of which, according to its proponent, underlies the same body of rules, and neither of which has yet been blessed with judicial recognition. Dworkin would say that that principle is a 'legal' one which follows from the best political theory, having regard to institutional fit and moral truth. I have myself argued that neither would be 'legal', since principles acquire the status of legality only once they are accepted as part of the tradition of a body of officials. It is not clear how MacCormick would deal with this problem. On the one hand, he tells us that legal principles explain and justify legal rules, which suggests that both candidates are already legal principles. On the other hand, he speaks of drawing analogies from 'existing principles', which suggests that some kind of authoritative formulation is necessary before a norm 'exists' as a legal principle.

MacCormick expresses disagreement with the House of Lords' decision in the *Ealing Borough* case. He thinks that the minority were right to prefer the principle underlying the Race Relations Act – that discrimination in general is undesirable – to the common law principle which influenced the majority – that freedom of action is to be upheld unless curtailed by clear statutory language. He does not, however, deal with the more general question: should judges always prefer legislative analogy to common law analogy? Presumably, this sort of general issue would be fitted into the 'political theory' which Dworkin attributes to his superhuman judge. Seventy years ago, Roscoe Pound listed four ways in which courts might deal with legislative innovation: (1) reason from it by analogy in preference to analogies based on judge-made rules, on the ground that it is a later and more direct expression of the will of a superior authority; (2) reason from it by analogy, but regard it as of equal authority with judge-made rules; (3) refuse to reason from it by analogy, but nevertheless give it a liberal interpretation to cover the whole field it was intended to encompass; (4) refuse to reason from it by analogy, and insist on giving it a narrow interpretation limited to cases which it covers expressly. Pound said the fourth approach represented the orthodox common law attitude, but that there was a tendency towards the third; and that the course of legal development should lead to the second and eventually the first.[9] Certainly, we have not yet reached the first approach, and some would argue that considerations of stability tell against it. If all arguments from common law principles are to give way before analogical extensions of legislation promoted by the parliamentary majority of the day, what price legal continuity? It is by no means clear that we have reached the second approach, that is, that judges will derive a principle from the general tenor of legislation and apply it analogically. The Court of Appeal has recently refused to extend the principle which prohibits discrimination on the ground of sex beyond the categories of conduct specifically declared unlawful in the Sex Discrimination Act 1975; and it accordingly held that immigration regulations could not be challenged on this ground.[10]

Other questions may be raised about MacCormick's theory of legal reasoning. He says that no line can be drawn between easy and hard cases, yet maintains that there are situations in which strict deduction is possible. Why should not the limits of deduction constitute the line? Is he right about deductive justification? In his example of the *Daniels* case, he says that the judge rightly dismissed out of hand counsel's submission that the sale of the bottle of lemonade was not a 'sale by description'. But could not Lewis J have concluded, faithful to the requirements of universalisability and consistency, that this category did not apply to sales by sellers who had no means of verifying the quality of goods? That might have led to incoherence with the rest of the law: and probably strict liability in contract has good consequences; but such coherence and consequentialist arguments are not dictated by logic. One might even wonder whether the very fact that an issue is litigated as to the law demonstrates that it is not one as to which indisputable deductive logic gives only one answer. In *Law and Legal Science*, I suggested that deductions in law are never formally valid, but that legal reasoning is for all practical purposes deductive when all that is needed to make it watertight is the exclusion of ludicrous purposive interpretations. Since Lewis J was sympathetic to the seller it might be argued that he should have at least tried to discover whether some purposively coherent explanation of existing statute and case law might be given which would let her off. A possible

---

9 (1908) 21 Harv L Rev 383.
10 *Kassam v Immigration Appeal Tribunal* [1980] 2 All ER 330. Leave has been granted to appeal to the House of Lords (*Times* 21 May 1980).

litigated instance where no such endeavour was warranted (so that the decision was, for all practical purposes, deductive), is the Canadian case of *R v Liggetts-Finlay Drug Stores Ltd.*[11] There a byelaw directed that 'all drug shops shall be closed at 10 p.m. on each and every day of the week'. The Appellate Division of the Supreme Court of Alberta rejected peremptorily the contention that there was no infringement if a drug shop closed at 10 p.m. and opened a few minutes later.

As a statement of the interrelationship between what I call 'legal models of rationality', MacCormick's theory may be considered as on the whole descriptively accurate, so far as the reasoning of United Kingdom judges is concerned. But his theory is intended to be normative as well as explanatory, and on the normative side, some may regard it as complacent. He accepts that doctrine-model reasoning should limit utility-model reasoning. Analogy with existing rules, or conformity with principles underlying existing rules, should restrain the proposed rulings which are candidates for utilitarian comparison. That is required, MacCormick argues, by the need to do 'justice according to law'. Judges should not make new rulings, however desirable in terms of corrective justice, community morality and public policy, unless they are authorised by analogy or existing principle. It might be argued that 'justice according to law' is satisfied so long as new rulings are consistent and coherent with the rest of the system. In *Malone v Metropolitan Police Commissioner*,[12] Megarry VC held that telephone tapping is not a legal wrong. Supposing he had laid down a new rule of tort law to the effect that a citizen may sue those who tap his telephone, unless the defendants are specifically authorised by statute or statutory instrument, and had justified this new rule by enunciating a new legal principle that 'privacy is to be respected'. That principle would not, I think, be incoherent with other principles underlying existing legal rules, but the new ruling would not be authorised by any such principle. Would such an innovation overstep the conception of 'doing justice according to law' which we wish to defend? That must depend on our appraisal of the proper constitutional distribution of power between legislature and judiciary, and the conception we have of the rule of law – does it exclude decisions justified by wholly innovative judicial rulings? For Dworkin, coherence ('institutional fit') is all that is needed, so long as the new principle reflects a 'background' moral right.

MacCormick appears to regard the 'natural meaning' model of rationality as merely an aspect of the 'will' model, and consequently

11 [1919] 3 WW R 1025.
12 [1979] Ch 344.

he accepts uncritically the view that there should always be a presumption in favour of plain meaning.

'Whether or not all the members of the legislature have the least
idea of the contents of clauses of Bills, the least unsuccessful way of
securing that the will of elected legislators will prevail will be to
take the words enacted by them at their face value and so far as
possible apply them in accordance with their plain meaning.'[13]

The presumption in favour of plain meaning may be justified, not
because of assumptions about Parliament's intention, but because
giving effect to it avoids judges entering into politically controversial
questions – that is, it supports the objectivity of the rule of law. On the
other hand, it may be condemned as arbitrary ('mechanical',
'legalistic'). These are important normative issues about legal
reasoning which MacCormick's failure to recognise the natural-
meaning model as a distinct model of legal reasoning prevents him
from investigating.

MacCormick also accepts uncritically the view that speculations
about legislative intent never permit you to go beyond some meaning
which statutory words can bear. Utility and doctrine can prevail over
plain meaning, but never over possible meaning.

'There is a justified presumption in favour of applying statutes in
accordance with their more obvious meanings, but provided there
are other *possible* meanings the presumption can be displaced by
good arguments from consequences and/or from legal principles.'[14]

But supposing we are confident that the legislature did intend
something which the words it ineptly chose cannot achieve? In *Inland
Revenue Commissioners v Hinchy*, a statute provided that a person making
an incorrect tax return shall forfeit the sum of £20 'and treble the tax
which he ought to be charged under this Act'. The taxpayer in his
return understated some interest he had received, the tax payable on
the amount omitted being £14 5s 0d. The tax payable on his entire
income for the year was £139 11s 6d. The House of Lords held
unanimously that the wording of the Act left them no alternative but
to award a penalty of £438 14s 6d, treble his whole tax not just treble
the underpaid tax. Lord Reid said that, since the words were not
capable of a more limited construction, 'we must apply them as they
stand, however unreasonable and unjust the consequences, and
however strongly we may suspect that this was not the real intention
of Parliament.[15]

13 *Legal Reasoning and Legal Theory* p. 204.
14 Page 213.
15 [1960] AC 748 at 767.

To an English or Scottish lawyer, this view may seem so obvious as to make critical examination of it a waste of time. How could legal reasoning justify giving an enactment a meaning which the words *cannot* bear? But that, as the House of Lords has recently stressed, is a parochial view. In *R v Henn*[16] convictions for importing obscene articles were challenged by reference to the Treaty of Rome. The Court of Appeal refused to refer to the European Court of Justice the question whether an absolute prohibition on importation could be a 'quantitative restriction on imports between member states' contrary to article 30 because it was plain that the words could not bear that meaning. The House of Lords referred the question, expecting (and getting) from the court the answer that absolute prohibitions were 'quantitative restrictions'. As Lord Diplock pointed out, the European Court seeks to give effect to the spirit rather than the letter of the treaties, sometimes indeed to an English judge it might seem to the exclusion of the letter. (Convictions were none the less upheld as the United Kingdom legislation came within the 'public morality' exception in article 36.)

Because of his uncritical assumption that words in the statute are the only evidence of legislative intent, MacCormick does not deal with some of those controversial issues discussed in chapter 12, above. Whatever its practical difficulties, would examination of parliamentary history facilitate legal reasoning? Would it be facilitated if the courts assumed the power to fill in gaps? For the same reason, broader questions are neglected. What is the proper relationship between will-model reasoning and the utility and doctrine models? Should speculation as to legislative purpose be considered a ground for authorising new rules, distinct from principle and analogy? Was Pound right when he argued that principles introduced by legislation should not merely be used as a basis for analogical reasoning in the way common law principles are, but should (in deference to their democratic origin) be given priority over common law principles?

Bibliography

Cardozo B.	*The Nature of the Judicial Process* (1921)
Denning Lord	*The Discipline of Law* (1979)
Devlin P.	'Judges and Lawmakers' (1976) 39 MLR 1
Eckhoff T.	'Guiding Standards in Legal Reasoning (1976) 29 CLP 205

16 [1980] 2 All ER 166.

Edmund-Davies Lord	'Judicial Activism' (1975) 28 CLP 1
Friedmann W.	*Legal Theory* (5th edn, 1967) ch 32
Fuller L. L.	'The Forms and Limits of Adjudication' (1978) 92 Harv L Rev 353
Golding M. P.	'Principled Decision-making and the Supreme court' in Summers (ed) *Essays in Legal Philosophy* (1968)
Gottlieb G.	*The Logic of Choice* (1968)
Griffiths J. A. G.	*The Politics of the Judiciary* (1977)
Guest A. G.	'Logic in the Law' in Guest (ed) *Oxford Essays in Jurisprudence* (1961)
Harris J. W.	*Law and Legal Science* (1979) ch 5 –
Hodgson D. H.	*Consequences of Utilitarianism* (1967)
Hook S. (ed)	*Law and Philosophy* (1964) Pt 3
Jensen O. C.	*The Nature of Legal Argument* (1957)
Levi E. H.	*An Introduction to Legal Reasoning* (1948)
Llewellyn K. N.	*The Common Law Tradition* (1960)
MacCormick D. N.	*Legal Reasoning and Legal Theory* (1978)
Perelman C. H.	*Justice, Law and Argument* (1980)
Perry T. D.	*Moral Reasoning and Truth* (1976) pp. 75–112, 196–216
Pound R.	'Common Law and Legislation' (1908) 21 Harv L Rev 383
Radcliffe Lord	'The Lawyer and his Times' in Sutherland (ed) *The Path of the Law from 1967* (1968)
Reid Lord	'The Judge as Law Maker' (1972) 12 JSPTL 22
Sartorius R. E.	*Individual Conduct and Social Norms* (1975) ch 10
Shuman S. I.	'Justification of Judicial Decisions' (1971) 59 Calif L Rev 723
Stoljar S. J.	'The Logical Status of a Legal Principle' (1953) 20 U Chi L Rev 181
Stone J.	*Legal System and Lawyers' Reasonings* (1964) chs 6–8
Summers R. S.	'Two Types of Substantive Reason: the Core of a Theory of Common Law Justification' (1978) 63 Cor L Rev 707
Twining W. and Myers D.	*How to do Things with Rules* (1976) ch 7
Wasserstrom R. A.	*The Judicial Decision* (1961)

16   The duty to obey the law

Is there a moral duty to obey the law? Most public men say there is. In the history of speculative thought, adherents of widely different social perspectives have said that there is. Socrates went to his unjust execution proclaiming such a duty. St Paul, writing to the Christians at Rome, affirmed a religious obligation to obey the secular law. St Thomas Aquinas states that human law ought to be obeyed unless it contravened natural law, and even then it was generally right to obey 'to avoid scandal'. Bentham, who rejected natural law and advocated that all law should be subject to criticism by reference to the standard of utility, recommended the following maxim: 'Obey punctually, censor freely.'

Yet, if you look around you, you find people of impeccable character who break the law and see nothing morally objectionable in so doing. An acquaintance of mine tells me that he drives to work every day in excess of the speed limit; it does no one any harm, and he'd never be on time if he did not. People I know, of the highest respectability, enter into informal transactions with builders and decorators on a cash basis, so as to avoid the value added tax which they are legally obliged to pay, and see nothing wrong with it. And, of course, radical critics of our political and legal institutions see nothing morally objectionable in breaking the law; it may be 'imprudent', but never 'wrong', to defy the establishment by flouting its laws. On the other hand, the same critics will be heard condemning official acts, or the actions of employers, on the specific ground that what they do is 'illegal' and therefore 'wrong'.

If someone affirms that there is a moral duty to obey the law, or implies that there is by the nature of the criticisms he makes of others, but at the same time breaks the law and sees nothing wrong with it, is he a hypocrite? Some believers in the duty might say this, or, more charitably, that he has made a mistake about the moral position in his own case which reflection and discussion might correct. If he dwells on the advantages which we all derive from legal institutions, he will come to understand the importance of cooperation and setting a good example. In this way moral education will at last lead him to realise that it is wrong (and not just illegal) to break traffic and tax laws.

But nowadays there are writers who take an opposite view. Our good citizen – be he supporter of the establishment or radical critic – is not mistaken when he says that there is nothing wrong with breaking the law. There is nothing wrong with it – not, at least, just because the law is broken. The only mistake lies in the belief that there is ever any moral duty to obey the law as such. The root cause of this mistake is a failure, so it is argued, to distinguish the act from its legal quality. Of course, there are good moral reasons against many acts which also happen to be illegal – like murder or theft – but it is not because they are illegal that we are morally obliged to abstain from them.

To assert that there is a moral duty to obey the law means affirming that there are moral grounds why one ought to perform any act which the law prescribes or abstains from any act which the law prohibits. Affirming this proposition leaves open the question whether the duty is absolute or qualified in some way. There are probably few people who would support the duty in its absolute form – that is, assert that the moral reasons for obeying the law could never be outweighed by moral reasons pointing towards disobedience. It is implausible to attribute to Socrates or St Paul the view that an ordinance of the state flatly contrary to one's religious duty should be complied with. St Thomas was explicit on the point. Democratic politicians would allow that it might be right to disobey the laws of undemocratic regimes, and probably also that protest against unjust laws of democratic regimes can sometimes legitimately include some kinds of lawbreaking. So the real issue is whether there is or is not a prima facie duty to obey. If I have in my left hand a book of Jubbjubb etiquette – something totally unknown to you – and in my right hand a book of your country's law, and I announce that I am going to open each at random, will you allow that there are moral reasons indicating obedience to whatever comes out of my right hand which plainly do not obtain in the case of the left-hand book? Or is your conscience equipoised between the two books – that is, until you hear the prescription read out, there is no way of knowing whether there will be moral reasons to comply? And remember: the question is not just one of probabilities. You might allow that, given your previous acquaintance with English law, there is more than a fifty-fifty chance that something required by it is something which there are moral grounds for performing. That is not enough. For one to be able to affirm that a prima facie moral duty to obey English law exists, one must be satisfied that, whatever comes out of the English law book, there are reasons (stateable in advance) why it is morally right to comply – albeit that, once the prescription is known, other moral reasons may tell against.

Arguments of five sorts are typically in play when this issue is debated. The first, generally wielded only by speculative theorists, is conceptual in nature. It suggests that, given that what we are talking about really is 'law', it would be some kind of contradiction to deny that it is 'binding' or 'valid'. The other four seek to establish that the duty exists by relating it to other moral concepts, whose existence as part of critical morality is assumed – the moral concepts in question being gratitude, promise-keeping, fairness, and the promotion of the collective good. Arguments two to five can carry nothing for one who denies moral status to any of these four concepts.

The conceptual argument has been advanced, in different ways, by adherents of some kinds of natural law doctrine and by formalist-positivists. If positive enactments contrary to natural law are not 'law' at all – because not morally binding and therefore not 'valid' law – then, by definition, everything which is valid law is binding (see chapter 2, above). Among positivists, Kelsen asserted that, the citizen who interprets the prescriptions of those who monopolise force in a territory as 'valid law', thereby attributes bindingness to the whole system (see chapter 6, above). A technical point might be made about such conceptual arguments, suggesting that they do not seek to establish a duty to obey the law as such. They equate the quality 'legal' with the quality 'binding' ('valid'); the quality of 'you ought to obey' is somehow inherent in true law. This, it might be argued, is not the same thing as providing an extra-legal platform on which a distinct duty, directed towards the law, can be stood – contrast the four succeeding arguments. But this is a distinction which merely points out that the argument is conceptual, not one based on substantive moral criteria. If it is true, as the natural lawyers and Kelsen argue, that all 'law' has an inherent ought-to-be-fulfilledness about it, then, once we acknowledge that an act is illegal, we have recognised that we ought not to do it.

Many will find this kind of conceptual argument unhelpful, as not speaking to the discriminations which daily life presents. In the everyday case of the tax or traffic law, the citizen has no difficulty in recognising what the law is, but he may still be perturbed as to the moral issue of compliance. So, for him, any theory which says that: if it really is law, it ought to be obeyed – will be unhelpful. Such a theory either defines law in some way inept for his problems, or it excludes moral debate by *fiat*.

The appeal to gratitude is conservative or romantic. Your country and its laws have conferred great benefits on you. The least you can do is to obey all its laws, unless some good ground for not doing so can be shown. As to this, it may be argued in reply that the concept of gratitude, as ordinarily understood, does not carry us so far. One may be grateful to one's parents, and obligations of many kinds may be said to flow from such gratitude – but not the obligation to do everything they tell you to do, nor even to give reasons why you should not do what they say. Even supposing one accepts that there is a prima facie duty to obey a benevolent parent – that is, to comply with his directions unless some countervailing reason exists – the relationship to legal authorities is different. Gratitude to them, if such there be, is more like the gratitude we owe to a friend who has conferred a favour in the course of a cooperative relationship. Certainly, we should do as much for him, but there is no question of taking his orders even as a prima facie moral guide.

The argument from promise-keeping is as old as the concept of the social contract, which for something over three hundred years has been toted about in political philosophy. Men who enter into a political compact with a government promise obedience in exchange for protection and other benefits – figuratively speaking. Anyone receiving the benefits commits himself to this social contract, and so impliedly promises obedience. Variants of this argument allege that anyone who takes part in democratic processes, for instance by voting, impliedly promises to obey the law. Granted that promise-keeping, in the absence of good reasons to the contrary, is morally required, it follows that obedience to the law is morally required.

The most sophisticated version of the social contract in modern political philosophy is contained in John Rawls' theory of justice, discussed in chapter 20, below. As we shall see, Rawls argues that a society is just if it is governed by principles which people would have agreed to in a state of ignorance about their particular position in society. Where a society is just or nearly just by this test there is, he says, a 'natural duty' of all citizens to support and further just institutions. This natural duty includes doing what is required of one by society's institutions, including the law. The duty exists independently of any actual promise to obey because, behind the veil of ignorance about their own situation, people would have agreed to it. So long as the basic structure of society is reasonably just, the duty extends to obeying unjust particular laws – provided they do not exceed certain limits of injustice, such as by making unjust demands only of a particular group or by denying basic liberties. When these limits are exceeded, conscientious refusal to obey the particular law is justified; and, in the case of blatant injustice, 'civil disobedience' of it or other laws may be warranted. Civil disobedience is a public, non-violent act aimed at bringing about a change in the law or the policies of the government. Unlike 'conscientious refusal', civil disobedience may warrant breaking laws which are not themselves unjust in order to draw attention to those which are.

Opponents of such lines of argument usually point to the simple 'fact' that receiving benefits, or voting, or getting the social set-up you would have agreed to in advance of knowledge of your position, are not equivalent to promising to obey. If you join a club and promise to observe the rules, you are acting wrongly, prima facie, if you break them. But a state organised under law is not like a club. We have no choice about belonging. In this context, there may be a difference between ordinary citizens and persons exercising official roles. If we accept that nothing a citizen does, and nothing that happens to him, is equivalent to a promise to obey the law, we might wish to distinguish the case of someone taking up a position as a judge or a minister or a town councillor or a policeman. Perhaps, given the nature of their legally-defined roles, taking up office is for them equivalent to a promise to obey all the laws – or, at any rate, all the laws directed to them in their official capacity. Rawls argues that, quite apart from the natural duty of citizens to obey the laws of a reasonably just society, officials have a special 'obligation' to do so. All obligations arise from[1] the 'principle of fairness', which is a distinct principle to which people would have agreed from behind the veil of ignorance.

> '[T]his principle holds that a person is under an obligation to do his part as specified by the rules of an institution whenever he has voluntarily accepted the benefits of the scheme or has taken advantage of the opportunities it offers to advance his interests, provided that this institution is just or fair.'[1]

Some may find a principle of fairness of this sort acceptable, independently of the contractarian basis Rawls offers for it, and might wish to extend it to all citizens. For them, 'fairness' would be a moral ground for the duty to obey the law, distinct from promise-keeping. Society may not be like a club in the sense of an association people join voluntarily, but it could be argued that a comparatively beneficent state has other qualities of non-political associations: it confers benefits and, in order to do so, imposes burdens. Those who support the closed shop in industry – that is, compulsory union membership for all employees – often do so on the ground that it would be unfair if people took the benefits of higher wages and improved conditions negotiated by the union without paying subscriptions. The argument is not that they ought to pay because they have promised to, but that they ought to promise to pay because it would be unfair if they did not. Similarly, some would argue, you ought not to take the benefit of a well-managed traffic system, or the benefits derived from tax expenditure, without submitting to the laws. You have a duty to obey the law, not because of anything you owe the government, but

1 *A Theory of Justice* p. 342.

because of something you owe your fellow citizens. If they all comply and you benefit, it is unfair if you benefit without complying.

To this argument, various sorts of answers are possible. An anarchist would, of course, deny that the legal institutions confer any benefit at all. Those who regard the state's institutions (at least in a democracy) as on the whole beneficial, counter the argument of fairness by pointing out that it cannot apply where submitting to a legal restraint in fact does no one any good. If I am driving along a deserted road, how can it be unfair in me to exceed the speed limit, even if I know that other people have regularly observed it? What one makes of this sort of example depends on how typical one thinks it is. If it is commonly the case that occasions of law-compliance benefit no one, then the analogy with the 'fairness' implications of day-to-day cooperative transactions breaks down. If, on the other hand, one supposes that compliance with the law usually confers some benefit, even if the benefit is not immediately obvious to the actor, then one can make out a case for saying that fairness requires that you obey the law (whatever it is) unless on the particular facts its total uselessness is made evident. You have to be satisfied of two things before a prima facie duty to obey the law can be said to be founded on the moral concept of fairness: first, that laws have generally beneficial effects; second, that most other people obey, so that you would be taking an unfair advantage if you do not. Just as, in the closed shop case, for the fairness argument to be appropriate – and there too, as with the law, it might be outweighed – you have to be satisfied, first, that the union does confer benefits, and second, that all other employees (or the great majority) are paying their subscriptions. It is rumoured that there are industries in which theft of material by workers, or misappropriation of resources for private purposes by managers, is so common that such conduct is no longer thought of as 'wrong'. If that is true, it might well be that someone whose conventional law-breaking actions are challenged on moral grounds would say: 'but everybody does it'. That would presuppose a fairness justification for a moral obligation to obey the law.

Perhaps the commonest justification for the duty to obey the law is appeal to the public good. If people break the law, the collective welfare of society is diminished: therefore, we are morally obliged to obey. In the parlance of moral philosophy, such arguments are called 'utilitarian', and their soundness is often challenged. It is not difficult for critics of the argument to think of examples where (on the face of it) total welfare would be diminished rather than increased by obedience to law. The law requires everyone to declare every item of income in his tax return. Supposing a man has received a small payment from a friend for performing some minor service, such as mowing a lawn or decorating a house. (Suppose also that he knows that most people do not declare such income, so that no argument of fairness would be relevant.) How is the public good affected if he breaks the law by omitting this item from his tax return? If he did comply, a little more tax would be collected from him by the authorities, and incremental benefits flowing from expenditure of state revenue would accrue. But against that would have to be set the disadvantage to himself and his family of having to forego the money collected – this, like all consequences to individuals, is a relevant consideration for the purpose of a utilitarian calculus in a way in which it is not for a fairness argument. He might claim that the loss to him and his family would outweigh any trivial benefit to others; and he could certainly make out this claim if he could show that the increase in administration costs required by collecting the extra sum would actually swallow up the addition to the state's revenue.

Those defending a utilitarian basis for the duty to obey the law may challenge this sort of hypothetical case on the ground that it naively limits those consequences which have to be taken into account. In particular, it ignores the effects of bad example. Even if my law-breaking directly does more good than harm, indirectly the reverse may be true because, following this example, others may break the law in circumstances where manifest harm is done, or I myself, on other occasions, may follow my own bad example with bad effects on the public good. *Ex hypothesi*, the man concealing the extra income will not produce bad consequences by way of bad example in the particular context of tax evasion, because I have assumed that he knows that most other people already cheat in this way. But his impressionable children, for instance, may get the idea that you need not obey the law where your own resulting loss will be greater than any tangible benefit to others. Dad will have explained that point when filling in his tax return last night, and so today they will shop-lift from large stores, calculating (perhaps mistakenly) that their gains will be greater than the losses to the company which owns the store. (If they were familiar with the terminology of theoretical economics, they would base such a view on 'marginal utility'. They would point out that, given their comparative poverty and the comparative wealth of the company, the next pound gained by them has more value than the next pound lost by the company.)

The argument from bad example attempts to justify the duty to obey the law on the basis of what is known as 'act-utilitarianism'. An act is morally wrong if it will have worse consequences than some other act open to the actor on the occasion. The argument suggests that an act of law-breaking is wrong by this test because its consequences include imitation in the way of further law-breaking, and some of the further acts of law-breaking will have bad consequences. Its plausibility depends on one's assessment of the generalisability of the effects of 'law-breaking' as a class of activities. If one takes the view that breaking some kinds of laws in no way leads, through bad example, to breaking other kinds of laws, this argument cannot found a duty to obey the law as such.

Sometimes consequentialist arguments for a duty to obey the law are stated in a particular form which makes it easy for the moral philosopher to shoot them down, as when someone says: 'You shouldn't evade your taxes, for what would happen if everybody did it?' To this the moral philosopher can answer that the wrongness of an action can never be established merely by pointing out that, if everyone did it, the consequences would be bad: if everyone caught the 9 a.m. train to Paddington tomorrow, there would be chaos; but that does not show that my catching it is in any way morally questionable. This misses the difficult but crucially important question, which is whether law-breaking is potentially imitative behaviour, in a way which train-catching is not. The argument should not be stated: 'What if everyone did it?' but: 'Other people will do it if you do.' This is an empirical proposition, whose truth cannot be tested in the philosopher's armchair. Is it in fact plausible?

Everyone would agree that some acts of law-breaking have bad effects on the collective welfare (whether through imitation of bad examples or otherwise), and that some do not – like the lone car driver exceeding the speed limit on the deserted road. It could be argued that everything turns on the particular situation, so that, before I open the law book, there is no way of knowing whether it will be right or wrong to obey any particular prescription; therefore, there is no prima facie duty to obey the law as such. To this it might be answered that, in many cases, it will be impracticable for the actor to assess the consequences of obedience or disobedience, that the consequences of disobedience are usually worse than the consequences of obedience, and that therefore one ought to obey the law (whatever it says) unless the consequences of doing so can be proved to be harmful. One's judgment on the question must turn on one's impression of whether consequences of law-breaking are or are not easily assessable at the moment when the issue of obedience or disobedience arises.

The other typical form of utilitarian argument is 'rule-utilitarianism': an action is right if required by a rule, where general observance of the rule would have best consequences. The difficulty with this kind of argument in the particular context of obedience to law is that it is hard to exhaust all possible formulations of rules about obedience in order to compare their respective consequences. Clearly, a rule that one should always obey will have better consequences than a rule that one should always disobey – the latter rule would be too onerous even for the most dedicated rebel, for one could not move about without being morally obliged constantly to smash things, hit people and break contracts. However, a rule requiring one to obey (with certain exceptions) would probably have better consequences than a rule requiring one always to obey. The problem is to formulate all the exceptions. They would presumably relate to occasions on which law-breaking did no harm, either directly, or indirectly through setting bad examples. In other words, on the issue of obeying the law, there are no considerations relevant to rule-utilitarianism which are not involved in a discussion of act-utilitarianism. The important points concern the actual consequences of obedience or disobedience to different kinds of laws, whether influence through bad example is a plausible source of consequences, and whether assessment of consequences is likely to be so impracticable that one ought to assume a moral presumption in favour of obeying the law.

Bibliography

Dworkin R. M.	*Taking Rights Seriously* (revised edn, 1978) chs 7–8
Fortas A.	*Discerning Dissent and Civil Disobedience* (1968)
Hart H. L. A.	'Are There Any Natural Rights?' in Quinton (ed) *Political Philosophy* (1967)
Hook S. (ed)	*Law and Philosophy* (1964) Pt 1
Kant I.	*The Philosophy of Law* (Hastie trans, 1887) pp. 255–258
Kelsen H.	'Why Should the Law be Obeyed?' in *What is Justice?* (1957)
Pennock J. R. and Chapman J. W. (eds)	*Political and Legal Obligation* (1970)
Pitkin H.	'Obligation and Consent' in Laslett, Runciman and Skinner (eds) *Philosophy, Politics and Society* (4th series, 1972)
Puna N. W.	'Civil Disobedience: an Analysis and Rationale' (1968) 43 NY U L Rev 651
Rawls J.	*A Theory of Justice* (1972) pp. 350–356, 363–391
Raz J.	*The Authority of Law* (1979) Pt 4
Ruben D. H.	'Positive and Natural Law Revisited' (1972) 49 Mod Sch 295
Sartorius R. E.	*Individual Conduct and Social Norms* (1975) ch 6
Singer P.	*Democracy and Disobedience* (1973)
Smith J. C.	*Legal Obligation* (1976) ch 5

Smith M. B. E.	'Is There a Prima Facie Obligation to Obey the Law?' (1973) 82 Yale LJ 950
Tussman J.	*Obligation and the Body Politic* (1960)
Walzer M.	*Obligations* (1970) chs 2, 6, 8–10
Wasserstrom R. A.	'The Obligation to Obey the Law' in Summers (ed) *Essays in Legal Philosophy* (1968)
Williamson H.	'Some Implications of Acceptance of Law as a Rule Structure' (1967) 3 Ad L Rev 18
Zinn H.	*Disobedience and Democracy* (1968)
Zwiebach B.	*Civility and Disobedience* (1975)

17   The historical school and non-state law

Jurisprudential controversies about the nature of law commonly assume, expressly or tacitly, that the law we are talking about is the law of the modern state. Is that not perhaps too parochial? Should we not be careful to ensure that our conception of law is wide enough to encompass the 'law' under which man lived before the modern state evolved, as well as the 'primitive law' of non-state communities? Besides these, are there not other systems of non-state 'law' for which our conception must account, such as the laws of churches, universities, clubs and, above all, public international law and other supra-state international legal orders?

The literature of jurisprudence speaks of a movement of thought amongst legal theorists of the nineteenth century as the 'historical school'. The members of this school, like the legal positivists, rejected natural law, but not for the same reasons. They agreed with the positivists that law was not discoverable by abstract reason, but they did not accept that it was the product of deliberate choice. Law was the outcome of historical processes, and could only be understood in their light.

Membership of this school is usually said to include German 'romantic' writers, like C. von Savigny (1779–1861), on the one hand, and Sir Henry Maine (1822–1888), on the other. In fact, Savigny and Maine had little in common, beyond the view that history matters in our understanding of what law now is. There is, of course, nothing unusual in those who agree that we should learn lessons from the past finding that they have quite different views of the lessons it teaches.

The central tenet of the German romantic school was that law resides in the spirit of the people, the *volksgeist*. It was an error to suppose that a legislator stood above the community and imposed his will. He was an organ of the people, giving effect to its intuitions. This entailed that law both did and should vary from one country to another, since different peoples had different spirits. The romantics resisted – ultimately without success – the move towards codification on the model of the *Code Napoléon*. For them, the idea of a code based

219

rationalistically upon universal features of human nature contra-
dicted the lesson of history, that a people's law resides in its own
peculiar customs. Their treatises are seldom cited today in connection
with the problems which preoccupy modern jurisprudence, such as
the controversy between positivist and non-positivist conceptions of
law, the nature of legal reasoning, the relations between law and
morals, the proper attitude for citizens to take to the law's claims and
the respective roles of legislature and judiciary. But two of their
underlying contentions still matter. First, if they were right, then both
'higher law' theorists and Benthamite utilitarians are wrong when
they claim that good law is everywhere the same; and comparative
lawyers should not assume that legal systems can learn from each
other. Secondly, they provide one reason for revering customary law.
As we shall see in chapter 19, below, there are social theorists who
value customary law because it contributes to 'community'. The
historical romantics valued it because it expresses national
uniqueness.

The romanticism of the German historical school should be
contrasted with the contemporary historicism of G. W. F. Hegel
(1770–1831). The romantics were backward-looking, seeking the true
roots of a people's law. Hegelian idealism is forward-looking,
prophesying the inexorable realisation of the spirit of history until
true justice (as embodied in the modern state) is achieved. As we shall
see in chapter 19, below, this prophetic historicism was taken over
and given a materialist interpretation in Marxist theory.

Many of the romantics stressed specifically Germanic features of
the law. Savigny, however, was both a historical romantic and a
Romanist. He traced the historical unfolding of German law back to
its sources in the *Corpus Juris* of Justinian. Many critics see this as a
paradox. If the universal source of law is custom, why focus our
interest upon those Roman texts which continental lawyers had
received in displacement of local custom? Savigny's answer is that
jurists are another organ of popular consciousness, alongside the
legislature. In expounding legal science, they are articulating the
volksgeist.

A less dramatic version of this seeming paradox, and its alleged
resolution, infuses debates about the value of the common law. It is
less dramatic, because England never experienced a wholesale
reception of a foreign system, requiring to be explained or explained
away. (It may be otherwise with former parts of the British Empire
which have received segments of the common law in displacement of
earlier law.) The common law is sometimes referred to – for instance,
by Blackstone – as the general custom of the realm. A romantic
outlook contrasts legislation with the common law: whereas the

former is produced by the parliamentary majority of the moment, the latter has evolved from the peculiar genius of the English people. On the other hand, its content can be discovered only by what Coke called 'the artificial reason of the law'. Thus, the common law is at once the product of the people and a technical achievement of lawyers. For a Bentham, this is a confidence trick. For an English Savignyan, there is no contradiction. Law is not, or should not be, what rationalistic bureaucrats conceive to be for our good. It should express the people's peculiar intuitions and needs; and, in so far as law must deal with technical matters on which overt consciousness is silent, the proper agent for the spirit of the people is legal science.

For Sir Henry Maine, the significance of history was the light it shed, not so much upon the nature of law, as upon its content. It was a mistake, he urged, to take the legal provisions in force at any time and to explain them in terms of some rationally coherent set of aims and functions. The law always contains deposits of institutions, principles and distinctions which reflect ideas of earlier ages. We may think we have wills and testaments because of the function they serve, in allowing people to determine how their property is to be distributed on death. The truth is that we have wills because we inherited this device from Rome, and historical research reveals that the Romans originally saw them as conveyances to heirs; like the fiction of adoption, these conveyances had as their object the continuance of the family, not satisfaction of property control from the grave. The principle of primogeniture was usually explained in feudal-functional terms – it kept the land together and so was a source of strength. But that, argued Maine, was only part of the story. Why was this particular device chosen? The answer, he suggests – with rather more speculation than evidence – was that the Germanic tribes who invaded the Roman empire carried with them memories of an ancient form of family government in which continuity was preserved through single chieftain heads. An idea which was, in its distant origins, concerned with devolution of responsibilities was thereafter impressed with Roman conceptions of absolute property. Maine noted the difficulty Blackstone had experienced in rationalising the common law rule which prohibited brothers of the half blood from inheriting on intestacy. The explanation, he said, lay in an ancient conception of property devolving on death only to agnatic male kin. This would exclude sons of a common mother.

Whatever the truth of these particular contentions, no one today would quarrel with Maine's historical method as applied to particular provisions. Pollock, Maitland, Holmes, Pound and many others have demonstrated that a law which now serves one purpose arose originally to meet quite another. It is on the level of historical generalisation that Maine has come in for most criticism. In this regard, he put forward hypotheses about legal forms and the social forces producing legal change, as well as about content. As to form he appears to suggest a sixfold developmental thesis. In the infancy of law, there were kingly judgments supposed to be divinely inspired. Next comes custom. This is followed by the age of codes, like the twelve tables of ancient Rome. These three stages, Maine believed, were common to all the Indo-European races. Thereafter, some peoples, like those of India, cease to evolve new legal forms, whereas the 'progressive' peoples, like the Romans and the English, proceeded to three further stages: fictions, equity, and legislation. The social forces behind this development concern the emergence from an archaic type of society in which communities are based solely on kinship, through larger units consisting of collections of familial groups, to the modern state where community is founded on territorial contiguity.

It is not clear how rigidly sequential Maine supposed his six stages to be. He stresses that the earliest communities of which we have any knowledge regarded themselves as descended from a common stock even though they were aware that strangers had been introduced through the 'fiction' of adoption. This suggests that fictions need not come after codes. In any event, his sixfold classification of forms is difficult to accept without qualification. Homeric texts are not an adequate basis for suggesting that royal judgments precede the development of custom. The invention of writing did lead to codification in ancient Mesopotamia, but apparently not in ancient Egypt. As to the later stages, the remarkable parallel between 'fictional' devices employed by the Roman jurisconsuls and by common law courts, and between the establishment of a supplementary 'equitable' body of rules by the Praetorian edict and by English chancellors, has often been drawn. Are we entitled to regard this as a symptom of 'progress'?

On the level of legal content, Maine asserts that in early law most of a man's obligations were fixed from birth by his status. Through many gradual stages, and despite the law of any one time being encumbered with inherited archaic notions, modern law comes to regard a man's free choice as the chief source of his obligations. His most often quoted generalisation runs:

'All the forms of Status taken notice of in the Law of Persons were derived from, and to some extent are still coloured by, the powers and privileges anciently residing in the Family. If then we employ Status, agreeably with the usage of the best writers, to signify these personal conditions only, and avoid applying the term to such conditions as are the immediate or remote result of agreement, we may say that the movement of the progressive societies has hitherto been a movement from *Status to Contract*.'[1]

Critics of this formula have pointed out that, since Maine's day, the law has tended to attach rights and obligations much more to status than to contract: witness the statutory protected tenancy, which supervenes when a contractual tenancy is terminated; and the right not to be unfairly dismissed from employment even when the employer is not in breach of contract. To this it may be answered that Maine did say 'hitherto'. He may have been a believer in progress, but there is little indication that he believed in historical inevitability. Another type of criticism accuses him of paying too much attention to the form of the law, at least in his analysis of modern law. He had been at pains to suggest that ancient provisions were dictated by belief in kinship community, and how this was fostered by the fiction of adoption. Might it not be said that the contract of employment of his own day was a similar 'fiction', in that it stressed obligations flowing from free consent whereas economic reality and class status denied any true freedom?

Maine was no antiquarian, examining the past for its own sake. He believed that historical research could expose modern error. He argued that the belief in natural law had arisen historically from confusions in Roman thought. The *Ius Gentium*, which had been devised to deal with disputes involving foreign residents in Rome, had been worked out on the basis of elements common to Italian tribes. Later, under the influence of Greek philosophy, it had come to be identified with *naturalis ratio*. In particular, *occupatio*, as a means of acquiring property, was just one of the provisions of the *Ius Gentium*. Political philosophers who alleged that, in the state of nature, individuals made things their own by occupying what was previously owned by no one, were anti-historical. All the evidence pointed to common ownership as the oldest proprietary institution, and to long possession of what had belonged to another as the typical title. Similarly, social compact theories were anti-historical, since the very notion that men could acquire obligations by agreement alone was a late development. It is a controversial question whether historical information of this sort has a bearing on theories of justice which rely on a 'notional' state of nature or a 'notional' contract. As we shall see in chapter 20, below, Rawls' contractarian theory of justice requires no assumptions about any real contract. On the other hand, Nozick's entitlement theory of justice is avowedly historical, requiring that all

1 *Ancient Law* pp. 181–182.

'just' property-holdings should be derived from an original proprietor whose acquisition was just. Can that be squared with Maine's contention that private titles arise from trespass on the common domain? So far as natural law is concerned, does the fact that the Romans appealed to it to meet a certain historical contingency prove that it does not exist?

Nor was Maine a romantic. Legal forms and codes of thought of the past should be investigated, but not necessarily revered. Natural law theory had served a good turn, with its insistence on symmetry and generality, but we moderns could do without it. Fictions had been an intelligent device for combining necessary change with respect for the written word, but they could not be supported today. Maine objected to Bentham's lack of historical perspective, but he had no objection to proposals for codification based on rational calculation of needs. He rejected Blackstone's view that the common law was custom; it was, he said, just another, rather unwieldy form of written law.

Maine is perhaps most respected today for the impetus he gave to the study of contemporary primitive law. He applauded Montesquieu (1689–1755) for having the right idea about explaining laws in terms of social forces, but complained at his lack of empirical research. Montesquieu's *L'Esprit des Droits* contained 'guesses' about the effect on the laws of different peoples of such matters as climate and racial characteristics. The thing to do (Maine said) was to look carefully at the records of ancient peoples, and also to investigate surviving communities still in a primitive stage of development. For Maine, the major source of information of this latter sort were the village communities of India. Since his time, anthropological research has accumulated information about a wide variety of pre-state communities. Generally, what Maine said about the importance of kinship groups and the absence of wholly executory contracts has been borne out. Not surprisingly, however, the content of the laws of primitive communities has been found to exhibit enormous variation, depending on the stage of development and the environmental conditions and economic mode of life.

What should the jurist ask of the anthropologist? Does the anthropologist have any obligation to deliver? The anthropologist investigates his chosen community in all its facets of life. Should he be hamstrung by a search for 'law'?

Perhaps the jurist can derive generalisations from the detailed information provided by anthropological research, about the contents of primitive law, or about the nature of primitive 'legal' institutions, or about the functions served by 'law' in primitive societies. We saw in chapter 2, above, that Hart was able to deduce a 'minimum content of natural law' from certain 'truisms' about man –

a society must have rules restricting force, theft and deception. Being 'necessary', such rules should appear in all societies, past, present and to come. It does, indeed, appear that there are such rules in all primitive societies; but there is no question of uniform provisions about these things. Homicide rules vary greatly. Because of their harsh conditions of life, Eskimo law, not merely permits, but requires suicide and senillicide in certain circumstances. 'Property', and so theft, exists everywhere in some form; but private property in land is rare, and modern conceptions of ownership – in the sense of an exclusive and unlimited right to do what one likes with one's own – is often absent (there may not even be a word for it). Although deception of some sort is proscribed, the law will not – as Maine pointed out – concern itself with all the forms of dishonesty which sophisticated institutions make possible.

Apart from filling in the details in Hart's list, does anthropological evidence add anything? Are there other types of rules which, though not necessary for all societies at all times, are universally found in primitive societies? E. A. Hoebel concludes from a survey of a wide variety of primitive societies that the one assumption of over-whelming importance underlying all primitive legal systems is the postulation of magico-religious forces as being superior to men; but there is no consistency as to whether magico-religious practices are permitted, required, or prohibited as the crime of 'sorcery'. He also says that primitive societies generally recognise the social inferiority of women and the relative exclusiveness of marital rights; but again, details vary. If Hoebel and Hart are right, early societies have rules 'about' the supernatural, sexual relations, violence, property and deceit; but developed societies could drop the first two.

The institutions employed in primitive legal systems vary also. The survey reported by R. D. Schwartz and J. S. Miller shows that they may use mediation, police and counsel, or some or none of these. They may even have 'courts', as does the Lozi society investigated by M. Gluckman.

Perhaps more illuminating generalisations will be discovered if we concentrate on functions, rather than content or institutions. Hoebel lists four functions which, he maintains, are served by the law of primitive man: defining relationships amongst the members of society; taming naked force and directing it to the maintenance of order; the disposition of trouble cases; and the redefinition of relationships as the conditions of life change. These may be contrasted with the wider range of functions which modern law is supposed to serve (see chapter 18, below). In connection with the fourth function, Hoebel criticises Maine's assumption about the static nature of customary law. It will be recalled that Hart, too, spoke of the static character of rules (owing to absence of rules of change) as one of the 'defects' of a 'pre-legal' society (see chapter 9, above). As we shall see in chapter 19, below, the social theorists' 'ideal type' of a customary society is one in which there is no perceived tension between what is practised and what is thought right, and no self-conscious creation of rules. It seems, however, that in many non-state societies people may recognise that a rule with a certain content exists and at the same time withhold moral approval from it; and may indeed, on occasion, make deliberate changes in their rules.

'Custom' is sometimes regarded as a separable topic in juris-prudence or legal theory, parallel to precedent or statutory interpretation. Such treatment is not to be recommended. Lawyers describing the contents of a modern legal system support their statements by reference to sources, one of which may be 'custom'. It is usually low down in the ranking of sources. English courts sometimes give effect to local customs, or to commercial customs. One is considering 'custom' in a quite different sense when it is urged that constitutional practices rest on custom. Then custom is not just another source, but the basis upon which some or all sources are fitted together. The most fundamental tenets of the United Kingdom constitution are, in this sense, 'customary'. Even where the consti-tution is written, it does not necessarily dictate the relationship between judge-made law and legislative enactments, nor indeed the criteria for the recognition of judge-made law. In the United States, for example, these vital matters rest on the practices of the courts and other officials. As we saw in chapters 12 and 13, above, canons of statutory interpretation and rules of precedent involve mixed questions of particular practices and analytic issues. Thirdly, as we saw in the discussion of Savigny's theory at the beginning of this chapter, 'custom' may be employed as an approbative juristic classification, as a 'hurrah' word. Then law is seen to be good so far as it truly reflects custom. Fourthly, when social theorists compare whole systems, describing some as systems of written law and others as systems of customary law, the topic of 'custom' is raised in yet another light. Finally, 'custom' may be appealed to as a ground for modifying the concept of law itself. To this issue we now turn.

A special battery of jurisprudential problems has been raised by attempts to include primitive law and public international law within, or exclude them from, an overall conception of law. Austin excluded them by defining law as the command of the sovereign (see chapter 3, above). Kelsen included them, by terming a victim's relatives and states 'organs', and blood revenge and war and reprisals 'sanctions' (see chapter 6, above). One view is that, so long as we have appraised our systems rightly and are aware of all the similarities and differences, how we choose to employ the label 'law' is a matter of small importance. What can be said on the other side? One ground for holding that labels do matter is frankly pedagogic: only if primitive law and international law are called 'law' will they get included within courses of instruction for law students. I doubt whether anyone recommending an inclusive concept would rest his case on this argument alone.

So far as primitive 'law' is concerned, the arguments for an inclusive concept of law are of two, totally incompatible kinds. The first holds that if we bring to bear on primitive societies some conception of law derived from our own society, we will learn more about them. The converse of this is that, if we mould a conception of law broad enough to encompass the ways in which primitive peoples themselves see their own social arrangements, we will learn more about ourselves. The first ('labels matter') line of argument calls for a discriminating concept of law to be used for slicing up the undif-ferentiated normative arrangements of primitive societies. Primitive communities generally have no specialist vocabulary for distin-guishing legal from non-legal rules in the way we do. As observers of them, we can bring out some crucial feature of their social life by applying some distinguishing characteristic of 'law'. For B. Malinowski, this distinguishing characteristic was reciprocity:

> 'The rules of law stand out from the rest in that they are felt and regarded as the obligations of one person and the rightful claims of another. They are sanctioned not by a mere psychological motive, but by a definite social machinery of binding force based as we know, upon mutual dependence, and realised in the equivalent arrangement of reciprocal services.'[2]

P. Bohannan criticises Malinowski's reciprocity criterion as being too undiscriminating between customary norms as a whole and law in particular. We should instead define law in terms of institutionalised customary norms. In the same vein, M. Gluckman isolated Lozi 'law' from Lozi custom and morality by reference to recognition by the judges. Of course, institutional criteria will not be of much assistance where the society in question lacks law-applying institutions. L. Pospisil suggests that primitive law can be isolated by reference to a cluster of differentiating criteria, such as authority, universality, the sense of obligation and sanctions. Depending on the extent to which these criteria were met in the disposal of disputes, the solution should be regarded as more or less 'legal'. Hoebel takes coercive enforcement to be the sole badge of law.

2 *Crime and Custom in Savage Society* p. 55.

'A social norm is legal if its neglect or infraction is regularly met, in threat or in fact, by the application of physical force by an individual or group possessing the socially recognized privilege of so acting.'[3]

Many anthropologists find that they can do their work perfectly well without any such discriminating concept of law. If the people being studied did not distinguish law from other customary norms, why should the observer? Indeed, insisting on fitting their rules into our preconceived pigeonholes, with all our inappropriate conceptual paraphanalia, may be distinctly unhelpful.

If the question were simply whether a concept of law helps or hinders the understanding of primitive communities, the issue would be entirely internal to anthropology. Nothing relevant to the concept of law appropriate to modern states could turn on it. At this point, however, we turn to the second and converse ('labels matter') argument. The argument runs: not only should we not try to distinguish legal from other social rules when studying primitive societies, it is a mistake to do so in our own society. This is a view which, as we shall see in chapter 18, below, is advocated by Ehrlich's sociology of law. The contention now under consideration regards the existence of primitive law as providing ammunition for the 'living law' approach. The call of the primitive is added to the call of the social.

M. Barkun argues that our 'common sense' notion of law is too professionally oriented. We need a conception of law which would apply to primitive law and to international law. Such a wider conception would provide us with a better picture of state law. He suggests that we should view law as a 'set of interrelated symbols', a 'means of conceptualising and managing the social environment'.

'The loci of power, the ties that persons and groups have with one another, the forces that deter and that attract decision-makers – all these are the "underground" questions of legal analysis ... If "legal system" is not limited to the parochial confines of courtrooms and law offices, it is – in the end – merely a product of its society.'[4]

I suggest the following exemplary proof as a test for the strength of this argument:

Demonstrandum: Social rules governing English family life are 'laws'.
(1) Any definition of law which cannot be applied, without distorting the subject, to primitive societies is parochial and unacceptable.

3 *The Law of Primitive Man* p. 28.
4 *Law Without Sanctions* p. 44. For a similar argument see Ehrlich (1922) 36 Harv L Rev 130; and Roberts *Order and Dispute*.

(2) Any definition of law which distinguishes among social rules (by reference to source, sanction, courts or any other criterion) results in distortion when applied to primitive societies.
(3) Any definition of law which distinguishes among social rules is parochial and unacceptable.
(4) All social rules are laws.
(5) Social rules governing English family life are laws.
   Q E D

Are you convinced?

International law, like primitive law, differs from state law in not possessing a legislature, and in the non-central significance of sanctions, and courts. Both may suffer distortion if definitions of law emphasising these features are applied to them. On the other hand, there is not the same distortion when state-law concepts, like right, duty, delict and property are applied. It may be true of many primitive societies that these words have no counterpart in the local language; but those who deal in international law have derived their vocabulary from municipal law contexts. Moreover, there are professional and normative arguments for calling international law 'law' which do not apply to primitive law.

International tribunals and government advisers have to use some term to distinguish the rules they wish to appeal to from other rules, such as those of 'comity' or 'policy'. They have to do that because 'legality', to put it at its lowest, plays a distinctive role in diplomatic exchange. Whereas, if some primitive societies successfully settle disputes without a clear-cut legal/non-legal distinction, why should they change? Colonial governments or their successors may wish to introduce the distinction with its accompanying battery of specifically legal concepts, but then that will bring the 'primitive law', in its undifferentiated condition, to an end.

Special normative claims also cluster round the law-label issue in the context of international law, which are not relevant to primitive law. They are connected with the rule-of-law ideal. One common reaction to international law is disappointment and frustration. Why should we call it 'law' when it does not bring us peace? The assumption is that law's supreme claim to respect is its shield against the chaos which Hobbes depicted in the state of nature where 'the life of man is solitary, poor, nasty, brutish and short'. To this it is answered that international law serves many of the other functions for which we value law – dispute-mediation, co-ordination of plans, and so forth. Further, it is argued, teach our leaders and their servants to think of international law as 'law', and the world will be a better place. Many of the arguments which we considered in chapter 11, above, for the view that 'principles of legality' have to be observed for law to work apply equally to international law. The same, as we saw, can be said of other non-state systems which do not have the special virtue of bringing peace, such as the 'laws' of churches, universities and clubs.

If we believe that there is a moral duty to obey the law – or at any rate that officials are so obligated (see chapter 16, above) – we may wish to argue that the same applies to international law. On the other hand, we may take the view that this crucial aspect of the rule-of-law ideal – compliance with declared rules by officials – has value only in the municipal context. When, in 1968, Sir Harold Wilson ordered the bombing of the stranded oil tanker, the *Torrey Canyon,* he justified the action as essential to prevent disastrous pollution, and indicated that the question of its international legality was a minor matter. When, in 1979, President Giscard D'Estaing justified breach of the law of the European Economic Community in relation to importing British lamb, he appealed to urgent French interests. Neither man would advocate breaking municipal law in pursuit of government policy, would they?

Bibliography

Allen C. K.	*Law in the Making* (7th edn, 1964) pp. 87–129
Barkum M.	*Law Without Sanctions* (1968)
Bohannan P.	'The Differing Realms of the Law' (1965) 67 Am Anth 33
Campbell A. H.	'International Law and the Student of Jurisprudence' (1950) 35 GST 113
Carter J. C.	*Law: its Origin, Growth and Function* (1907)
Diamond A. S.	*Primitive Law, Past and Present* (2nd edn. 1971)
Ehrlich E.	'The Sociology of Law' (1922) 36 Harv L Rev 130
Friedmann W.	*Legal Theory* (5th edn, 1967) chs 18–19
Fuller L. L.	*Anatomy of the Law* (1971) pp. 71–82
Gluckman M.	*The Judicial Process Among the Barotse of Northern Rhodesia* (2nd edn, 1967)
Hoebel E. A.	*The Law of Primitive Man* (1954)
Jones J. W.	*Historical Introduction to the Theory of Law* (1956) ch 2
Kantorowicz H. U.	'Savigny and the Historical School of Law' (1937) 53 LQR 326
Llewellyn K. N. and Hoebel E. A.	*The Cheyenne Way* (1941)
Lloyd D.	*Introduction to Jurisprudence* (4th edn, 1979) ch 9

MacCormack G.   'Professor Gluckman's Contribution to Legal
                     Theory' (1976) Jur Rev 229
Maine H. J. S.   *Ancient Law* (Pollock edn, 1930)
Malinowski B.   *Crime and Custom in Savage Society* (1932)
Patterson E. W.   'Historical and Revolutionary Theories of
                     Law' (1951) 51 Colum L Rev 681
Pospisil L.   *Anthropology of Law* (1971)
Pound R.   'Law in Books and Law in Action' (1910) Am
                     L Rev 12
Roberts S.   *Order and Dispute* (1979)
Robson W. A.   'Sir Henry Maine To-day' in Jennings (ed)
                     Modern Theories of Law (1933)
Savigny F. C. von   *On the Vocation of our Age for Legislation and
                     Jurisprudence* (2nd edn, Hayward trans, 1831)
                     System of the Modern Roman Law (Rattigan
                     trans, 1884) ss. 7–16
Schapera I.   'Malinowski's Theories of Law' in Firth (ed)
                     Man and Culture (1957)
Schwarz R. D. and
Miller J. S.   Legal Evolution and Societal Complexity' in
                     Schwarz and Skolnick (eds) *Society and the
                     Legal Order* (1970)
Twining W.   *Karl Llewellyn and the Realist Movement* (1973)
                     ch 8
Walton F. P.   'The Historical School of Jurisprudence and
                     Transplantation of Law' (1927) 9 JCL (3rd
                     series) 183
Williams G. L.   'International Law and the Controversy
                     Concerning the Word "Law"' in Laslett (ed)
                     Philosophy, Politics and Society (1956)

18   Sociological jurisprudence

'Law is a social phenomenon.' That is the universal cry of progressive law schools. But what precisely does it mean? Against what view of law is it directed? To what new vision is it a banner? The sociological approach to law is generally contrasted with the analytic. Yet analytical jurists purport to convey sociological information. Austin tells us that in every political society there is some sovereign person or body who receives habitual obedience and renders it to none. Kelsen says that in all societies lawyers make systematic descriptions of norms which are by and large effectively enforced. Hart explains what sorts of practices and attitudes are involved when a society lives by rules – and, indeed, describes his book as 'an essay in descriptive sociology'. Would any of these authors, if pressed to give a yes/no answer, deny that law is a social phenomenon?

The quarrel of sociological jurists with the analytical school is not so much that the latter's sociological assumptions are wrong – for after all, they disagreed with each other. It is the use they made of concepts drawn from the law itself in setting down information about society. There was too much talk about legal rights, duties, powers, property, persons and so forth. We should instead employ societal concepts, like interest, function, role, group and class. This will enable us to make the crucial break with the professional lawyer's view of law.

'Legal sociology' is a burgeoning research enterprise. As its practitioners are the first to admit, however, there is as yet little agreement about its proper subject matter. Just as general jurisprudence embraces debates about the nature of 'law' when it is the subject of legal science – what do lawyers mean by 'law'? – so it should concern itself with 'law' as the subject of legal sociology – what do sociologists of law mean by 'law'? There are two broad questions: What is the proper business of the sociology of law? and Does a sociological approach lead to a vision of law which is in some way better than that provided by other schools?

As things are, works proclaiming their concern with the social aspects of law lie across a spectrum from the law-out-to-society end, to the society-into-law end. At the nearer end, the researcher takes

232

legal materials or legal institutions – identified by a legal-positivist criterion – and asks what are their social implications, effects or causes. He might find, for instance, that some rule of contract law to be found in the books has precious little influence on the way businessmen actually arrange their affairs; or that the moral implications of 'fault' in the law of tort do not correlate with community attitudes; or that statutory rights to welfare benefits or to legal aid are taken up more by some social classes than by others; or that an attempt to compromise a clash between certain interest-groups is the historical explanation for the passing of a certain Act; or that what directs the exercise by the Lord Chancellor of his powers to nominate judges is an old-boy network. Detailed studies of this kind are commonly called 'socio-legal research', and generalisations from them 'sociological jurisprudence'. Yet such research turns out not to presuppose any concept of law different from that investigated in analytical jurisprudence. It requires that we identify 'law' just as lawyers do; but then we move out to society. Nonetheless, accurate generalisations which this 'moving out' provides might supplement or correct the sort of sociological information which analytical jurists provide.

The writers dealt with in the next two sections, on interests and functions, have been close to this end of the spectrum. So too, in practice, has most of the research carried out in the name of 'realism'. At the mid-point of the spectrum comes the view that we need to set alongside a conception of law as something contained in books a quite different conception of law, as a spontaneous social product. To this we turn in the third section, under the heading of 'living law'. At the further end of the spectrum, there are social theorists for whom conceptions of law must be subsumed under conceptions of society. For them, you cannot define law without a social theory which defines society. Some of these writers are discussed in the next chapter. Speculations from the mid-point to the further end of the spectrum are often termed 'the sociology of law', in contrast to 'sociological jurisprudence'. But there exists no uniformity in the use of such expressions.

As to the first of the two broad questions – what is the proper business of the sociology of law? – controversies within theoretical sociology have to be taken on board. In particular, should a socio-logical study of law be value-free and 'positivistic', as D. Black argues? Or should it – as writers like P. Selznick and P. Nonet maintain – elucidate the working of the law in terms of social ideals? ('Positivism', for sociologists, is not the same thing as 'positivism' for legal theorists; it refers to the view that social phenomena can be causally explained, as natural phenomena are causally explained in

234 Sociological jurisprudence

the natural sciences.) Legal sociology also has its own peculiar methodological problems. Should our focus be the behaviour patterns of governmental officials, or wider behaviour patterns? Or should it be, not behaviour at all, but abstract legal rules and principles?

As to the second broad question – does a sociological approach yield a better vision of law? – there appears to be an aspiration towards a sociological conception of law which would transcend or replace conceptions arrived at in the analytic mode: an aspiration which, as yet, no one has fulfilled. At any rate, competing analytical conceptions of law may be tested in the light of the demands of legal sociology – or so I have argued in the context of the 'problem of structure' (see *Law and Legal Science*). One of the reasons for defining law may be that we want to isolate a phenomenon about which we can then raise empirical questions.

1 Social interests

The phrase 'sociological jurisprudence' is most often associated with the work of the prolific American jurist, Roscoe Pound (1870–1964). He gave this label to the new approach to legal studies which, he said, was the culmination of the legal philosophy of the past. In 1912, he set down a six-point programme for sociological jurists. First, study of the actual effects of legal institutions and legal doctrine. Second, sociological study in preparation for legislation – particularly, the effects of comparative legislation. Third, study of the means of making legal rules effective: 'The life of the law is in its enforcement.' Fourth, a 'sociological legal history', which would consider what effects legal doctrines had had in the past. Fifth, advocacy of reasonable and just solutions of individual cases, too often sacrificed in the name of certainty. Sixth, making effort more effective in achieving the purpose of law.[1]

This mixture of rather vague methodological and normative precepts is all too typical of Pound's writings. His work comprises a massive survey of legal philosophy, researches into legal history and discourses on particular legal problems. It is collated in the five volumes of his *Jurisprudence*, published in 1959, but the principal themes were laid down in the early years of the century. He can be regarded as an advocate for socio-legal studies, although researchers in this field are unlikely to derive much nourishment from his writing. They are interested in problems like devising efficient questionnaires and statistical techniques, not in the comparative history of juristic speculation. So far as his own contribution to theory is concerned, the

1 (1912) 25 Harv L Rev 489 at 514–516.

focal points for Pound are 'legal interests' and 'jural postulates', ideas which he derived respectively from R. von Jhering and J. Kohler.

The sociological jurist should engage in a survey of 'social interests', that is, of those 'claims or demands or desires' which have pressed or are pressing for legal recognition. He should distinguish 'individual interests', which are asserted in the title of individual life; 'public interests', which are asserted in the title of politically organised society; and 'social interests', which are asserted in the title of social life. It is a matter of controversy whether Pound conceived of these three types as different entities or as different levels of generality for the same entity. At any rate, he indicates that, when we are considering whether some interest ought to be preferred to some other, they must be weighed on the same plane (generally the social plane). Our appraisal will be distorted if we conceive of a clash as one between an individual interest and a social interest. Consequently, individual interests should be subsumed under broader social interests for the purposes of comparative evaluation. Social interests include: first, general security in safety, health, peace and public order, acquisitions, and transactions; second, security of social institutions – family, religious, political, and economic; third, general morals; fourth, conservation of social resources; fifth, general progress – economic, political, and cultural; sixth ('and most important'), the social interest in individual life – that each individual be able to live a human life according to the standards of the society.[2]

Thus, the sociological jurist, unlike the traditional legal scientist, is not to engage in logical reconstruction of the meaning expressed by legal texts, but is to survey and classify social interests to which those texts do, or should, give effect. But his source of information about claims, demands and desires is still lawbook-bound. The most he looks at, apart from statutes and reported judgments, are claims which the courts have rejected, and possibly proposals for legislative reform. Pound rejects the idea of a Benthamite felicific calculus – a survey of all human needs measured by an objective scale. In his early writings, he accepted the 'pragmatic' philosophy of William James. James had said: 'Everything which is demanded is by that fact a good.'[3]

Pound's pragmatic jurisprudence equates justice with quietening those who are banging on the gates. We should not attempt an all-embracing blue-print for legal reform. We should record the demands which people have made or are making on the law, and achieve the best balance we can. 'Social engineering' consists in

2 (1943–44) 57 Harv L Rev 1–39.
3 *The Will to Believe* (1897) p. 205.

giving effect to as much as possible of such claims. Where there are irreducible value-conflicts, we can rely on the 'trained intuition' of the judge. Later, Pound extended the concept of social interest to include 'desires' as well as 'claims' and 'demands'; and he expressed misgivings about pragmatism. Perhaps we should take account of reasonable expectations which no one has articulated, and not give countenance to unreasonable claims. But he never achieved a theory of justice by which such decisions could be measured.

> 'I have come to feel that instead of putting the task of law, as William James did, in terms of satisfying as much as we can of the total of human demands, we do better to speak of providing as much as we may of the total of men's reasonable expectations in life in civilised society with the minimum of friction and waste.'[4]

Where the legal technician cannot accommodate interests, there is no objective way of resolving conflicts. There are, however, 'jural postulates' by which new interests may be tested. These are 'presuppositions' of legal reasoning. They involve what men must be able to assume 'in civilised society' – no intentional aggression by others; beneficial control over what they acquire under the existing social and economic order; good faith in dealings; due care not to injure; control over dangerous activities. These jural postulates are similar to Dworkin's 'background rights' (see chapter 14, above), except that, for Pound, their sole basis is what Dworkin calls 'institutional support'. There is no question of testing them against objective morality. Pound formulates a jural postulate by generalising some value protected by the existing law. He then tells us that entirely novel claims are to be judged by reference to jural postulates. This suggests that creative legal reasoning must be incremental: new claims will be recognised only if claims of that sort are already recognised. On the other hand, Pound takes note of the fact that jural postulates change, that they are relative to stages in social evolution. In 1942, he recorded the emergence of new jural postulates, relating to job security, enterprise liability, and social insurance.[5]

Pound's pragmatism and relativism resemble much work-a-day discussion of law reform. You set out the law as it is. You note suggestions for change in dissenting judgments and law reform committees, and consider whether they are incompatible with some underlying principle of the system ('jural postulate'). You put competing considerations in different pans of the scales. And you do your best to give as much satisfaction as possible, having regard to all

4 (1954) 68 Harv L Rev 19.
5 *Social Control through Law* (1942).

technical limitations. If one is sceptical about theories of justice, or about the desirability of wholesale change, then perhaps this will do. But if law reform is to be piecemeal, relativist and pragmatic, is there any point in broad-scale classifications of interests and jural postulates? Why not employ detailed socio-legal research to problems one by one, as they arise? Pound believed that his theory was of practical value in relation both to problems of 'law reform', and to the sorts of problems of 'legal reasoning' discussed in chapter 15, above. Was he right in either respect? If not, should we draw the conclusion that 'sociological jurisprudence' means the death of theory altogether?

2 The functions and limits of law

Sociological jurisprudence is sometimes referred to as 'functional'. In a broad sense, all legal theories make assumptions about 'functions'. As we saw in chapter 6, above, Kelsen's pure theory of law assumes that all legal systems tend to a monopoly of violence. We may think of 'function' as an overall legal goal, or as an attribute of particular legal rules. On the most abstract plane, some would claim that the function of law is to keep the peace, to stop us from killing or injuring each other: or to prevent 'free riders' from taking unfair advantage of the rest of us by not playing their part in schemes of social cooperation; or to resolve disputes between individuals; or to provide a balance between the claims upon social resources of different interest groups; or to impose on society the interests of a ruling class; or some combination of some or all of these. On the plane of individual rules, we may suggest that particular kinds of rules have typical social functions. We saw in chapter 9, above, that Hart gives as a reason for distinguishing power-conferring rules from duty-imposing rules that not to do so would distort their social function.

R. S. Summers has argued that abstract and particularistic functional analyses can be reconciled if we distinguish the overall functions of law from the 'technique element'. In Summers and Howard's *Law: its Nature, Functions and Limits*, he applies this distinction to modern American law. The book contains a comprehensive survey of the social functions which legal institutions 'help' to serve. They help: (1) to promote human health and a healthy environment; (2) to reinforce the family and protect private life; (3) to keep community peace; (4) to protect basic freedoms; (5) to secure equality of opportunity; (6) to recognise and order private ownership; (7) to exercise surveillance and control over persons in power, including lawyers. The authors see all these functions as subserving the ultimate end of individual self-realisation − a concept much stressed by Pound who derived it from the Neo-Hegelianism of Kohler. Like Pound, their legal critique is in terms of 'social engineering'; but they clarify the relation between means and ends. The seven functions of law are served by five legal 'modes' ('instrumentalities', 'techniques'): (1) the grievance remedial instrument; (2) the penal instrument; (3) the administrative regulatory instrument; (4) the government benefit-conferral instrument; (5) the private arrangement facilitating instrument. Various combinations of these instrumentalities are used to further the law's functions. For instance, in furthering a healthy environment, the grievance remedial mode comes in by allowing actions for certain kinds of deleterious nuisance, negligence or breach of treatment or insurance contracts; there are penal prohibitions; conduct bearing on health is subjected to administrative regulation and licensing; benefits are conferred through revenue law and health care law; and private arrangements relating to health and facilitated by contract law, and charity law. Summers and Howard invite the reader to consider whether particular legal instruments are efficiently employed towards achieving the social goals. They stress the fact that each instrumentality is a 'process', involving the cooperation of legislators, administrators, law-enforcement officers, lawyers, private citizens and courts; and they draw attention to 'process values', similar to the principles of legality mentioned in chapter 11, above. They suggest that the nature of these processes imposes inherent limits on the extent to which law can further its functions. For example, the penal mode should not be employed where conduct cannot be effectively policed. Prohibition was an instance of an abuse of this instrument. And there are limits flowing from the fact that excessive zeal in fulfilling one function may derogate from another. Providing uniform education (through the benefit-conferral technique) in the interests of the function of securing equality of opportunity might derogate from the function of securing basic freedoms, as when it takes away a parent's right to choose schools.

Such a survey of the functions of law has the merit of providing much more sociological information than does the standard analytic approach. It avoids certain kinds of distortions. The authors stress that law is not just about rights, duties, powers and sanctions. The mass of modern law devoted to what they call the administrative-regulatory and benefit-conferral modes makes that clear. They might have added that their analysis (if accurate) also falsifies Hart's assumption that it is possible to 'individuate' laws by reference to social function. Not only is it not true that one type of law corresponds with one legal function; it is not even the case that one type of law corresponds with one legal technique. 'Power-conferring' rules have their place in the private arrangement facilitating instrument, but they crop up in other instruments as well.

Nevertheless, this functional survey is still at the near end of the sociological–jurisprudence spectrum. Summers and Howard make clear that law 'helps' to achieve the seven goals, that there are other coordinating 'non-legal' factors – psychological, moral, political, economic, religious and so on. The law then is a distinct means of social control, and it is assumed that one identifies it by reference to legal-positivistic criteria. It consists of legal rules and legal institutions.

It may be objected that the entire picture is artificial, that the law has been cut to fit clothes it does not deserve to wear. Seven desirable end-points are conceived. Then swathes are hacked through legal materials to find those that appear to tend in a desired direction. Anything that tells against the achievement of some end is called a 'non-legal factor'. For example, in the context of securing equality of opportunity, 'the rule of law' is exemplified by reference to law relating to welfare, education and restrictions on discrimination; while the non-legal factors are said to include wealth, athletic ability, economics and considerations of justice and utility. Might one not stand the picture on its head and say that the law helps to secure inequality of opportunity, in that it facilitates arrangements which confer privileges on the wealthy and the well-endowed; but it is hampered in its unequalising function by a multiplicity of social and economic forces?

There are two problems for the idea of 'function of law'. First, by 'function', do we mean simply 'effects' or 'intended effects'; and if the latter, whose intention is crucial? Secondly, which segments of legal material shall we select before attributing to them any 'function'? It seems likely that the select-and-collect procedure we apply will be illuminated by normative presuppositions we ourselves bring to the task. A radical social critic who engages in legal-functional analysis will make different segmental selections out of the law from those made by Summers and Howard; and no doubt will read the effects differently.

The expression 'the limits of law' appears to be even more ambiguous. Sometimes it is used as a label for the positivist thesis that there are criteria of validity by reference to which legal standards can be distinguished from non-legal ones. More often, it has to do with limits on what the law can (or ought to try to) achieve – as in the essays contained in Pennock and Chapman (eds) *The Limits of Law*. Some issues relate to alleged ethical limitations, such as the questions whether the law should be employed to enforce popular morality or paternalistically to save people from harming themselves (discussed in chapter 10, above); or whether coercion should be exercised according to a retributive principle, or according to an analogy with medical treatment, or merely for community self-defence (discussed in chapter 5, above). Issues may, however, be viewed instrumentally. Granted that a certain goal is desirable, nevertheless 'you can't make people good by legislation'. Illuminating generalisations seem hard to come by. Ingrained attitudes may frustrate an enterprise of law reform; or law may have an 'educative' role. Some kinds of behaviour cannot be effectively policed; but which these are is not static, given developments in data collection, bugging, telephone tapping and the like. Perhaps all limits on law's effectiveness should be seen as ultimately ethical rather than instrumental: there are things the law could achieve, but only by unacceptedly intrusive means. Measuring the effectiveness of law raises obvious methodological problems connected with sampling technique and statistical correlation, but also difficult conceptual problems. How do we identify 'the law' before assessing its effects? Is it a system of rules or a pattern of official behaviour or a process conceived in terms of 'governmental' functions? If it is rules, should we individuate them into different types before measuring their effectiveness? And do we determine effectiveness by reference to outward compliance, conscious obedience, or achievement of goals? If there are any necessary limits to what the law can achieve, they must flow either from our conception of man or from our conception of law. The former is the basis of what Hart calls 'the minimum content of natural law' (see chapter 2, above). The latter underlies Fuller's 'inner morality of law' (see chapter 11, above). If man's altruism is ineradicably limited, the law cannot make it unlimited. If the law is necessarily something that operates through rules, then its contributions to social organisation are limited by the requirements of formal justice (rule justice); and it cannot achieve the sort of individuated justice which requires every problem to be treated exclusively on its merits.

3 The living law

Supposing we take the view that the effects normally attributed to the law are really brought about by spontaneously generated social norms. Business is carried on, family life and education fostered, antisocial violence kept within bounds, all because of the effective operation of rules; but the rules in question have no necessary relation to the rules in the law books. We might then conclude that law is socially unimportant; or we might change our view of what law is. The latter is the course recommended by Eugen Ehrlich.

Pound indicated that there was a distinction between 'the law in books' and 'the law in action', but he paid little detailed attention to the latter. Ehrlich, on the other hand, is preoccupied with what he calls 'the living law'. He believed that social associations have an 'inner order' which is the true determinant of action. He does not recommend that book law should be ignored. It contains 'norms for decision' addressed to officials and may well affect what they do. Individual citizens, however, follow the 'living law', the spontaneous norms of the social associations to which they belong. It is the business of juristic science to press for alterations in the norms for decision so as to bring them into line with the living law.

> 'The inner order of the associations of human beings is not only the original but also down to the present time the basic form of law. The legal proposition not only comes into being at a much later time but is largely derived from the inner order of the associations.'[6]

That social groups may have customary rules is true. Why should we call them 'law'? Two arguments are implicit in Ehrlich's writings. The first is the analogy with primitive 'law' mentioned in the last chapter. The second is the more important. Lawyers are supposed to be people who convey chunks of useful rule-information. What is the good of them reading rules out of books, when social life actually goes by other rules?

Suppose a trainee manager comes to a factory and is told to bone up on some relevant law. The traditionalist would refer him to the Factory Acts, where it would say that certain kinds of machine should be fenced. The Ehrlichian 'living' lawyer would tell him, say, that, in the life of this factory those machines are not to be fenced, but on the other hand there is a very rigid 'law' about tea-breaks. In *Law and Legal Science* I argue that, since legal science is supposed to be useful precisely because it informs one of the rules officials will apply consistently with the values of legality and constitutionality, there is no special point in calling anything but the first sort of information 'law'. That is not to say that the Ehrlichian information should not also be passed on to our trainee. He ought to be told that the machinery-fencing law is a dead letter in this factory – a significant legal-sociological detail. And he ought to know about the tea-breaks, even though, *pace* Ehrlich, they have nothing to do with the law. The fact that the established practice is not to fence machines, or that it is to take tea-breaks at fixed hours, may be given as a reason for altering existing regulations, or existing labour contracts, respectively. But there may be arguments against such changes; and the debate should

6 *Fundamental Principles of the Sociology of Law* pp. 37–38.

not be pre-empted by saying that, because these things are already the subject of group practices, they are already 'law'.

A variant of the 'living law' approach sometimes appears in attitudinal socio-legal research. Whereas Anglo-American studies in legal sociology tend to be oriented either to behavioural or to effectiveness surveys – that is, they assess the behaviour patterns of officials, or consider whether particular legal measures achieve their objectives – continental scholars appear to regard the 'sociology of law' as a discipline which inquires whether norms have been 'internalised', and whether there is a match between book law and internalised norms. Professor A. Podgorecki insists that such research requires a conception of law which is wider than the traditional one. This is so because there may be 'legal sentiments' or 'legal attitudes' which do not correlate with formal law. The existence of such sentiments is established if people answering questionnaires indicate that they believe conduct ought to be punished. They may evince such an attitude towards conduct which is not formally proscribed.[7]

That attitudinal research, like behaviour research, is a proper activity for legal sociology may readily be accepted. I have suggested that book-law rules ('pure-norm rules') should be compared with internalised rules ('rule-ideas') as well as with behavioural patterns ('rule-situations').[8] It is not clear to me that any non-traditional conception of law is required by such research. On the contrary, living law notions can result in useful information being presented in tendentious terms. One of Podgorecki's colleagues, B. Kutchinsky, summarises the results of research into the attitudes of criminals towards penalisation of conduct in the following words:

> 'Contrary to expectations criminals apparently do not have criminal attitudes – they are, at best, slightly more tolerant towards crimes than non-criminals.'[9]

Kutchinsky uses 'criminal attitude' as the opposite to 'legal attitude'. If your view about whether conduct should be punished coincides with that of the majority, you have a legal attitude. If it does not, you have a criminal attitude.

In my view, no new conception of law is required by socio-legal research. It remains for consideration whether different conceptions of law are required for more fundamental social critiques, a topic dealt with in the next chapter.

---

7 Podgorecki et al *Knowledge and Opinion about Law* pp. 65ff.
8 *Law and Legal Science* ch 6.
9 *Knowledge and Opinion about Law* p.118.

Bibliography

Aubert V. (ed)	*Sociology of Law* Pts 4 and 5
Black D.	'The Boundaries of Legal Sociology' (1972) 81 Yale LJ 1086
	The Behaviour of Law (1976)
Campbell C. and Wiles P.	'The Study of Law and Society in Britain' (1976) 10 LS Rev 547
Gibbs J. P.	'Definitions of Law and Empirical Questions' (1968) 2 LS Rev 429
Harris J. W.	*Law and Legal Science* (1979) ss. 12, 23
Hunt A.	*The Sociological Movement in Law* (1978) ch 6
Lloyd D.	*Introduction to Jurisprudence* (4th edn, 1979) ch 6
MacCormick D. N.	'Challenging Sociological Definitions' (1977) 4 Br J L Soc 87
Nonet P.	'For Jurisprudential Sociology' (1976) 10 LS Rev 525
Ross A.	On Law and Justice (1958) ch 15
Schiff D.	'Socio-Legal Theory, Social Structure and Law' (1976) 39 MLR 287
Selznick P.	'The Sociology of Law' in Merton, Broom and Cottrell (eds) *Sociology To-day: Problems and Perspectives* (1959)
	'Sociology and Natural Law' (1961) 6 NLF 84
	'The Sociology of Law' (1968) 9 IESS 50
Stone J.	*Law and the Social Sciences* (1966)

Social interests

Braybrooke E. K.	'The Sociological Jurisprudence of Roscoe Pound' in Sawer (ed) *Studies in the Sociology of Law* (1961)
Hunt A.	*The Sociological Movement in Law* (1978) ch 2
Lepaulle P.	'The Function of Comparative Law with a Critique of Sociological Jurisprudence' (1921–22) 35 Harv L Rev 838
Morris H.	'Dean Pound's Jurisprudence' in Summers (ed) *More Essays in Legal Philosophy* (1971)
Patterson E. W.	'Pound's Theory of Social Interests' in Sayre (ed) *Interpretations of Modern Legal Philosophies* (1947)
Pound R.	'The Scope and Purpose of Sociological Jurisprudence' (1911) 24 Harv L Rev 591;

	(1912) 25 Harv L Rev 140, 489
	Social Control Through Law (1942)
	'A Survey of Social Interests' (1943–44) Harv L Rev 1
	'The Role of Will in Law' (1954) 68 Harv L Rev 19
	Jurisprudence (1959) vol III, chs 14–15
Stone J.	*Human Law and Human Justice* (1965) ch 9

The functions and limits of law

Allott A.	*The Limits of Law* (1980)
Aubert V. (ed)	*Sociology of Law* (1969) Pt 3
Cowan T. A.	'Law Without Force' (1971) 59 Calif L Rev 683
Friedmann W.	*Law in a Changing Society* (2nd edn, 1972)
Galanter M.	'Why the Haves come out Ahead: Speculations on the Limits of Legal Change' (1974) 9 LS Rev 95, 347
Honoré A. M.	'Real Laws' in Hacker and Raz (eds) *Law, Morality, and Society* (1977)
Pennock J. R. and Chapman J. W. (eds)	*The Limits of Law* (1974)
Pound R.	'The Limits of Effective Legal Action' (1917) IJE 27
Raz J.	*The Authority of Law* (1979) ch 9
Summers R. S.	'The Technique Element in Law' (1971) 59 Calif L Rev 732
	'Naive Instrumentalism and the Law' in Hacker and Raz (eds) *Law, Morality, and Society* (1977)
	Summers and Howard—*Law: its Nature, Functions and Limits* (2nd edn, 1972)

The living law

Aubert V. (ed)	*Sociology of Law* (1969) Pt 2
Ehrlich E.	*Fundamental Principles of the Sociology of Law* (Moll trans, 1936)
Fuller L. L.	*Anatomy of the Law* (1971) pp. 64–71
Lucas J. R.	'The Phenomenon of Law' in Hacker and Raz (eds) *Law, Morality and Society* (1977)
Partridge P. H.	'Ehrlich's Sociology of Law' in Sawer (ed) *Studies in the Sociology of Law* (1961)
Podgorecki A. et al	*Knowledge and Opinion about Law* (1971)

19 Law, social theory and Marxist jurisprudence

Our starting-point at the beginning of the last chapter was the aphorism that 'law is a social phenomenon'. We then discussed various ways of looking at society from the point of view of law. Might it not be better to try to explain the aphorism by first asking what we mean by 'social'? What is the bond that holds men together in societies and social groups? What part, if any, does the law play in the social bond? Such questions have been raised in the history of political and social philosophy from the time of the ancient Greeks. But towards the end of the last century, they came to be subsumed under what was conceived of as a new kind of discipline, that of 'social theory'. Political philosophers had generally not distinguished the questions as to what it was that did, and what it was that ought to, hold men together; and they had usually framed their answers in terms of a supra-historical conception of human nature. Social theorists sought to demarcate a value-free 'sociology'. Man was to be conceived, not as an entity in terms of which the justice of social arrangements could be measured, but as the product of forces which determined his relations with others. The social bond was different, and consequently the perceptions of the individual were different, depending on the stage of historical development of society. In particular, the society of contemporary western capitalism was unique. If social theory has any distinctive contribution to make to jurisprudence, it is by showing that different kinds of society produce, or correspond with, different kinds of law.

1 Law and social theory

Two of the most important progenitors of social theory, Durkheim and Weber, made just this claim — that different kinds of society correlate with different kinds of law. Emile Durkheim (1858–1917) distinguished primitive from modern societies. The former were characterised by 'mechanical', the latter by 'organic', social solidarity. Primitive societies were held together by shared values. The collective conscience of the group constituted the reality of society. In

245

modern societies, in contrast, economic specialisation had led to role-differentiation. The collective conscience was weakened to the extent that role values had emerged. Society was held together by the complex interrelation of roles. Durkheim insisted on a 'scientific' methodology, on establishing the social by reference to externally-observable phenomena: and nothing could be harder evidence of a society's collective values than its law.

'Since law reproduces the principal forms of social solidarity, we have only to classify the different types of law to find therefrom the different types of social solidarity which correspond to it.'[1]

The proof of the two types of social solidarity lay in the manifest existence of two kinds of law, distinguishable by their content. Primitive society had 'repressive' law in which sanctions were prescribed for violations of the collective conscience. Modern society had 'restitutive' law, which provided, through civil remedy, for the restitution of the balance between society's components.

Max Weber (1864–1920) provided more complex typologies and society/law correlations. He spoke of the social bond in terms, not of solidarity, but of legitimate domination. In different historical settings, people had accepted the right of others to control their lives for one of three kinds of reason: the charismatic qualities of a leader; the traditional sanctity of an office; or the fact that imperative power was clothed with legal rationality. Alongside this typology of authorities, he set a fourfold classification of laws distinguished by the kind of rationality they exhibited. Law is substantively irrational where every case is decided on its merits by the judge's intuition. Law is formally irrational where decisions turn on some test beyond human control, such as an oracle or an ordeal. Law is substantively rational where decisions are made by reference to general principles which are not confined to rules deducible from legal texts. Law is formally rational where every case is decided by logical deduction from existing legal rules and concepts constituting a gapless system.

In societies held together by charismatic domination, reliance is placed on substantive or formal irrationality. With traditional domination, substantive rationality may be added. The crucial correlation is between legal rational domination and logically formal rationality. The nineteenth-century west had evolved a unique system of power relations whereby allegiance was owed to the law itself. Ideally – unfortunately, the practice did not always match the ideal – each adjudication, accepted as legitimate, was the result of the logical application of legal rules. The hierarchy of legal institutions

1 *The Division of Labour in Society* p. 68.

matched that other product of western society, the rational bureaucracy. Just as a bureaucrat is an expert seeking given ends by rational means, so the legal expert is a master of the science of conceptual deduction seeking legally rational solutions.

The rationalism of the bureaucrat and the legal expert made life more predictable and secure for the capitalist entrepreneur. Weber, however, rejected any simple economic determinism. Formally rational law had not come about as a simple consequence of capitalism. He pointed to the English example, where capitalism had evolved before anywhere else although formal legal rationality was only partly present. The common law was substantively rational in so far as it incorporated non-legal standards like 'public policy'; and it had large elements of substantive irrationality, in that the facts of a particular case might affect a decision about the law, and of formal irrationality, in its reliance on oaths and its exclusion of relevant evidence through the adversarial system. Weber's historicism is multi-causal. The self-interest of the independent legal profession in England had inhibited the development of formally rational law. In continental countries, on the other hand, the combination of capital's need for predictability, and the princely bureaucracy's need for organisational planning, had provided the conditions for formal legal rationality. This tendency had also been favoured by the control over legal education of legal scholars. Above all, codification was a precondition of formally rational law.

'[I]t may indeed be said that England achieved capitalistic supremacy among the nations not because but rather in spite of its judicial system.'[2]

The literature of theoretical sociology devoted to critical examination of Durkheim and Weber is vast. For the most part, however, it has not centred on their views about law. Cultural anthropologists have chewed over what Durkheim had to say about the repressive nature of primitive law, generally rejecting it. So far as modern societies are concerned, the sociology of Talcot Parsons gives a special place to the court system as a sub-system within the total political order, whose specialist function is to integrate society. This theme is developed by H. C. Bredemeier in his *Law as an Integrative Mechanism*. Such 'consensus' models of the role of law are commonly contrasted with 'conflict' models, which see the law as a means for influential groups or, in the case of Marxist jurisprudence, for a ruling class, to impose their interests on the rest of society.

2 *On Law in Economy and Society* p. 231.

Jurisprudential concern with social theory should not be limited to writers who purport to engage in what Weber called 'the sociology of law'. It may be possible to set up different typologies of society and of law in critical reaction, not merely to these recent 'classics', but encompassing also the political and social philosophy which preceded them. Two recent authors, H. A. Hayek and R. M. Unger, have attempted to do this. In chapter 11, above, their views on 'the rule of law' were contrasted.

Hayek distinguishes two kinds of social order, 'grown order', and 'made order'. The former consists of the reciprocal expectations which spontaneously arise between men and which make social life possible. The 'rules' – that is, regularities in expected behaviour – which constitute such an order need not be known to those who observe them. A made order consists of a completely different kind of 'rules', namely, purposive prescriptions laid down to establish an organisation and to further its aims. A different kind of 'law' corresponds to each kind of social order. To the order of reciprocal expectations corresponds 'rules of just conduct'. These are abstract, negative rules, restraining individuals from invading the free domain of others. Such law originally grew up as customary law. But this was not necessarily the sort of customary law which legal anthropologists investigate. Its rules existed as regularities of behaviour and expectation long before they were consciously articulated as the basis of tribal mediation or enforcement.

'Although man never existed without laws that he obeyed, he did, of course, exist for hundreds of thousands of years without laws he "knew" in the sense that he was able to articulate them.'[3]

Rules of just conduct came to be articulated in the settlement of disputes. Eventually, this task becomes the specialist activity of lawyers. Their role is, in case of doubt, to find what the rules are by a test of consistency with all other rules of just conduct. Although rules are inevitably modified in the process of articulation, only aiming at consistency rather than a purposive creation can produce legal rules which serve the underlying social order of reciprocal expectations. The common law system of precedent provides the best institutional background for this process.

'It seems that the constant necessity of articulating rules in order to distinguish between the relevant and the accidental in the precedents which guide him, produces in the common law judge a capacity for discovering general principles rarely acquired by a

3 *Rules and Order* p. 43.

judge who operates with a supposedly complete catalogue of applicable rules before him.'⁴

To made social orders corresponds another kind of 'law', namely, the rules for the organisation of government. As mentioned in chapter 11, above Hayek sees a deplorable tendency for such organisational law to replace the rules of just conduct, owing to the legal positivist heresy that all law is made law. The likely outcome is totalitarianism.

Unger presents a similar match between forms of social life and types of law:

'A society's law constitutes the chief bond between its culture and its organization; it is the external manifestation of the embeddedness of the former in the latter.'⁵

But where Hayek offers two types of law, Unger offers three. This he does to account, in society/law correlation terms, for a cultural phenomenon which he believes in and which Hayek denies: an ineradicable sense of unjustified hierarchy, of illegitimate personal domination, as a pervasive attribute of the psychology of modern man. Unger's three types of law are customary law, which corresponds to tribal society; bureaucratic law, which is public and positive and corresponds to aristocratic society; and the 'legal order' of liberal society. The legal order has two further characteristics, besides being 'public' and 'positive'. It is 'general' and 'autonomous'. It is autonomous as to substance in that its norms are not restatements of non-legal norms; as to the institutions which administer it; as to its methodology, in that it incorporates a special manner of legal justification; and as to occupational specialisation of those who staff it. It arose uniquely in the west because of the conjunction of two necessary conditions: political compromise between three interest groups – the nobles, the merchants, and the princes and their bureaucratic staffs; and the belief in a higher law, which made the articulation of the compromise take the particular form of the rule of law. So far the analysis is not far different from Weber's. But Unger goes on to assert that the legal order did not and could not produce a sense of legitimate domination. The ideology of the rule of law is doomed to failure because the reality of subjection by dominant groups forces itself on people's consciousness. Whereas Hayek sees lawyers' law as the continuation of customary law, both being concerned with rules of just conduct, Unger regards feelings of unjustified hierarchy as the inevitable sequel to the loss of unreflective

4 *Rules and Order* p. 87.
5 *Law in Modern Society* p. 250.

legitimacy which is characteristic of customary law. Law is not properly customary law if people have critical feelings about it. (As mentioned in chapter 17, above, some writers on 'primitive law' have stressed that members of a tribal society sometimes do both acknowledge and criticise customs. But Unger deals in 'ideal types' with which actual societies need only partly correspond.)

Unger, like Hayek, sees the modern law of the west as 'post-liberal'. The legal order has been modified by the introduction of welfare law, which is neither general nor autonomous, and by state corporatist law (incorporating the 'living law' of associations), which is neither public nor positive. Unger compares post-liberal society with two other kinds of modern society, neither of which (he says) have solved the dialectic between the experience of personal dependence and the ideal of community. In traditionalistic society, like that of modern Japan, some aspects of the western legal order have been super-imposed upon the customary rank system and industrial bureaucratic law. In revolutionary socialist societies, there is a pervasive tension between the customary law of autonomous organisations and a vast amount of ruthlessly enforced bureaucratic law. The only way out for modern man, in Unger's view, is a reversion to a new kind of customary law of independent groups, which could restore a sense of legitimacy without destroying the possibility of free critical appraisal. Thus, both Hayek and Unger cry 'back to customary law'. But they mean quite different things by it: for Hayek, it is the lawyers' law; for Unger, the living law of equalised associations.

The models of society and of law offered by these various theorists are all what Weber called 'ideal types'. They are mental constructions designed to illuminate complex overarching elements in human history. They do not purport to be precise descriptions. Whether giving a central place to law is necessary to an understanding of the general problem of human social bonding is a question for social theory – just as it is arguable, as we saw in chapter 17, above, that whether rules of a primitive society can usefully be treated as 'law' is a question internal to anthropology. For jurisprudence, the question is whether the typologies of law which emerge from these social theorists are informative about law. Is Durkheim's contention about an evolutionary shift from repressive to restitutive law an accurate generalisation about the content of law? How do the contrasting commendations made by Weber of the rationality of conceptual deduction, or by Hayek of the compatibility-through-general-principle of the common law, compare with other discussions of legal rationality not based on a social-theoretical superstructure, such as those mentioned in chapters 14 and 15, above? The historical explanations of different legal systems offered by social theorists should be compared with those offered by the historical school and by Marxist jurisprudence. At the very least, social theorising of this kind goes beyond traditional jurisprudence by its attempt to specify the social and political setting of the lawyer's role. Is it his business to forward social solidarity, the implication drawn by L. Duguit from Durkheim's sociology? Is he the natural and creditable ally of rational bureaucratic government, as Weber suggests, or is that, as Hayek would have it, a perversion of his true role (as declarer of the community's rules of just conduct)? Or is Unger right, and the lawyer, when asked for the bread of impartial justice, offers only the stone of class-supremacist legality?

2 Marxist jurisprudence

Of the new breed of social theorists who broke away from the tradition of classical political philosophy in the nineteenth century, one writer has acquired a certain notoriety. If the reader of this book is new to social theory, he may not have heard of Durkheim or Weber, but I would lay very long odds that he has heard of Marx. 'Marxist theory' refers to any body of social thought which claims to be based on the writings of Karl Marx (1818–1883), and of Fredrich Engels (1820–1895). Half the world is ruled by governments who claim that these writings are uniquely 'scientific' and ought to be the basis for all governmental action, including the operation of legal institutions. In the rest of the world, some analysts of society express a commitment to these writings in a way in which commentators do not concede authoritative allegiance to other texts, except for the religious. These are reasons enough for jurisprudence to concern itself with what these writers had to say about law.

However, unlike the theorists discussed earlier in this chapter, Marx and Engels did not give law any centrality in their analysis of the social bond. None of their voluminous works contains a separate treatment of law. They elaborate sequential stages in the evolution of human society, but do not indicate whether different kinds of law correspond to each. One inference might be that, within Marxist theory of society, a theory of law is of little account. In the preface to *Contribution to Critique of Political Economy* (1859), Marx drew a famous distinction between the basis and the superstructure of social relations. The basis consisted of the relations between members of society and the means of production. This economic basis had a determining effect over all forms of social intercourse. Religion, philosophy, aesthetics and law were all but part of the superstructure resting on it. That being so, one might argue, so long as one has correctly appraised the relations of production existing at any particular historical period, one would be able to state all that really matters about the law of that period. A separate theory of law might suggest, what Marx and Engels denied, that law (an element of the superstructure) could have a separate history, that it was something with its own autonomy.

On the other hand, there are lengthy passages in their writings about law, now collected in M. Cain and A. Hunt *Marx and Engels on Law*. Is it possible (should one try) to build a distinct theory of law on these extracts? In this chapter, I shall merely draw attention to three aspects of Marxist theory which seem to have important jurisprudential implications, whether or not a distinct Marxist theory of law can be constructed: Marxist economism; Marxist critique of law in capitalist society; and Marxist prophetic historicism.

According to Marx and Engels, it is a fallacy to suppose that the content of law depends on 'will', on the arbitrary choice of a legislature. The relations of production control what the legislature can and does lay down. In primitive clan society, production of the means of life was spontaneously ordered on a communal basis. Since man emerged from this primitive stage, there has been class division: always a ruling class and one or more oppressed classes. These classes are defined in terms of relations of production, replacing one another as the mechanics of production have changed. In this way society has evolved from clan society, through slave-owning society and feudalism, to modern capitalist society. The law, like other instrumentalities of the state, does express the will of the ruling class at different historical epochs; but what they will is ultimately dependent on their class interests, themselves dictated by their definitional involvement in the means of production. Relations of production are thus the economic basis of law. Marxist economism should be sharply contrasted with the 'economic analysis of law' discussed in chapter 4, above. That view takes as the unit of value the satisfaction of wants, as evidenced by willingness to pay. The Marxist unit of value is productive work. So, for example, if you contract with me that you will do work and I will pay you a wage, according to the classical economists satisfactions are, prima facie, maximised: the work must be of more value to me than anything else I could have done with the money, or else I would not have hired you for that amount; and the money must be of more value to you than anything else you could have achieved with your time and effort, or else you would have done that other thing. According to Marxist economics, however, the relevant units are the thing you produced with your work and the products of labour-power stored up in my money. If you are a member of an exploited class and I an exploiter, we can be sure that what you have produced has cost more labour-power than the control over others' labour-power which the money will give you. The surplus I expropriate. In a capitalist society, the ruling class (the bourgeoisie) are in just this relationship to the exploited class (the proletariat). The latter produce goods with their labour; the former take the goods and give the proletariat only so much as is necessary for them to maintain bare existence. The surplus value of the workers' labour is expropriated by the capitalists.

It is far from clear how specific Marx and Engels believed the determination of law by relations of production to be. Their comments on historical legislative events suggest that not every statute can be read off as directly caused by some shift in relations of production. Marx discusses legislation in England from the end of the middle ages up to the nineteenth century, and argues that much of it did assist the rising bourgeoisie, by driving the poor from the land so as to provide a ready army of exploitable proletariat. But he also mentions the early legislation which tried, ineffectually, to prevent enclosure. Perhaps the point is, not that each legislative choice is directly motivated by the interests of the ruling class, but that the economic basis of class interests will filter out and render ineffective all laws which are not.

What about the fact that the same laws sometimes stay on the books after some Marxist-significant economic change, or the fact that different societies at the same stage of economic development have (on the face of it) different laws? It seems clear that Marx and Engels did not suppose that every detail need have an economic explanation, and Engels at least indicates that the law may react on its economic base – may, to some extent, warp or temporarily halt the inexorable march of the relations of production. The Austrian Marxist, K. Renner (1870–1950) has elaborated a theory according to which the functions of law may change, consistently with economic determination, although the form remains the same – feudal Europe employed the same Roman law concept of ownership as does capitalist Europe, but it now serves as the vehicle for capitalists to give orders to workmen, whereas in feudal law the duty of feudal inferiors to obey their lords was explicitly laid down. The Russian Marxist, E. B. Pashukanis (1891–1937), produced a more abstract theory, showing that the form of law is essentially capitalist, so that 'law' as such reached its highest flowering in capitalist society – it is of the essence of a juridical interpretation of human effort that it regards what a man does as an exchangeable commodity, not as something intrinsic to his personality.

The critique of capitalist society which bulks so large in Marxist theory is both moral and functional-economic. Marx claimed that his theory was scientific, that it showed how changes in the material world in the modes of production, inevitably produced the evolution into class society in general, and changes from one form of class society to another in particular. But this alleged objectivity was not divorced from ethical comment. The capitalists were both historically inevitable and ruthlessly cruel. The coercive machinery of the state, including all law, was used to further their class interests. Workers were kept down by the brute force of law to the minimum of subsistence so that profits could be maximised. The capitalist economic system had achieved an enormous increase in total human wealth; but, in late capitalism, it was now hindering a much greater output which would only come when the proletariat took over the means of production.

Modern Marxists accept this critique of nineteenth-century capitalism, and believe that it is applicable at least to all those societies of the present day which have not yet undergone a Marxist revolution. They differ sharply, however, in the implications to be drawn for our view of modern law. Particularly problematic is the immense burgeoning, since Marx's time, of welfare law in capitalist societies. If Marx was right, such law must be fitted into his critique. One way of doing this is to regard all welfare law as a trick, with which no good Marxist should have anything to do. In their book, *Images of Law*, Z. Bankowski and G. Mungham direct a polemical attack on all those engaged in welfare law or poverty law programmes. They regard the demand for new university courses on such subjects as a bad mistake, and warn students against being misled into involvement in legal advice services. The demand for welfare and poverty law courses is, they argue, itself economically determined. Legal work in traditional areas is already catered for, but there are pickings to be made in these new areas both by practitioners and by academics; that is why they have arisen. No doubt, these authors would accept that their own book was similarly motivated. They urge that all law is slavery, and that diverting attention from traditional law subjects might obscure this fact.

This view should be contrasted with that of other modern Marxist writers, like Cain and Hunt, who maintain that involvement in such new law areas is fully warranted by Marxist theory. They point to the fact that Marx and Engels mentioned that particular pieces of legislation had been wrested from the bourgeoisie by the proletariat. In capitalist society, class struggle continues until the revolution is achieved. We should not sit back until then, but rather, as part of the class struggle, make demands for legal change and encourage the oppressed to claim whatever rights bourgeois law affords.

Marxist theory is historicist – that is, it explains social evolution in terms of inexorable forces. This historicism was derived from Hegelianism; Hegel saw historical development in terms of ideas – a 'dialectic' involving a thesis, its opposite (an antithesis), and the resolution in a synthesis. Marx and Engels envisaged historical forces operating on the material plane – so that the dialectic consisted of a struggle between classes, producing a revolutionary synthesis. The bourgeois revolution had been the outcome of the struggle between the ruling feudal class and classes opposed to it. They prophesied that the next revolution would occur when the forces of production unleashed by capitalism could no longer be kept within the bounds of bourgeois domination, when the proletariat would throw off its chains and seize the means of production for itself. The result of this revolution would be that the proletariat, the overwhelming majority of the population, would itself become the ruling class for a time. But at the end of a transition period, the 'dictatorship of the proletariat' would be succeeded by a society in which all classes had been abolished and 'communism' would be achieved. At this final stage there would be no classes, no domination, no exploitation, and hence no coercion.

What about 'law' after the revolution? Critics of Marxism often construct the following argument. Marx had said that a proletarian revolution would lead to a classless society in which there would be no need for a coercive state. Engels expressed this by stating that the expropriation of the bourgeoisie by the proletariat would be its last act as a proletarian class, and that thereafter the state would 'wither away'. Now, there have been a number of Marxist revolutions and the result has universally been that the state, far from withering away, has become ever stronger. Instead of there being less law, there has been more. (Ivo Lapenna denies that even Yugoslavia is an exception. As himself a Yugoslav exile, he claimed that the decentralisation of economic functions which Yugoslav leaders claim as evidence of 'withering away' in fact devolves less power than is devolved in England on local authorities.) Therefore, Marx's and Engels' prophecies have been proved false, and this suggests that their whole analysis was faulty.

This argument can be met in various ways. One could say that their prophecies were false, but nonetheless their analysis of capitalist society was basically correct, in so far as it showed how the mass of people are in a constant state of being dominated by others. This seems to be Unger's view. Alternatively, one could deny that the revolutions which have occurred were truly Marxist, so that the prophecy will some day come true. Finally, one could claim that the prophecy has been partially fulfilled, but that 'withering away' has not yet begun because revolutionary socialist societies are still going through the period of the dictatorship of the proletariat.

The official view expounded by the governments of revolutionary socialist states has varied. Those within the Soviet sphere accept Lenin's interpretation (expounded in *State and Revolution*) as authoritative. According to Lenin, Engels did not mean that the bourgeois state would wither away. That was to be entirely smashed by the revolution. The proletariat, under the leadership of the communist party, would then establish a proletarian state and it was that state which would wither away, once its enemies had been crushed. Lenin's book was written in 1917 and Pashukanis, writing in 1924, claimed that the law to be used during the transition period was bourgeois law – there could be no other sort. This view has since been repudiated, and a novel concept has been evolved, that of 'socialist legality'. It has been claimed, since the 1930s, that there are two reasons why law is essential to a socialist state, even after all counter-revolutionary classes have been crushed. The first is 'capitalist encirclement': a state apparatus and coercive law are needed until at any rate most of the world has undergone a socialist revolution; for until then the socialist state has to defend itself against capitalist foreign enemies. Secondly, law is needed as an instrument for constructing the new society.

It is this second function of law which, if anything, gives a specific flavour to the legal systems of Marxist states. Professor H. Berman has termed it 'parental law'. The communist party, as representing the entire proletariat class, educates the population into communist morality and brings about the increase in productive forces foretold by Marx and Lenin, inter alia through the medium of law. In different communist countries, at varying stages of political development, either the first or the second of the words in 'socialist legality' has been stressed. Sometimes it is insisted that our legality is 'socialist', that is, that it has nothing to do with the bourgeois concept of the rule of law. Consequently, informal tribunals may undertake re-educating tasks in which they need not stick within the letter of the law. At other times it is urged that socialist administration insists on 'legality', that is, the strict observance of the law by citizenry and even party officials.

Before there can be 'withering away', human nature must be transformed in the way Marx believed it could (and would) be. Man in class society is alienated from his original social nature. When all traces of this alienation have been removed, each person will see himself, not as the isolated, right-bearing individual which bourgeois justice focuses upon, but as an integral member of a community. Its life will be his life. All will spontaneously observe what Lenin called the 'elementary rules of social life' and should any isolated individual step out of line, he will be dealt with by the spontaneous reaction of his fellows. There will be no need for rule-makers, no need for coercion, and so no 'law' in the bourgeois sense. Can you believe it?

Bibliography

Law and social theory

Albrow M.	'Legal Positivism and Bourgeois Materialism – Max Weber's View of the Sociology of Law' (1975) 2 Br J L Soc 14
Aubert V. (ed)	*Sociology of Law* (1969) Pt 1
Bredemeier H. C.	'Law as an Integrative Mechanism' in Evan (ed) *Law and Sociology* (1962)
Chambliss W. and Seidman R.	*Law, Order and Power* (1971)
Clarke M.	'Durkheim's Sociology of Law' (1976) 3 Br J L Soc 246
Cotterrell R. B. M.	'Durkheim on Legal Development and Social Solidarity' (1977) 4 Br J L Soc 241
Duguit L.	'Objective Law' (Grandgent and Gifford trans) (1920) 20 Colum L Rev 817, (1921) 21 Colum L Rev 17, 126, 242
Durkheim E.	*The Division of Labor in Society* (Simpson trans, 1964)
Grace C. and Wilkinson P.	*Sociological Inquiry and Legal Phenomena* (1978)
Hunt A.	*The Sociological Movement in Law* (1978) chs 4–5
Morris C.	'Law, Reason and Sociology' (1958–59) 107 U Pa L Rev 310
Parsons T.	'The Law and Social Control' in Evan (ed) *Law and Sociology* (1962)
Schwarzenberger G.	'The Three Types of Law' (1949) 2 CLP 103
Stoljar S. D.	'Weber's Sociology of Law' in Sawer (ed) *Studies in the Sociology of Law* (1961)
Trubeck D.	'Toward a Social Theory of Law: an Essay on the Study of Law and Development' (1972) 82 Yale LJ 1 'Max Weber on Law and the Rise of Capitalism' (1972) 3 Wis L Rev 720
Weber M.	*On Law in Economy and Society* (Rheinstein edn, Shils trans, 1954)

Marxist jurisprudence

Bankowski Z. and Mungham G.	*Images of Law* (1976)
Beirne P.	'Marxism and the Sociology of Law: Theory or Practice?' (1975) 2 Br J L Soc 78

Berman H. J.   *Justice in the USSR* (revised edn, 1963)
Cain M.   'The Main Themes of Marx' and Engels'
                      Sociology of Law' (1974) 1 Br J L Soc 136

Cain M. and
Hunt A.   *Marx and Engels on Law* (1979)
Engels F.   *Socialism Utopian and Scientific* in *The Essential
                      Left* (1968)

Kamenka E. and
Tay A. E.   'Socialism, Anarchism and Law' in Kamenka,
                      Brown and Ray (eds) *Law and Society* (1978)
Kinsey R.   'Marxism and the Law: Preliminary
                      Analyses' (1978) 5 Br J L Soc 202
Lapenna I.   *State and Law: Soviet and Yugoslav Theory* (1964)
Lenin V. I. U.   *The State and Revolution* in *The Essential Left*
                      (1968)
Li V. H.   'The Role of Law in Communist China'
                      (1970) China Q 66
Lubman S.   'Mao and Mediation: Politics and Dispute
                      Resolution in Communist China' (1967) 55
                      Calif L Rev 1284

Marx H. K. and
Engels F.   *The Manifesto of the Communist Party* in *The
                      Essential Left* (1968)
Marx H. K.   *Value, Price and Profit* in *The Essential Left* (1968)
Pashukanis E. B.   *Law and Marxism: a General Theory* (Einhorn
                      trans, 1978)
Renner K.   *The Institutions of Private Law and Their Social
                      Functions* (Kahn-Freund (ed), Schwarzschild
                      trans, 1949)

Robson P.   'Renner Revisited' in Attwooll (ed) *Perspectives
                      in Jurisprudence* (1977)
Rudden B.   'Law and Ideology in the Soviet Union'
                      (1978) 31 CLP 189
Sawer G.   'Law as Socially Neutral: Karl Renner' in
                      Sawer (ed) *Studies in the Sociology of Law* (1961)

20 Justice

Men have talked about justice for as long as they have talked about law. The scope of justice is, however, wider. A man may be just or unjust in his dealings with his family or his friends. For legal philosophy, we are interested only in couplings of assertions about justice with those about law. Three sorts should be distinguished. Justice may be claimed to be something inherent in law, or law may be contrasted with justice, or justice may be a measure for testing law.

If law is a system of rules, then some aspects of 'procedural' and of 'formal' justice may be inherent to it. If a rule stipulates that all motorists exceeding a speed limit shall be fined, but those exacting fines take no (or insufficient) steps to find out whether people have fulfilled the condition of the rule, then both procedural justice is violated and, it may be, the rule becomes an empty formula which does not deserve the designation 'legal'. If, during a period of political turbulence, a revolutionary 'court' selects victims for execution on an ad hoc basis, without announcing any universalisable criteria for distinguishing those subject to punishment from those not, it violates formal justice and may, for that reason, be said not to be operating under any system of law. Questions of procedural and formal justice are comprised within the concept of the rule of law, discussed in chapter 11, above. It should be borne in mind, however, that they are only part of that doctrine. If a revolutionary court announces that all those who voted for an ousted regime are to be shot, and takes diligent steps in each case to find out whether or not a person had so voted, it meets the requirements of both formal and procedural justice; but it still might be claimed to be violating the rule of law, because of the opposition between that doctrine and totally retroactive rules. Questions of procedural and formal justice also overlap with the topic of legal reasoning, discussed in chapter 15, above. Legal reasoning, whatever it comprises, is supposed to exclude personal bias. If a judge were to announce: 'The evidence about the defendant's negligence is inconclusive, but I shall find against him because I don't like his type', his decision could be described as procedurally unjust – it would not lack formal justice if he laid down that all people of this 'type' should, in similar circumstances, be held negligent. It is *[handwritten margin notes at top: "procedural" "admin — law" "no bias, law — hearing etc" "formal justice — (universality)"]*

controversial, as we have seen, to what standards a judge should appeal in deciding a case not clearly covered by a valid legal rule; but it may be that the reasons he gives must at least be 'universalisable' so that his reasoning is circumscribed by the requirements of formal justice. If that is true, then it would be 'unjust' in a judge to say: 'For the following reasons I find that this manufacturer should pay damages, but I do not lay down that any other manufacturer, to whom the reasons would equally apply, should also be liable.' If formal justice is a requirement of legal reasoning, it raises problems in the context of 'prospective overruling', as we saw in chapter 13, above.

[handwritten margin note: "② contrast law w/ justice"]

The second of the three distinctions to which I referred concerns an alleged contrast between 'law' and 'justice'. From Aristotle onwards, it has been a controversial question whether all law must be contrasted with one's sense of 'justice' or 'equity'. Is it the case that legal rules, however good in themselves (however 'just' in terms of the third distinction), may nonetheless lead to injustice in particular cases? If that is so, it is because the features of some situations in which individuals confront the law are so unique that they cannot be captured by any rule (including any universalisable exception to any rule), but can be captured by this particular sense of justice. We know what solution would be just in all the circumstances of the case, but we cannot frame any rule which would stipulate this solution. If we can frame such a rule but the existing legal rules do not include it, then we are making a point falling under the third distinction: we are saying that the existing rules are unjust and should be replaced by our new rule. We are then using justice as a measure for the law. In terms of the second distinction, the allegation is that no rule can do justice. The conception of justice appealed to is intuitive. I know that it would be unjust to hold this party liable, although I cannot give reasons which could be generalised and form the basis of a new rule or a new exception.

In *An Introduction to the Philosophy of Law*, Roscoe Pound argued that 'executive justice' has to be reconciled with 'justice according to law' by giving proper allowance to individualisation. The former, he says, relies on 'trained intuition', and is particularly important where judgment has to be passed on human conduct and moral issues, less important in the area of property and commercial law. He lists seven agencies for giving effect to executive justice, to be found in Anglo-American legal systems: discretion in the application of equitable remedies; general standards, like reasonableness; jury general verdicts; judicial latitude in finding the law; penal treatment; informal methods of judicial administration in petty courts; and administrative tribunals. These are curious bed-fellows. The fourth (judicial latitude in finding the law) deserves special attention. If the more extreme of the American realists are right, judges always have latitude, and all they can ever do is to administer intuitive 'executive justice'. This being so, as Frank argued, the way forward is for judges to be as forthcoming as possible about the factors which guide their intuitions, and to give up the pretence of rule-bound decisions, of 'justice according to law' (see chapter 8, above). On Pound's own view, however, judges have latitude in finding the law only some-times. When they do, why should their decisions be guided by individualising 'executive justice'? If judges exercise 'discretion' in finding the law, they may balance competing considerations in an intuitive way, but the considerations weighed may still be general in nature rather than the individual circumstances of the parties. As to the first, second and fifth of Pound's agencies (discretionary remedies, general standards, and sentencing), individual circumstances are often stressed, but usually in a principled way. That is, judges giving reasons in such contexts do not normally indicate that they are reasons which can have no bearing on any other case. So far as that is true, principled reasoning appeals to rule-like standards, to 'justice according to law'. Perhaps jury general verdicts are the best illustration of what Pound intends by 'executive justice'. If Lord Devlin's view of the sovereignty of the jury is correct no one may question the jury's right to render an acquittal verdict, however clear the law and however strong the prosecution evidence. This suggests that the jury is entitled to give preference to its own view of the justice of the case as against justice according to law.

For the most part, when men speak of the law and of justice together, they are not concerned with any alleged inherent justice of law, nor with any alleged inherent contrast between law and justice, but with my third distinction – justice as the measure of law's virtue. If a court applies a legal rule conscientiously according to its terms or, in an unclear case, justifies its decision by reference to accepted standards of legal reasoning, it may do justice according to law; but the outcome may still be unjust because the rules and other legal standards are themselves unjust. When justice is used as the measure of the law, the assumption is that the law either does or could be made to conform to justice; 'justice' in this context stands for a substantive moral criterion, sometimes called 'distributive justice', or more recently, 'social justice'. The law ought to distribute rights and duties in a certain way, and if it does not it is unjust. In the view of classical natural law, an unjust law does not merit the name 'law' at all, but is a mere exercise of illegitimate power. On many a non-natural law view, the justice or injustice of the law is a crucial factor in determining whether it deserves the citizen's support or whether it should be obeyed.

According to classical political philosophy, the substantive justice of the law had to do with providing just remedies, civil and penal. The law was just if it afforded remedies for, and only for, all true wrongs by one man to another; and if it attached the just, and no more than the just, retribution to crime. It was the law's sole business to lay down what Hayek calls 'rules of just conduct' (see chapter 19, above). This remedial or corrective conception of justice presupposes some extra-legal means of identifying 'true wrongs'. Natural law and contract-arian theorists believed that this could be done by reason. Locke, for example, argued that each man is by nature entitled to a certain inviolability of the person and of property, invasion of which is a wrong to him, and that the compact giving rise to civil society builds upon this basis. The arch anti-naturalist, Hume, maintained that wrongs could be identified by conventional opinion: the maintenance of existing property relations, through rules which treated inter-ference with them as 'wrongs', was all the 'justice' at which the law could or should aim.

Substantive remedial justice is sometimes what is meant by a judge who appeals to 'justice' as a ground for laying down some new rule. It is commonly assumed that such and such conduct is obviously a wrong, and such and such redress obviously the right remedy. In so far as a ground is given, it is Humean consensus of public opinion rather than Lockian a priori reasoning. For example, in *Pickett v British Rail Engineering Ltd*,[1] the House of Lords laid down a new ruling, that damages for an injury which had shortened a person's life should include the earnings which would have accrued to him during the 'lost years'. The primary justification for the decision – which overruled earlier authorities – was stated to be that this new rule would accord with the ordinary man's expectations about claims against tortfeasors, and was for that reason 'just'.

Those debating the merits of a proposed bill, or criticising legis-lation, in terms of 'justice' may, however, have a quite different conception of substantive justice in mind. The justice of the law is dependent on how it, along with other social arrangements, allocates all the good things of life – such as wealth, power, and liberty. The distributive justice appealed to in the case of tax, welfare or planning law is 'social justice' rather than 'remedial justice'.

It is possible to be sceptical about all conceptions of substantive justice. Alf Ross writes:

'To invoke justice is the same thing as banging on the table: an emotional expression which turns one's demand into an absolute

1 [1980] AC 136.

postulate. That is no proper way to mutual understanding. It is impossible to have a rational discussion with a man who mobilises 'justice', because he says nothing that can be argued for or against. His words are persuasion, not argument. The ideology of justice leads to implacability and conflict, since on the one hand it incites to the belief that one's demand is not merely the expression of a certain interest in conflict with opposing interests, but that it possesses a higher, absolute validity; and on the other hand it precludes all rational argument and discussion of a settlement.'[2]

If one is to be constructive rather than sceptical about social justice, it behoves one to state criteria for judging the justice of social arrangements and to have some way of meeting the charge that the choice of such criteria is purely subjective (and, likely as not, motivated by one's own interests). One might conclude that there is a plurality of such criteria – such as need, desert or talent – but no objective way of choosing between them. Or one might take the utilitarian view sketched in chapter 4, above, and argue that those social arrangements are best which maximise human satisfactions. Or one might adopt what philosophers call a 'perfectionist' approach, by advancing some criterion of human excellence as the social touchstone. The most celebrated of recent theories of justice is that advanced by Professor John Rawls, who rejects pluralism, utilitarianism and perfectionism in favour of a refined version of the social contract theories of Locke and Rousseau.

Rawls asks his reader to do two things. First, he must reflect on what it is about people's judgments of justice which gives them either authenticity or else the appearance of self-interested special pleading. He should construct an imaginary situation in which people are making judgments about society from the outside, without personal bias, and consider what such neutral outsiders would decide. The principles they would choose, having been arrived at by a fair procedure, constitute 'justice as fairness'. Secondly, the reader must match the principles which would be chosen in this way against his own considered judgments of justice. He may find that what his imaginary outsiders would choose does not gell with the considered judgments he is accustomed to make. If that is so, then either he should modify his considered judgments, or else he should go back to the construction and see whether it was defective in some way. In the end, Rawls hopes, the reader will reach a position of 'reflective equilibrium', in which his own considered judgments cohere with principles which the neutral outsiders would choose.

2 *On Law and Justice* pp. 274–275.

The constructive situation is called by Rawls the 'original position'. It consists of a congress of people, each representing a social class. They are placed behind a 'veil of ignorance'. They have only general information about human psychology and the laws of science. They do not know to which social class they are going to belong, nor even at what stage of development their society stands. They choose, by unanimous agreement, the principles which will regulate whatever society they belong to. In making this choice, they are guided only by rational self-interest. Each knows that he will have a plan of life (his own conception of the good), but he does not know what it will be. They will therefore agree to social principles which will give them the best chance of achieving each his life plan, whatever that may turn out to be. Since these are, by definition, principles which people would choose without taking into account special interests, they are objectively just.

Rawls concludes that the principles which the people in the original position choose are two in number:

'*First Principle*. Each person is to have an equal right to the most extensive total system of equal basic liberties compatible with a similar system of liberty for all. *Second Principle*. Social and economic inequalities are to be arranged so that they are both: (a) to the greatest benefit of the least advantaged, consistent with the just savings principle, and (b) attached to offices and positions open to all under conditions of fair equality of opportunity.'[3]

Rawls does not specify the 'system of equal basic liberties' precisely. He indicates that it includes political liberties (the right to vote and to be eligible for public office, freedom of speech and of assembly, liberty of conscience and freedom of thought); freedom of the person; the right to hold personal property; and freedom from arbitrary arrest and seizure, as defined by the concept of the rule of law. By their first principle, the people in the original position choose equality in these things, and they give this principle 'lexical priority' over the second principle; that is, they agree that the equal liberties of all are not to be sacrificed for any gain in respect of income, wealth or power (the matters dealt with in the second principle). They choose that the society to which they belong should have a basic structure of institutions which puts liberty first. Why should they? Because, says Rawls, it would be irrational for any of them to take chances with his liberty. He does not know what position he will hold in society, nor what things will be valued by the person he turns out to be. But he does know that there are 'social primary goods', that is, things which

3 *A Theory of Justice* p. 302.

every rational person wants whatever else he wants. These include liberty and opportunity, income and wealth, and the bases of self-respect. A person in the original position will choose the basic liberties in priority to any distribution of income, wealth and power, because he knows that, by so doing, he will have the best chance of obtaining for himself the social primary goods and of pursuing whatever other ends his particular plan turns out to encompass. He would not opt for principles which would allow a dictator to take away political liberties on condition that the dictator increased everyone's wealth, because, whereas he does not know whether he would value the increase in wealth (beyond the minimum which constitutes a primary social good), he does know that he would miss the political liberties, for they contribute to the social primary goods of liberty and self-respect.

Rawls makes one qualification on the priority of liberty. The people in the original position will choose the two principles which constitute the 'special conception' of justice, only on the assumption that their society has reached a stage at which liberties can be effectively secured. On the assumption that that stage has not been reached, they will choose a more 'general conception' of justice, which requires that all social primary goods, including liberty, are to be distributed equally unless an unequal distribution would be to the advantage of the least favoured. It is not clear what Rawls has in mind for the take-off point of the priority of liberty. Presumably, if conditions of a society are chaotic so that minimum security required as a basis of liberty and self-respect cannot be obtained, the people in the original position would allow that their basic liberties might be traded for firm government; and, presumably, if economic development is at such a low level that many people may starve without draconian, anti-libertarian measures, the same trade-off would be agreed to. But once this minimum stage has been attained, the people in the original position insist on their lexically-ordered two principles. The only limitations on liberty are to be justified for the sake of the total system of basic liberties, such as rules of order in debate. From behind the veil of ignorance, people would not agree to their liberties being restricted for the sake of economic prosperity.

The first clause of the second principle allows for social and economic inequalities, but only if they are for the benefit of the least advantaged. This is Rawls' famous 'difference' principle. The people in the original position would choose this, not knowing whether they would be favoured or disfavoured by any inequality, because the worst they could be would be 'least advantaged'. They would not opt for a set-up which allowed greater inequalities, because that would be risking being worse off, should they be the least advantaged; and it would be perverse to opt for complete equality even if that meant that everyone was worse off including the least advantaged. Rawls leaves open the question whether free enterprise or public ownership of the means of production does maximise the position of the worst off members of society; but claims that whichever does must, for that reason, be the more just – assuming the priority of liberty.

Try testing this feature of the special conception of justice, as Rawls tell us to do, against your considered judgments about justice. Suppose we have a rich man and a poor man arguing about whether their society is just.

> *Poor man*: How can it be just, when you can afford champagne and I only get beer.
>
> *Rich man*: But I get a higher salary than you because I'm cleverer and so contribute more to society; and also, my father was cleverer than yours and saved money which he left to me. Your lack of talent is not your fault, of course, but you can't complain that it's unfair if my greater contribution is more rewarded.
>
> *Poor man*: Your greater talents are not your fault either. They are just an accident of birth. If we all work our best, why shouldn't we be paid the same?
>
> *Rich man*: On that argument, why shouldn't we be paid the same whether we work or not? If people have to be paid to give them an incentive to work, isn't it right that those who happen to have talents and need long training should be given extra incentives? For if they weren't, there'd be less produced to pay for old-age pensions and so on. If my wealth were shared out, industry would collapse and you'd be worse off than you are now. Would that be worth it, just for the satisfaction of knowing that I was no better off than you?
>
> *Poor man*: I don't believe that industry would collapse.

Now Rawls constructs his original position on the assumption that the poor man is right in regarding being born with talents as morally irrelevant; hence he stipulates that the veil of ignorance hides from each chooser whether he has greater or less intelligence or abilities. He also constructs it on the assumption that the rich man is right in denying pure envy a legitimate place in reasoning about justice; hence each person in the original position is defined as the sort of individual who is concerned exclusively with his own maximum good, and consequently they choose what would favour them most should they be least advantaged over against a set-up which would give them less, but make men more equal. If, on reflection, you do not agree that ability and/or envy are morally irrelevant, you would construct the thing differently.

The rest of the second principle of Rawls' special conception of justice makes reference to two things which qualify the call for arrangements to be so ordered as to confer maximum benefit on the least advantaged. First, he makes reference to a 'just savings' principle. The people in the original position would know (knowing human psychology) that they would have some concern (once the veil of ignorance was lifted) for at least the next generation, so they will agree that all social assets should not be immediately squandered. Secondly, they will not debar anyone from attaining any office even if it carries special power or wealth, provided 'fair equality of opportunity' is guaranteed. Top jobs would be open to all, without reverse discrimination against the best endowed individuals. But it would be agreed that as much as possible should be done, by way of education provision and so forth, to counteract disadvantages such as those flowing from family background, so that the equality of opportunity will be 'fair'.

Rawls' theory envisages a four-stage unfolding of just institutions. The first stage is the original position itself, in which the two, lexically-ordered principles of justice are chosen. The second stage is a constitutional convention. The veil of ignorance is partly lifted, so that people now know what society they belong to; but they are still unaware which people they are. At this second stage they choose a constitution, which must embody the two principles of justice already chosen. The constitution will provide for some form of majority rule, since it must secure equal liberties to vote and stand for office. It will secure fair equality of opportunity, perhaps by providing for public funding of political parties. Whether or not it limits majority rule by a bill of rights will depend on the balance struck among the system of basic liberties – for example, freedom to control policy through one's vote against freedom of the person and of property. The third stage is that of legislation, at which the legislators are still ignorant of their personal circumstances. To be just, laws must comply with the two principles of justice and the constitution, and be the sort of laws which legislators would choose if not motivated by knowledge of their own individual circumstances. The fourth stage relates to the application of laws by judges and other officials, at which stage the veil of ignorance has been totally removed.

Unfortunately, Rawls tells us very little about this fourth stage, so that we cannot look to his theory for enlightenment about problems of adjudication or legal reasoning. His theory is concerned with the justice of 'institutions', that is, 'public systems of rules'. He discusses the justice of actions primarily only in so far as they affect the creation or operation of institutions. As we saw in chapter 16, above, he claims that all citizens have a natural duty to support the institutions of a just society, and that officials have a special obligation to do this as well. What guidance can the theory provide for judges in hard cases?

When judges appeal to 'justice' in a difficult case, they may mean 'executive justice' in Pound's sense, or some version of substantive remedial justice, as in Pickett's case. If they do have some conception of social substantive justice in mind, it will usually be a small-scale one – how resources ought to be distributed between two classes of people, rather than how distribution should be made across society as a whole. For example, judges lay down criteria for establishing just distribution of assets between husbands and wives on divorce. The broader question about what part the taxpayer should play in supporting deserted wives and their children is left to the legislature. There is no point in pressing Rawls' theory in hard cases unless the decision is going to establish, modify or support some institution. The law of contract is a public system of rules, and so an 'institution' within Rawls' definition. If the House of Lords were faced with a choice between affirming or negating some pretty fundamental contract rule – say, the rule that people are normally bound by the terms of documents they have signed but not read – it might be urged that a decision one way or the other would strengthen the system of basic liberties or, if the decision was indifferent on the liberty count, that choosing one way or the other would benefit the least advantaged class in society. Generally, Rawls' theory relates to large-scale social issues of the sort which, in England, do not turn on judicial decisions – it is otherwise, of course, with the American Supreme Court.

Since its publication in 1972, Rawls' *A Theory of Justice* has produced a wealth of critical commentary. 'Justice' (whatever it means) cannot be done in this short chapter either to the complexity of the theory itself or to the subtlety of the critical reactions. Very roughly, objections may be divided into two kinds. First, why should we play Rawls' contract game anyway? Why should the convictions about justice which we now have be tailored to meet the sort of principles which would be agreed to by imaginary people? Secondly, even if we do play Rawls" game, he has not demonstrated that the people in the original position would choose his two principles.

Objections to the game may be levelled at its alleged objectivity. Its merit is supposed to be that it provides a common check for people who now disagree. If I say to you: 'You only call this law just because it benefits you (or because it accords with some religious principle you have)', and you offer counter-jibes in terms of my subjective interests and views, we can both be asked whether people who did not know their own particular situation would have agreed to it. Then we shall have to give reasons which at least purport to leave out special pleadings. Against this it may be argued that Rawls' original-position people are not truly neutral. They have controversial evaluations built into them, and their conclusions must therefore be controversial.

One may cavil at the conception of the primary good of 'self-respect' which Rawls attributes to his people. In arguing for the priority of liberty, he says that this primary good leads them to favour freedom of conscience so much that they will not trade it for economic gain. But is this conception of self-respect, as he claims, something that all rational people desire – and hence a 'primary social good'? Perhaps people's self-esteem has more to do with the size of their car than their ability to engage in free moral and political speculation. Many, no doubt, hold that it is better to be a philosopher than a rational pig; but then such prior evaluations of human excellence were supposed to be eliminated from the original position. Further, self-respect may be a relative matter, depending on how far we fall short of others in achievement. If that is so, why should not 'envy' be taken into account? Conversely, self-respect may be impossible unless we feel that we are benefiting others; so why should Rawls assume that the people in the original position calculate only on the basis of self-interest? Some sort of 'service to others' may be a primary social good. Perhaps Rawls' people are too pig-like. Rawls makes it clear that his 'contractarian' approach to justice is open for adoption by someone who does not accept his particular version of the contract situation. 'Reflective equilibrium' may lead to modifications in the original position in order that principles emerging from it match our considered judgments. Can this process produce accord between those whose considered judgments differ, especially if they vary, not merely about what they regard as just, but about what is essentially 'human'?

The most far-reaching attack of the 'why should we play the game' kind comes from Professor Robert Nozick. He objects to all conceptions of justice whose object is to arrive at a proper distribution of social goods. Such views presuppose, without proper argument, that the abilities of all are a common asset, so that everyone has a claim on what anyone makes out of exercising his talents. Rawls contends that his difference principle accords to the least advantaged reasonable terms of social cooperation. But (Nozick replies) are the terms reasonable for the better off? Why should they be forced to engage in social cooperation with the least advantaged, unless they will be better off thereby than they would have been without such cooperation? Worse still, no conception of justice which makes a certain pattern of distribution its favoured end state (whether arrived at through an imaginary contract or otherwise), is compatible with anything less than a total suppression of liberty. Nozick asks us to imagine what is to happen if such a pattern has once been achieved, and then a talented sportsman enters into freely negotiated contracts which produce for him wealth out of line with the favoured pattern. Leaving him his new wealth would be acquiescing in an unjust distribution pattern; so the state must intervene, either by expropriating the sportsman's gains, or by prohibiting his contracts *in limine*.

Nozick offers an alternative theory of justice, 'the theory of entitlements'. According to this theory, the justice of social arrangements has nothing to do with the way in which the total wealth and power of a society is distributed, but is exclusively concerned with the justice of people's present holdings. There are three principles. The 'principle of acquisition' requires that holdings over resources, which were previously owned by no one, were acquired in a just way. The 'principle of transfer' requires that holdings devolved to the present owners through just transactions. The 'principle of rectification' comes into play only when either of the other two has been violated. As Nozick recognises, the theory is very sketchy. How are we to decide whether original acquisitions were just, what vitiating elements make transactions unjust, and what criteria to apply in directing rectifications? He criticises Locke's view that just property holdings begin when someone mixes his labour with material objects and that anyone may appropriate material from the common stock of unowned things so long as there is enough left for all; but he offers no alternative description of just acquisition. He does not appear to share Hume's view that the interests of society necessitate a conservative respect for conventional property law, whatever its content; but he does not tell us how far back along the line of transfers we may go to find a basis for just rectification. Nozick's theory depends on historical entitlements, and should therefore be viewed in the light of actual information about the history of property holdings. It is difficult to square it with Maine's contention that all individual titles begin with dispossession (see chapter 17, above).

As compared with Rawls' theory, the entitlements theory looks very conservative. The difference principle would support progressive taxation, up to the point at which further taxation of the rich, by removing incentives, would not improve the lot of the least advantaged. For Nozick, taxation of some to meet the needs of others is equivalent to forced labour. Taxation and all other coercive political measures are justified only to uphold a 'minimal state', one which merely protects each man's domain over his person and property holdings. On the other hand, an entitlements theory can be constructed which produces more radical conclusions than the difference principle. One advocate of it, M. Rothbard, suggests that much of the land in South America should be returned to the peasantry, to rectify past injustices. Supporters of 'reverse discrimination' in the United States sometimes claim that blacks should receive more than equality of treatment and more than fair equality of opportunity, to rectify the injustices done to their ancestors. The difficulty with any ameliorative programme, based solely on rectification rather than redistribution, is in identifying the claimant with the person originally wronged and the defendant with the original wrongdoer.

Objections to Rawls' theory of the second kind (framed in terms of the contract game itself) argue that *his* people in *his* original position would not necessarily agree on his two principles and their lexical ordering. Rawls says that they do know general facts about economics and human psychology. The psychological knowledge plays an important part in his argument, in relation to the assumptions he says they will make about stability. They will opt for the difference principle because they know that, even if they turn out to be among the favoured members of society and so will afterwards regret their choice, they can predict that they and the maximalised least advantaged will put up with the arrangement. But might they not prefer to opt for some version of average utilitarianism, a social arrangement which maximises total satisfactions averaged over the population? They might turn out to be worse off than under the difference principle, but the chances are that they will not. Why should their general knowledge of psychology lead them to conclude that a society is most stable if it complies with the two principles? There have been many stable historical societies which clearly do not, and presumably their psychological information is inferred from generalised historical information. If they know they may be people who cannot tolerate certain kinds of belief on the part of others, how can they honestly predict that they will be able to put up with the basic liberties? Does their general economic and psychological information enable them to pronounce on the truth or falsity of Marxist claims? If they believed they were true, then they would know either that they would be members of exploited classes, in which case they would know that they would engage in class war against their exploiters and in re-education of fellow class members whose consciousness was impaired by indoctrination (and to hell with the basic liberties and the difference principle); or they would be members of a ruling class, in which case they could predict that they would be unable to bring themselves to sacrifice their privileges in the way the difference principle requires. In other words, it seems that we must ourselves first decide, from within the world, that Marxist claims are false, before we can arrive at general information on the basis of which people behind a veil of ignorance could hope to agree.

NB

Bibliography

Barry B. M.	*The Liberal Theory of Justice* (1973)
	'Justice Between Generations' in Hacker and Raz (eds) *Law, Morality, and Society* (1977)
	'Is Democracy Special?' in Laslett and Fishkin (eds) *Philosophy, Politics and Society* (5th series, 1979)
Becker L. C.	*Property Rights: Philosophic Foundations* (1977)
Daniels N. (ed)	*Reading Rawls* (1975)
Devlin P.	*The Judge* (1979) ch 5
Dias R. W. M.	*Jurisprudence* (4th edn, 1976) ch 3
Eckhoff T.	'Justice and Social Utility' in Universitets-Forlaget *Legal Essays, a Tribute to Fried Castberg* (1963)
Finnis J. M.	*Natural Law and Natural Rights* (1980) ch 7
Fishkin J.	'Tyranny and Democratic Theory' in Laslett and Fishkin (eds) *Philosophy, Politics and Society* (5th series, 1979)
Hall J.	'Justice in the Twentieth Century' (1971) 59 Calif L Rev 752
Hart H. L. A.	*The Concept of Law* (1961) ch 8
Hayeck F. A.	*Law, Legislation and Liberty* vol 2
	The Mirage of Social Justice (1976)
Honoré A. M.	'Social Justice' in Summers (ed) *Essays in Legal Philosophy* (1968)
	'Property, Title and Redistribution' in Wellman (ed) *Equality and Freedom* (1977)
Hume D.	*A Treatise of Human Nature* (Mossner (ed), 1969) Book III, Pt 2
Locke J.	*Two Treatises of Government* (Laslett (ed), 2nd edn, 1970) Book II, ch 5
Lucas J. R.	*On Justice* (1980)
MacCormick D. N.	'Justice, an Unoriginal Position' (1976) 3 Dal LJ 367
	Legal Reasoning and Legal Theory (1978) ch 4
Miller D.	*Social Justice* (1976)
Nozick R.	*Anarchy, State and Utopia* (1974) ch 7
Pound R.	*An Introduction to the Philosophy of Law* (revised edn, 1954) ch 3

Rae D. W.   'A Principle of Simple Justice' in Laslett and
                         Fishkin (eds) *Philosophy, Politics and Society* (5th
                         series, 1979)
Rawls J.   *A Theory of Justice* (1972)
                         'A Well-ordered Society' in Laslett and
                         Fishkin (eds) *Philosophy, Politics and Society*
                         (5th series, 1979)
Ross A.   *On Law and Justice* (1958) ch 12
Rothbard M. N.   'Justice and Property Rights' in Blumenfeld
                         (ed) *Property in a Humane Economy* (1974)
Sartorius R. E.   *Individual Conduct and Social Norms* (1975) ch 7
Stone J.   *Human Law and Human Justice* (1965) ch 10
Wasserstrom R. A.   *The Judicial Decision* (1961) ch 5
Wolff R. P.   *Understanding Rawls* (1977)

Index

282   Index

Austin's commands ———

   4 elements — ① wish   ⎤

           ② sanction   ⎥

           ③ expression of a wish ⎦

           ④ generality — must be included

                        for law.

"all punishment is a mischief" Bentham

WK II quotes
- punishment is punishment only when it is deserved.

WK I
Mills harm principle. —

— " The only purpose for which power can be rightfully exercised over any member of a civilized community, vs. his will is to prevent harm to others. His own good, either physical or moral, is not a **sufficient warrant**. "

Command Theory WK III

Austin - " Our rules wd. be fashioned on utility; our conduct, on our rules. (Province)

Mr. Gibson

30
4

160
4